PENNY ARCADE™ 4

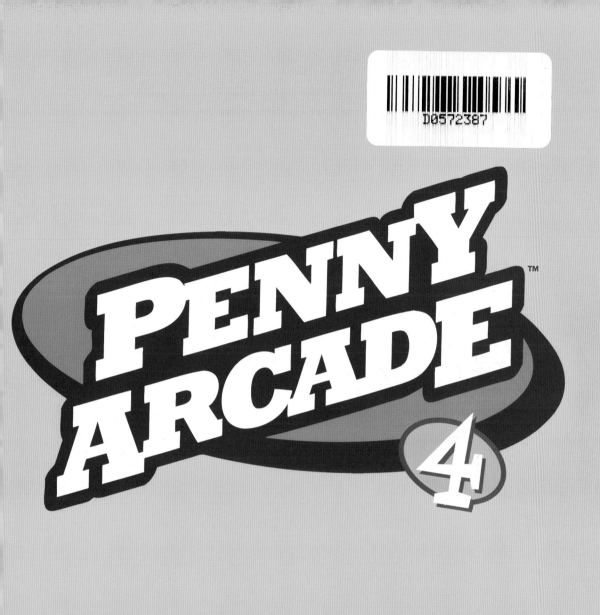

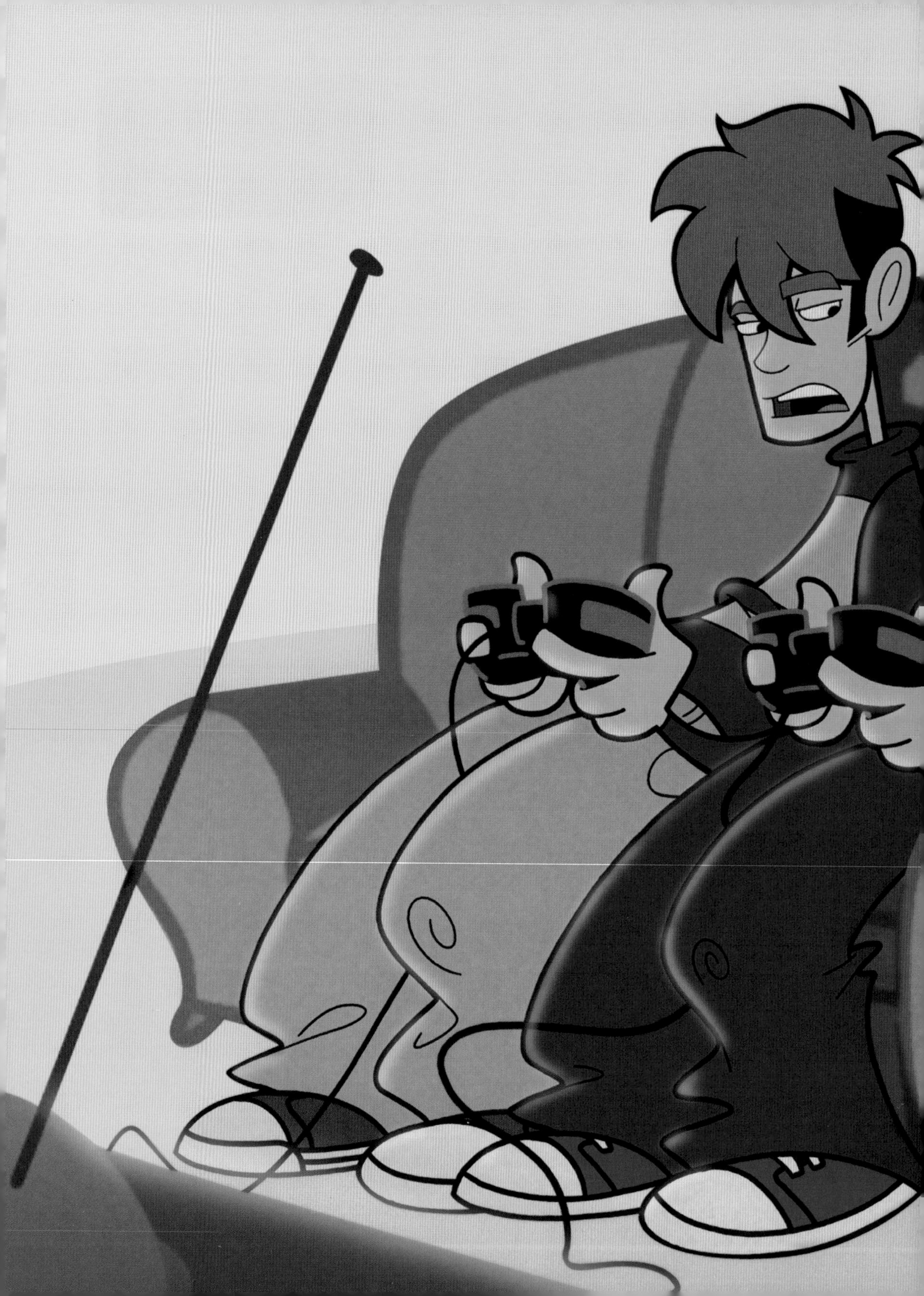

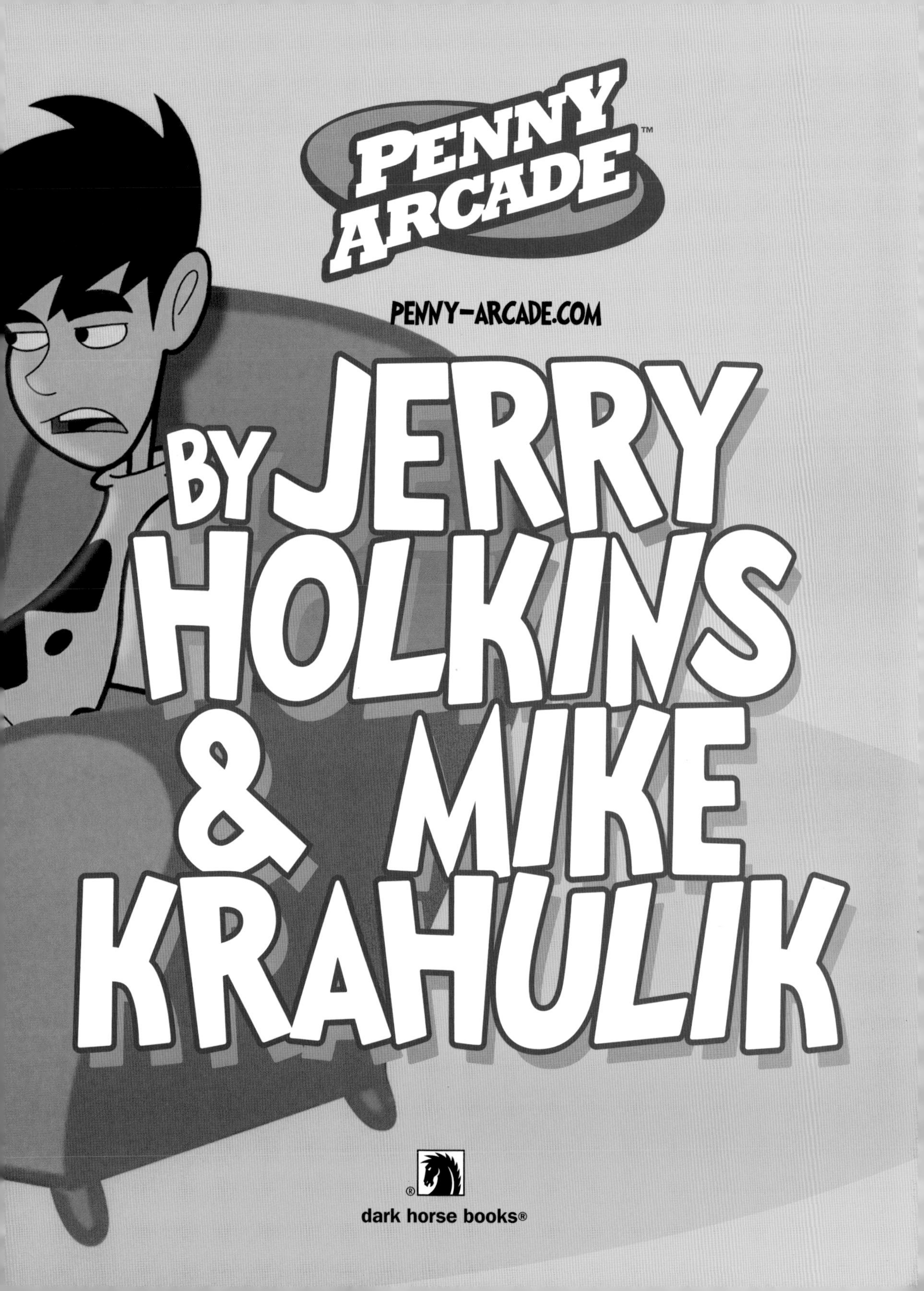

PENNY ARCADE™

PENNY-ARCADE.COM

BY JERRY HOLKINS & MIKE KRAHULIK

dark horse books®

Publisher
MIKE RICHARDSON

Editor
MIKE CARRIGLITTO

Editorial Assistant
SAMANTHA ROBERTSON

Designer
DAVID NESTELLE

Art Director
LIA RIBACCHI

Very special thanks to ROBERT KHOO at Penny Arcade!

PENNY ARCADE Volume 4: BIRDS ARE WEIRD

This volume collects comic strips from the Penny Arcade website, originally published online from January 1, 2003 through December 31, 2003.

Published by
Dark Horse Books
A division of Dark Horse Comics, Inc.
10956 SE Main Street
Milwaukie, OR 97222

darkhorse.com

To find a comics shop in your area, call the Comic Shop Locator Service toll-free at 1-888-266-4226

First edition: June 2007
ISBN 10: 1-59307-773-4
ISBN 13: 978-1-59307-773-0

10 9 8 7 6 5 4 3 2 1
Printed in China

Foreword by Karen Traviss

y acquaintance with *Penny Arcade* began with a Wookiee's penis, which is as good a way as any to start a relationship.

"I think you should see *this*," said a friend at Lucas-Arts. "Just remember, *Penny Arcade* is love."

I clicked a link to a webcomic depicting characters from a game on which we both worked—Republic Commando, for which I was writing the tie-in novels, in fact. (I write science fiction for a living, so I can cyberskive whenever I please.) I fell in love with *Penny Arcade* at that very moment.

Gabe and Tycho had captured the very essence of the RepCom characters. They also said words like "Wookiee penis." From that day on, I was hooked.

Okay, let me reword that. *Hooked* isn't quite accurate. I became an undiluted *PA* fangirl, making "squee" noises on my blog so much that my younger readers (actually, *all* my readers are younger than me, even the very old ones) said it was touching and even *miraculous* that I'd taken these pop culture icons to my aging black granite heart.

What kept me reading *PA*, once the joy of the Wookiee penis had passed? For me, the fact that it's both a comic and an unflinching trade journal. Look, you *know* it's wonderfully self-deprecating, entertaining, relevant, educational, unafraid, iconic, and pants-wettingly funny, or you wouldn't have bought this book. (And if you're just browsing this in a bookstore—buy it, you cheapskate, and stop pawing the merchandise.)

But for a pro like me, *PA* is also a benchmark of excellence. Gabe is a superb artist, whose full range is tantalizingly glimpsed in this book, showing just how many stylistic directions he could have chosen from; Tycho's smart script—and his elegant and relevant editorials, some of which appear here—make me envious in a narrow-eyed writerly way. Put simply, this is Good Stuff, produced by, well, there's no other way to say it: Good People. *PA* has become a phenomenon with real market clout, but stays clean, honest, and generous, and gives back to the community.

Having done a tasting of 2003's strips (smooth vanilla finish, with hints of cedar and spice, ideal with roast lamb), I feel this year of *Penny Arcade* shows most of the elements we've come to love—smacks in the mouth for the corporate world, characters like Frank and everyone's favorite ravisher of citrus fruits, surgical but affectionate dissections of games and gamers, unalloyed eccentricity, and the consolidation of the two superbly realized main characters.

It's sublimely entertaining. So buy it, as well as the rest of the series. The store CCTV is watching you, so I'll know if you don't.

—SF author and **PA** *fangirl*
Karen Traviss
December 11, 2006
Devizes, England

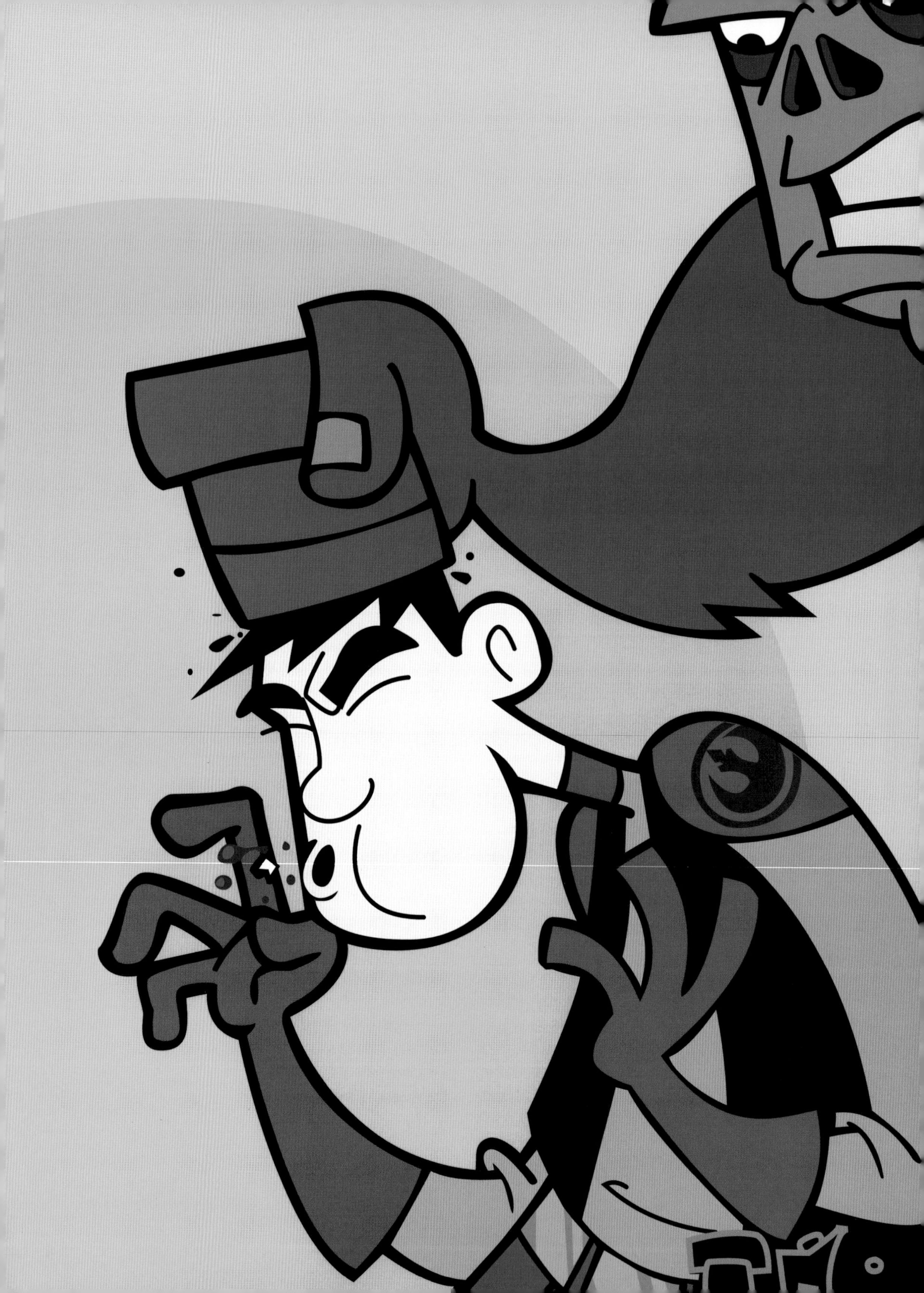

Introduction 4.0

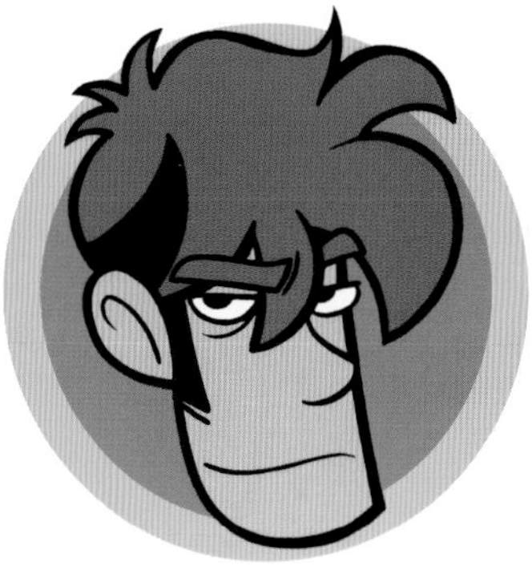

In this, our fourth nonsensically titled volume, we thought: let's just go *crazy.*

And we did, for a while.

We weren't satisfied with books that (like those of our *esteemed* competitors), were content merely to be read. What if our collections could hold sauces of various kinds? Condiments are always in great demand, and their close proximity to the reader would be a comfort. In practice, this proved unwise. Testers informed us that steak sauce, mayonnaise, or a commingling of the two would sometimes fire at the reader, pooling in (this is from the official report) "the crotchal region."

Briefly, we experimented with new "papers" we hoped would usher in the new era we envisioned, and comics were printed on thin strips of lean Angus beef. I can see you nodding yes, clearly moved by the power and wisdom of our vision. The problem? Dogs. Wild dogs, no doubt driven mad by the scent of freshly printed meat, managed to gain entry to our secure facility and devour forty thousand books in a single night.

Those were the boldest moves, but we did endeavor to innovate in other areas. Books daubed with aromatic mint. Living books that could feel pain and loneliness. I once suggested that we take out the "are" in *Birds Are Weird*, replacing it with a single, *backwards* R.

Ultimately, we settled on something very like this book. Hopefully you will not be disappointed by the humdrum, no sauce, no beef version of *Birds Are Weird*. You may be comforted to know that *this* version, for all its faults, is less likely to attract dingoes.

Against our better judgment, at the end of the book we've included a sampling of Gabriel's work before *Penny Arcade*. We thought you might want to see these pieces before they are all shoveled into a furnace. We apologize for any permanent damage these materials might inflict upon the *retinal nerve*.

—Tycho Brahe
January 9, 2007
Seattle, WA

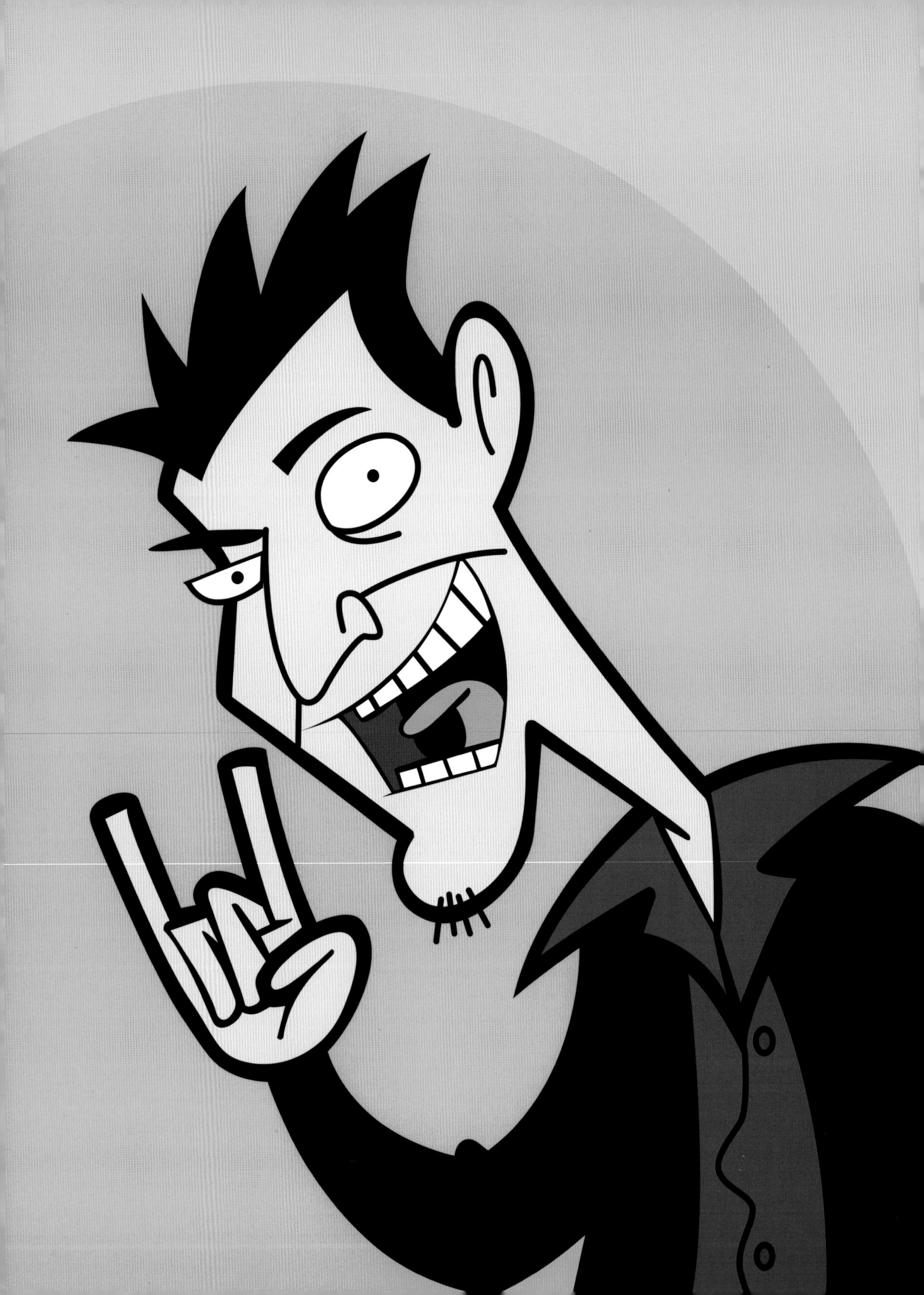

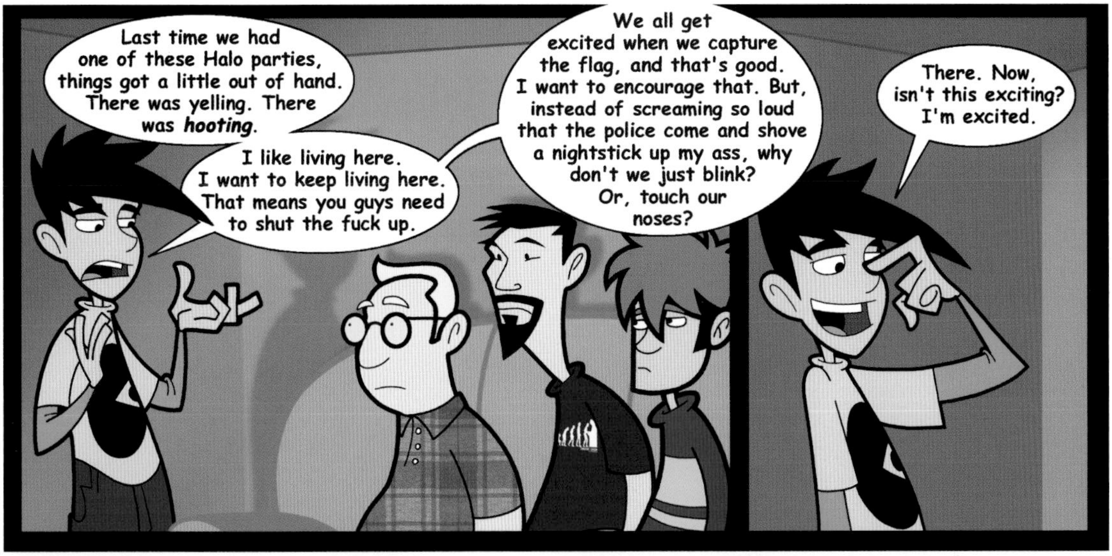
Last time we had one of these Halo parties, things got a little out of hand. There was yelling. There was *hooting*.
I like living here. I want to keep living here. That means you guys need to shut the fuck up.
We all get excited when we capture the flag, and that's good. I want to encourage that. But, instead of screaming so loud that the police come and shove a nightstick up my ass, why don't we just blink? Or, touch our noses?
There. Now, isn't this exciting? I'm excited.

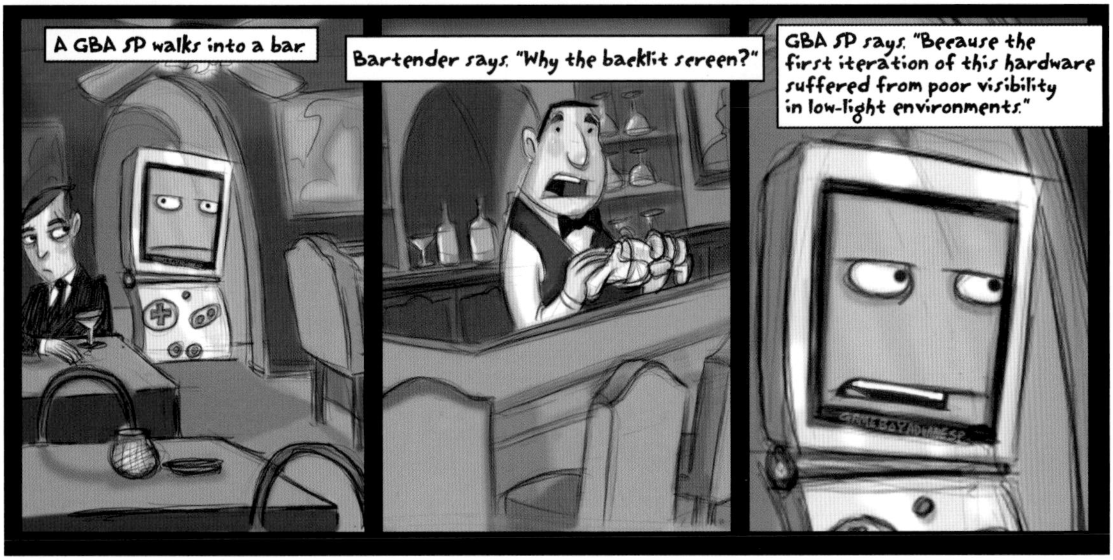
A GBA SP walks into a bar.
Bartender says: "Why the backlit screen?"
GBA SP says: "Because the first iteration of this hardware suffered from poor visibility in low-light environments."

EXHILARATING

January 3, 2003 After more than a year of Halo hatred (based on the almost fractally repetitive single-player experience), we were forced to admit that the multiplayer on this thing had *legs*. Many, many legs in fact, like a centipede. The ability to gin up unique modes and play tons of people on three or four boxes was a revolution to us, as we were used to hauling eight or more PCs across town in order to achieve a similar effect.

MINUS THE POPE AND A RABBI

January 8, 2003 Something happened to Gabriel during this period that (apparently!) caused him to reject his entire aesthetic, moving in a direction that I loved writing for. Altered art gave rise to experimentation in the dialogue as well, but reader outcry on one or both of these things was such that it didn't carry on this way for very long. I was sad to see it go.

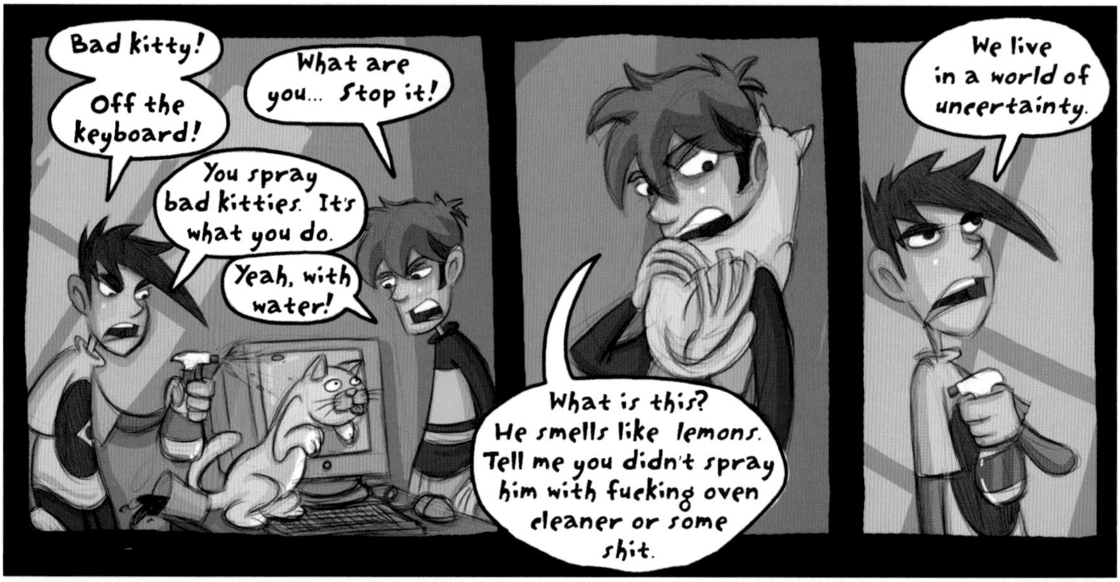
Bad kitty!
Off the keyboard!
What are you... Stop it!
You spray bad kitties. It's what you do.
Yeah, with water!
What is this? He smells like lemons. Tell me you didn't spray him with fucking oven cleaner or some shit.
We live in a world of uncertainty.

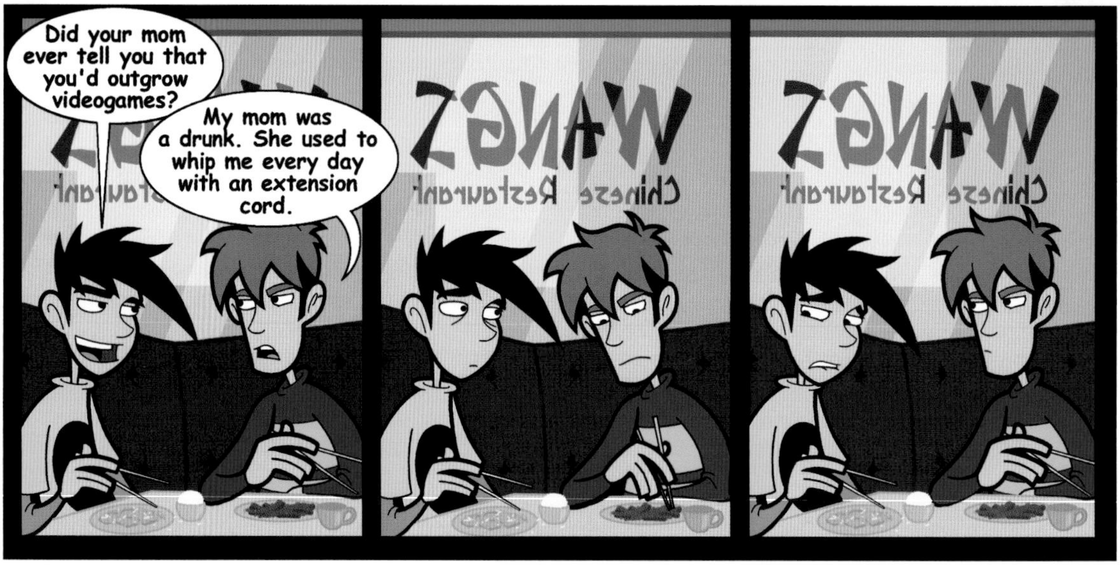
Did your mom ever tell you that you'd outgrow videogames?
My mom was a drunk. She used to whip me every day with an extension cord.

FELINITY

January 10, 2003 Unwilling to be yoked by convention, he even drew the panel *borders* in this one. You can see *here* that what began as a visual adventure became some kind of sitcom about cat punishment. So maybe it wasn't the change in the art that enraged readers, but rather the fact that we had gone completely *insane*.

SWEET AND SOUR

January 13, 2003 Mysteriously, the style shift skipped this strip. My mother did believe that I would eventually cast off our glorious pastime, that part is true—but those portions of the comic dealing with *strong spirits* or unique, improvised whips are (perhaps) less accurate. Presumably she thought I would take up a keen interest in *automobiles* or *belt buckles* or some other acceptably masculine endeavor.

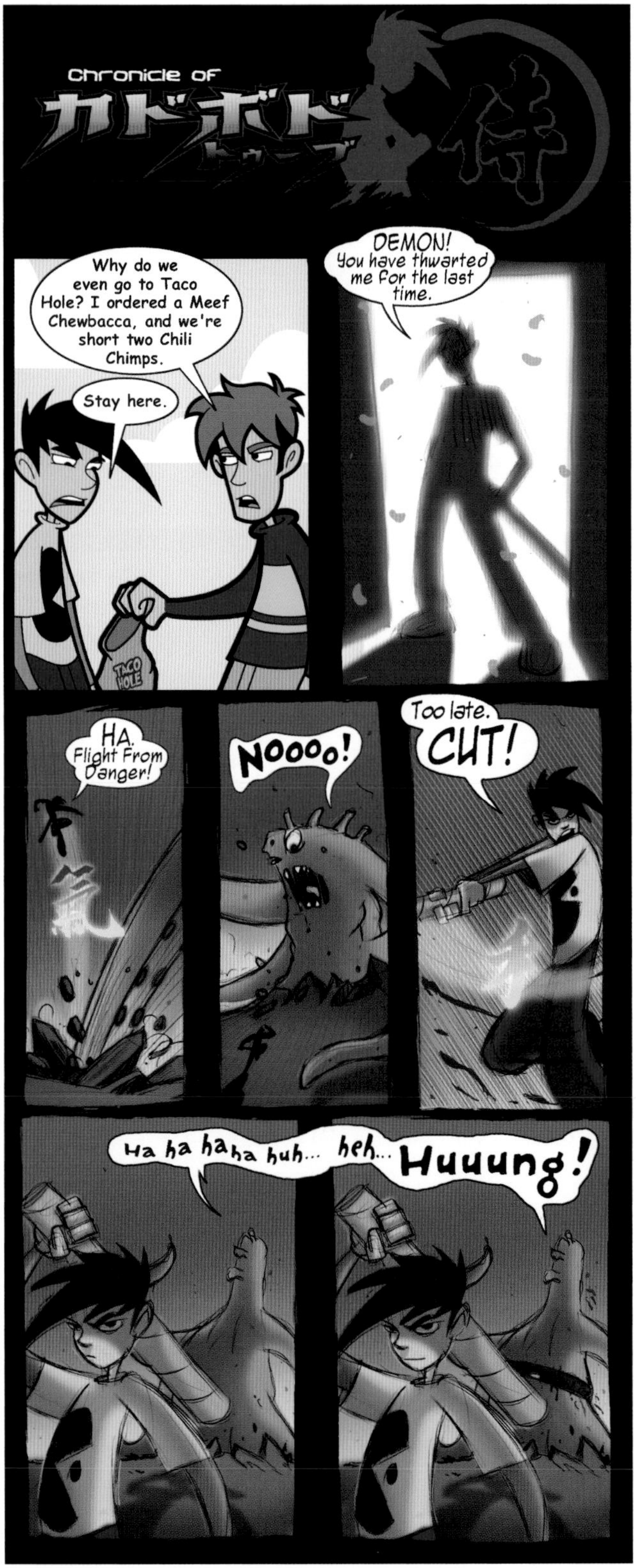
Chronicle of
カドボド
トゥーブ
侍
Why do we even go to Taco Hole? I ordered a Meef Chewbacca, and we're short two Chili Chimps.
Stay here.
TACO HOLE
DEMON! You have thwarted me for the last time.
HA. Flight From Danger!
Noooo!
Too late. CUT!
Ha ha haha huh... heh... Huuung!

CHRONICLE OF CARDBOARD TUBE SAMURAI

January 15, 2003 An attempt to hybridize the styles accompanies the return of the Cardboard Tube Samurai, before his activities took on their modern interpretation—back when he was still more parody than homage. The CTS is always understood—by us, at least—to be Gabriel's fantasy at some level. It's actually later in *this very book* that we stop taking the idea so literally, and give him a little room to breathe.

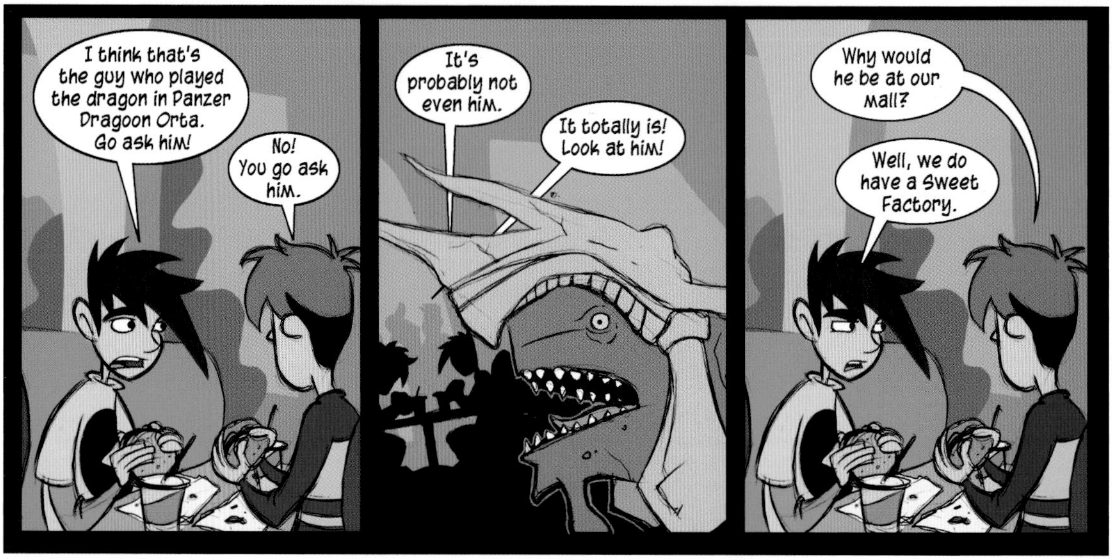
I think that's the guy who played the dragon in Panzer Dragoon Orta. Go ask him!
No! You go ask him.
It's probably not even him.
It totally is! Look at him!
Why would he be at our Mall?
Well, we do have a Sweet Factory.

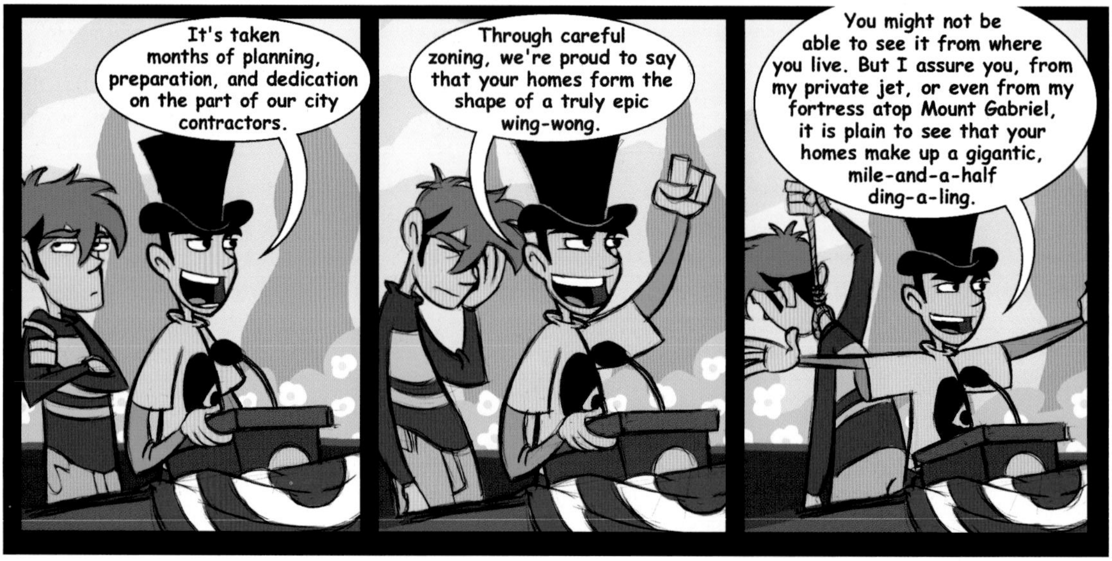
It's taken months of planning, preparation, and dedication on the part of our city contractors.
Through careful zoning, we're proud to say that your homes form the shape of a truly epic wing-wong.
You might not be able to see it from where you live. But I assure you, from my private jet, or even from my fortress atop Mount Gabriel, it is plain to see that your homes make up a gigantic, mile-and-a-half ding-a-ling.

ENTER THE DRAGON

January 17, 2003 Sweet Factory is such a fixture for us that I never paused to consider whether or not readers even knew what it *was*. For example, I feel comfortable referencing our Sun—secure in the knowledge that you'll know which star I'm talking about. It's really at that level—and, much like the Sun, Sweet Factory sustains the Earth.

PUBIC WORKS PROJECT

January 20, 2003 Sim City 4 was fine, but Sim City 2000 was the only one I ever really obsessed over. We used to play it on an ancient Macintosh that Gabe's mom had hauled home from work. This was before he really played PC games—before my nefarious influence had begun to take root.

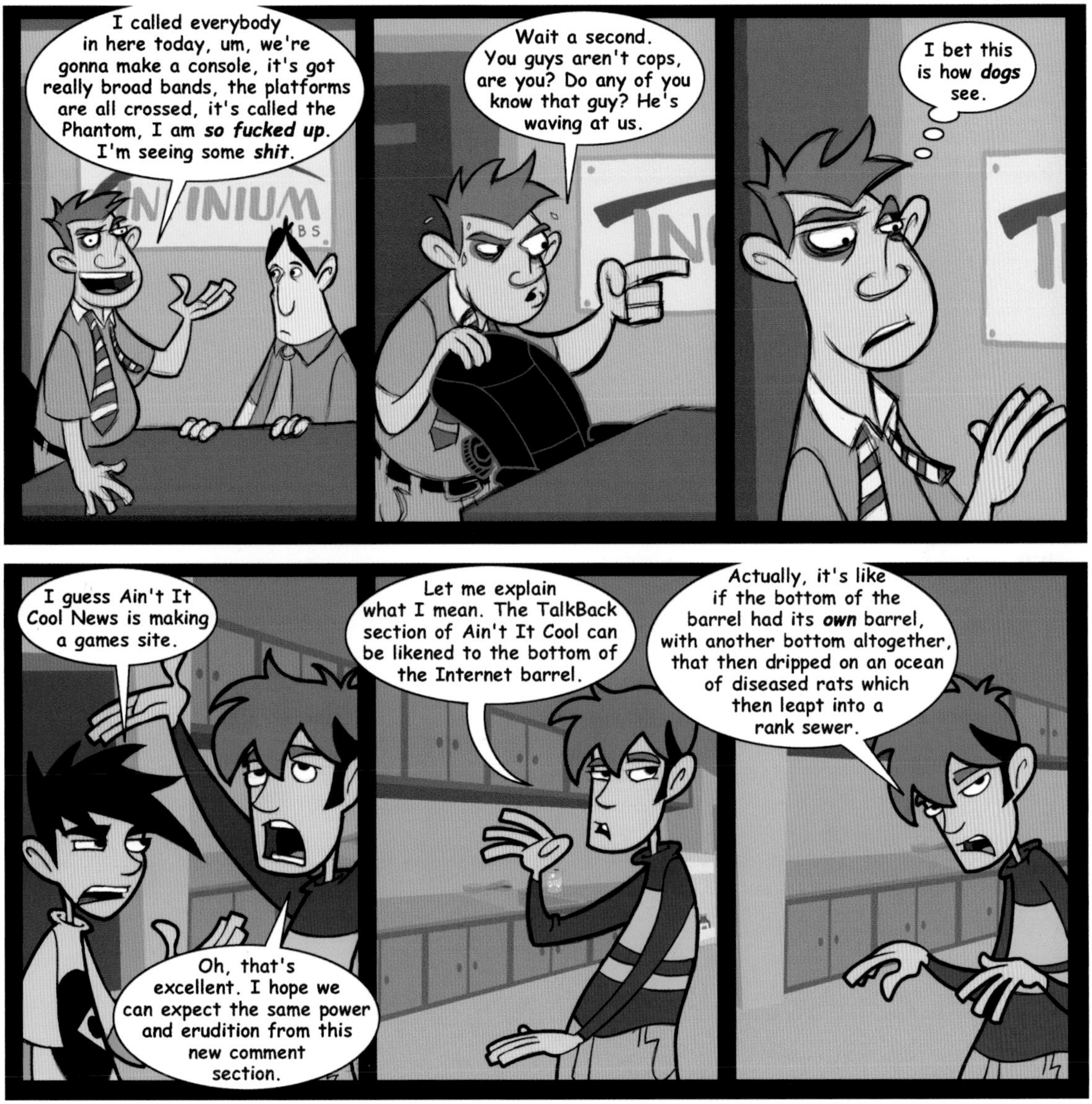
I called everybody in here today, um, we're gonna make a console, it's got really broad bands, the platforms are all crossed, it's called the Phantom, I am *so fucked up*. I'm seeing some *shit*.
INFINIUM
Wait a second. You guys aren't cops, are you? Do any of you know that guy? He's waving at us.
I bet this is how *dogs* see.
I guess Ain't It Cool News is making a games site.
Oh, that's excellent. I hope we can expect the same power and erudition from this new comment section.
Let me explain what I mean. The TalkBack section of Ain't It Cool can be likened to the bottom of the Internet barrel.
Actually, it's like if the bottom of the barrel had its *own* barrel, with another bottom altogether, that then dripped on an ocean of diseased rats which then leapt into a rank sewer.

DUDE, WHOA

January 22, 2003 I should emphasize that now, in 2007, there is still no Phantom console, and there never will be. The ridiculous caricature we have devised here for your amusement is more capable, honest, and *sober* than the men who steered that company off the edge of the map and into the Crazy Lands Beyond. Since then, new people have come in and made the best of a bad situation—selling their brilliantly engineered mouse/keyboard combo independently, and transforming their game streaming technology into a service rather than a hardware platform.

EXULTATION

January 27, 2003 It didn't last very long.

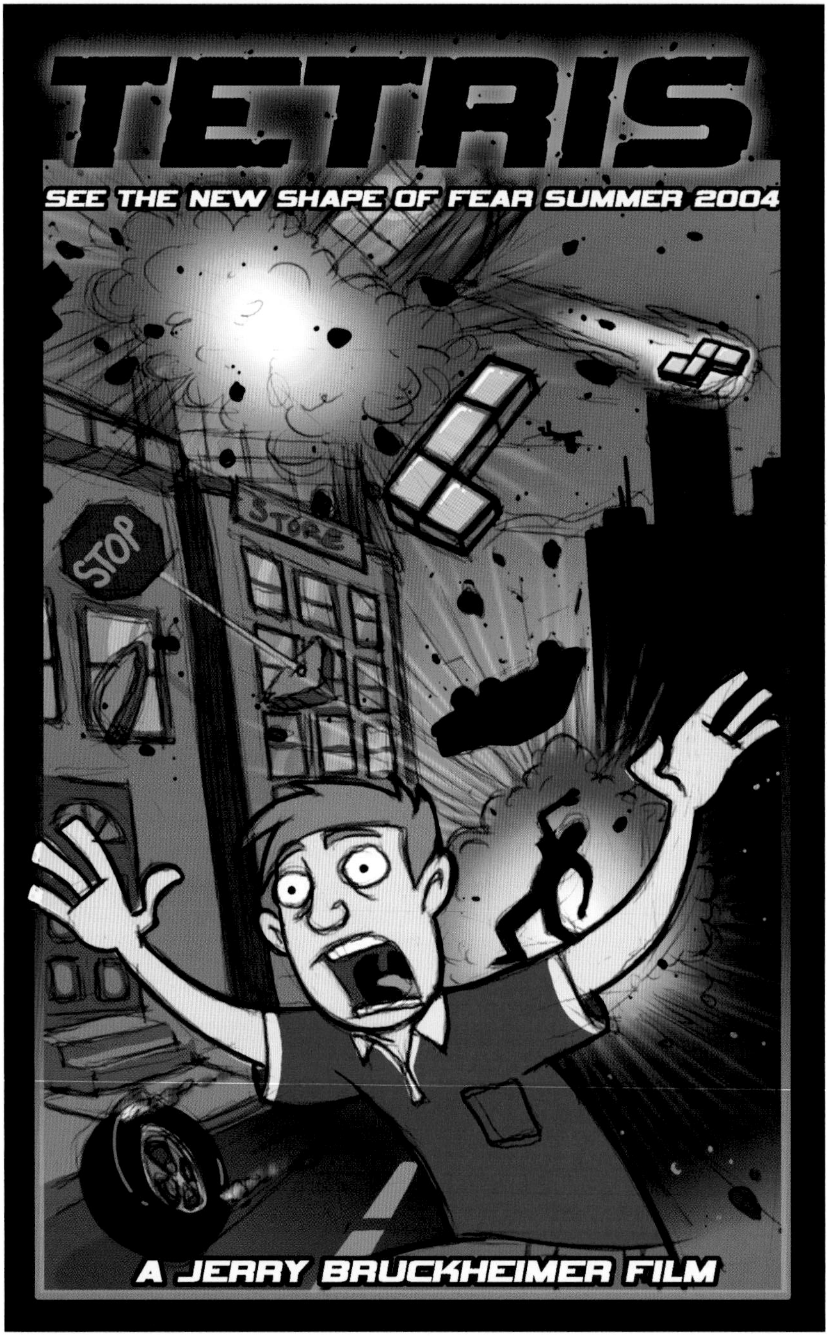
TETRIS
SEE THE NEW SHAPE OF FEAR SUMMER 2004
STOP
STORE
A JERRY BRUCKHEIMER FILM

WHY THE HELL NOT

January 24, 2003 When Hollywood got a whiff of the gaming industry's strong brands (and, no doubt, our radical devotion *to* them) they began to move in on them like jungle predators. It was around this time that the idea of a Metroid movie materialized, and it's something that pops up again every year or so. We countered with the notion of a big-budget Tetris movie, which I suggested would be a "blockbuster." *A-hem.*

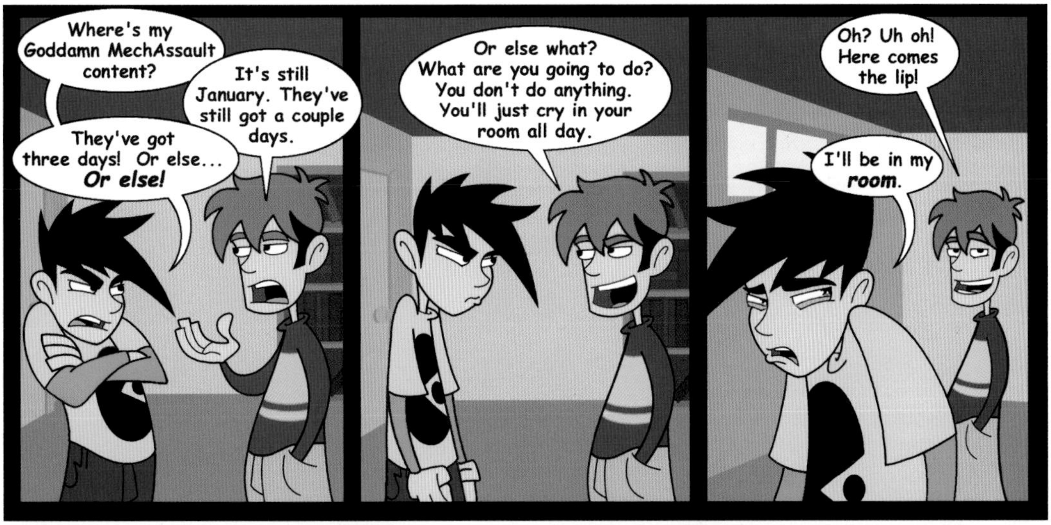
Where's my Goddamn MechAssault content?
It's still January. They've still got a couple days.
They've got three days! Or else... *Or else!*
Or else what? What are you going to do? You don't do anything. You'll just cry in your room all day.
Oh? Uh oh! Here comes the lip!
I'll be in my *room*.

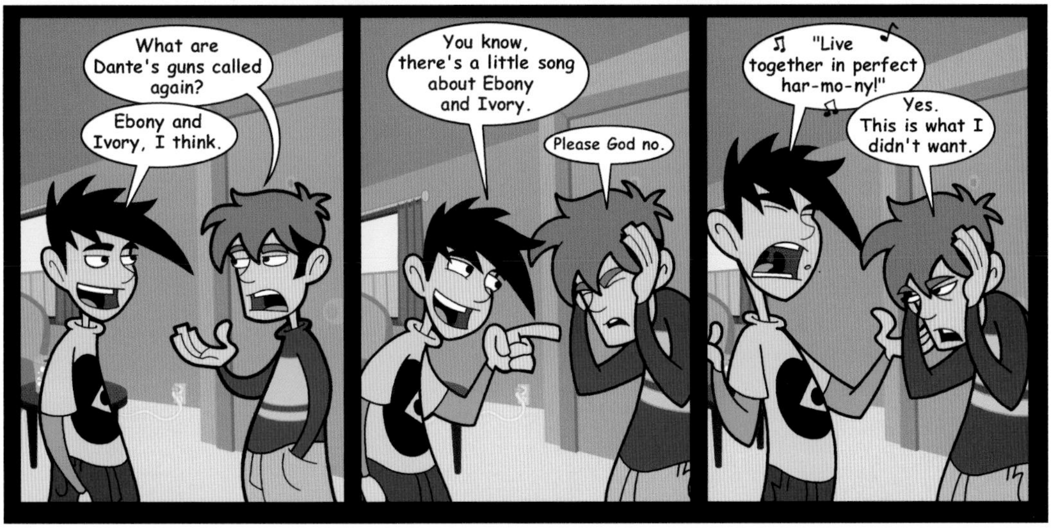
What are Dante's guns called again?
Ebony and Ivory, I think.
You know, there's a little song about Ebony and Ivory.
Please God no.
"Live together in perfect har-mo-ny!"
Yes. This is what I didn't want.

DISCONTENT

January 29, 2003 There is a lot of rage projected toward developers by our people, but other than refusing to buy games—something which goes sharply against my nature—shouting in the wilderness is often our only recourse. Then again, there have now been several instances when the community has stepped forward to literally *finish development* on a game—Vampire: The Masquerade, Temple of Elemental Evil, and Knights of the Old Republic II all saw significant work done to them after the official developers had washed their hands of the products.

WHY CAN'T WE

January 31, 2003 Well, you've never heard him sing. It's actually *dangerous*—it's like the Book of Goddamn Revelations coming to life in your living room. He was singing Rick Springfield's "Jesse's Girl" the other day, and when I went to get a glass of water out of the tap, instead of cool, refreshing water, it deposited a bat. I've never drank *bat* before—maybe it's good—but I felt confident that it wasn't a practice I wanted to invest a lot of time in.

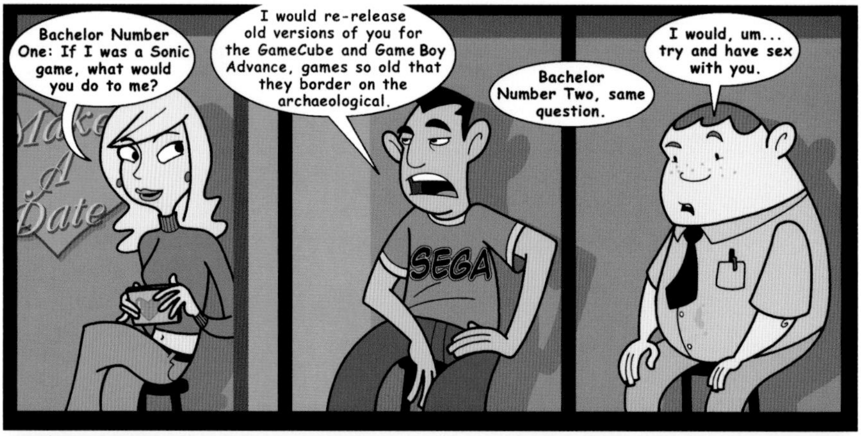
Bachelor Number One: If I was a Sonic game, what would you do to me?
Make A Date
I would re-release old versions of you for the GameCube and Game Boy Advance, games so old that they border on the archaeological.
SEGA
Bachelor Number Two, same question.
I would, um... try and have sex with you.

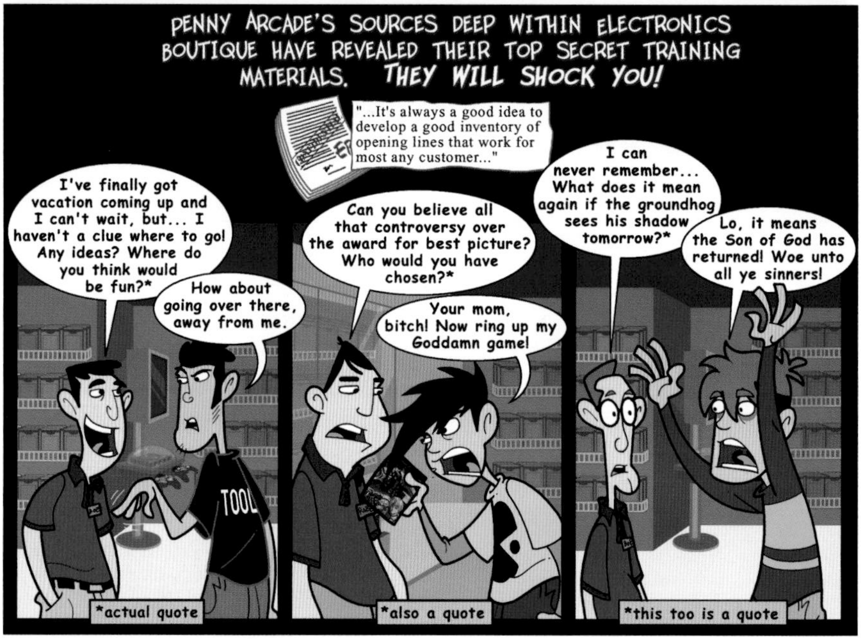
PENNY ARCADE'S SOURCES DEEP WITHIN ELECTRONICS BOUTIQUE HAVE REVEALED THEIR TOP SECRET TRAINING MATERIALS. THEY WILL SHOCK YOU!
"...It's always a good idea to develop a good inventory of opening lines that work for most any customer..."
I've finally got vacation coming up and I can't wait, but... I haven't a clue where to go! Any ideas? Where do you think would be fun?*
How about going over there, away from me.
TOOL
*actual quote
Can you believe all that controversy over the award for best picture? Who would you have chosen?*
Your mom, bitch! Now ring up my Goddamn game!
*also a quote
I can never remember... What does it mean again if the groundhog sees his shadow tomorrow?*
Lo, it means the Son of God has returned! Woe unto all ye sinners!
*this too is a quote

SOME KIND OF SHOW

February 3, 2003 As I have said on numerous occasions, the Sega we remember isn't really with us these days. The guys we have now are the ones grinding their brands into the earth and releasing toxic waste like Sonic Riders. Sega as a pure *publisher* is starting to make some interesting moves though, approaching Obsidian and Gearbox and letting them play in the classic Alien franchise, but that's two examples in a bucking, storm-tossed sea of bullshit.

EXPOSÉ!

February 5, 2003 These are not quality materials, no, and they don't inspire loyalty. But giving damning corporate materials to young men and women who aren't paid enough to *care* is a bad idea. This all happened (at the time of this writing) more than four years ago, and it *still* got circulation throughout the entire community. Nowadays, assuming you did not see it immediately on one of the *five* gaming blogs you read, it'd probably pop up via RSS on your mobile device, or via the LCD matrix implanted in your *palm*.

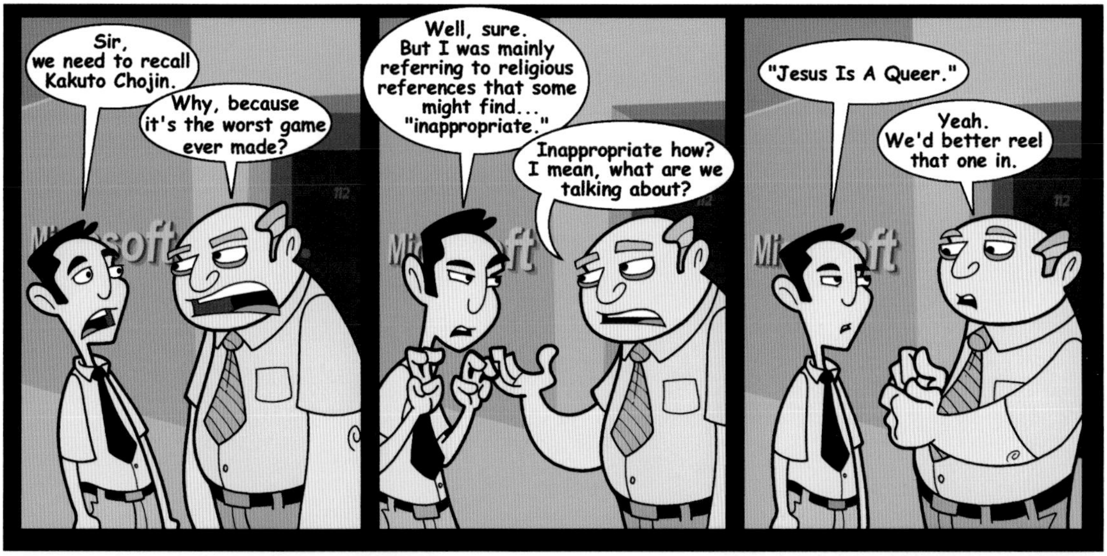
Sir, we need to recall Kakuto Chojin.
Why, because it's the worst game ever made?
Microsoft
Well, sure. But I was mainly referring to religious references that some might find... "inappropriate."
Inappropriate how? I mean, what are we talking about?
"Jesus Is A Queer."
Yeah. We'd better reel that one in.

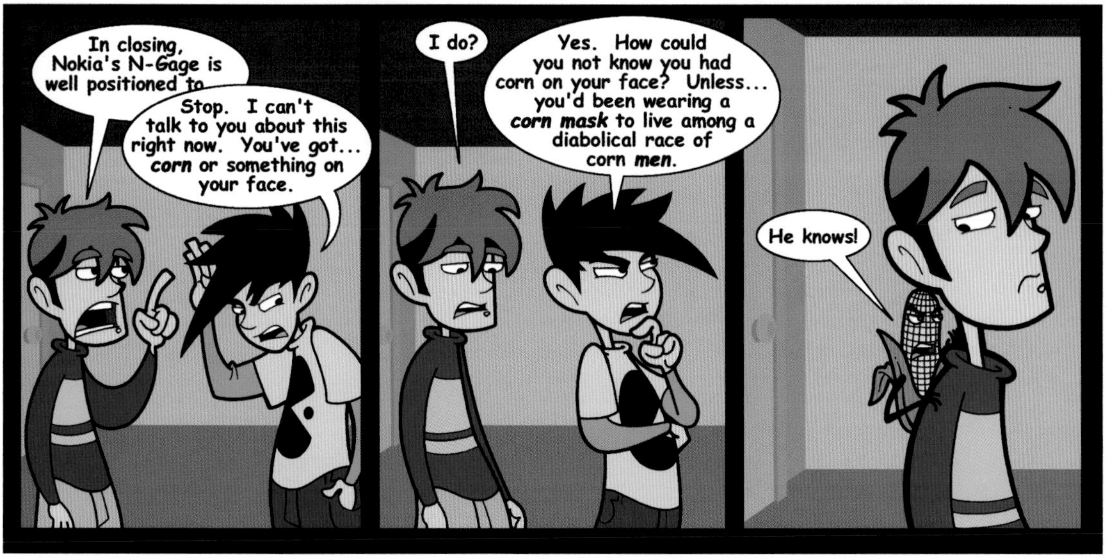
In closing, Nokia's N-Gage is well positioned to
Stop. I can't talk to you about this right now. You've got... *corn* or something on your face.
I do?
Yes. How could you not know you had corn on your face? Unless... you'd been wearing a *corn mask* to live among a diabolical race of corn *men*.
He knows!

KAKUTO CHOJIN IS SATAN'S CHILD

February 7, 2003 The "offensive religious material" apparently included a Muslim call to prayer, which . . . I don't know. It seems like that would be a good thing. Like if you put in Kakuto Chojin (presumably by accident!) and then you heard this call to prayer, maybe you'd be like, "Oh, I guess it's time to pray now."

"STALK" AS A DOUBLE ENTENDRE

February 10, 2003 Oh, N-Gage! I don't think the idea of a phone dedicated to gaming is all that weird, and once they altered the hardware so that you didn't have to *shut off your phone* every time you wanted to switch games, they were starting to get it. The emphasis on 3D games early on wasn't a great move—eventually, these were not the focus. In fact, there were even a handful of really fun strategy games that were unique to the system. Unfortunately, they learned all these things too late.

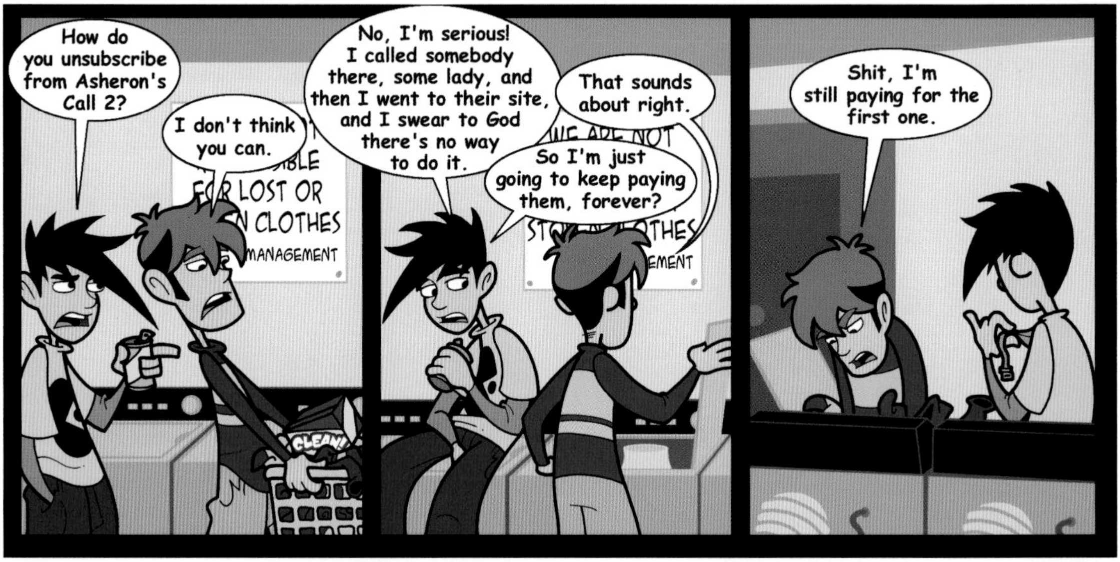
How do you unsubscribe from Asheron's Call 2?
I don't think you can.
No, I'm serious! I called somebody there, some lady, and then I went to their site, and I swear to God there's no way to do it.
That sounds about right.
So I'm just going to keep paying them, forever?
CLEAN!
Shit, I'm still paying for the first one.

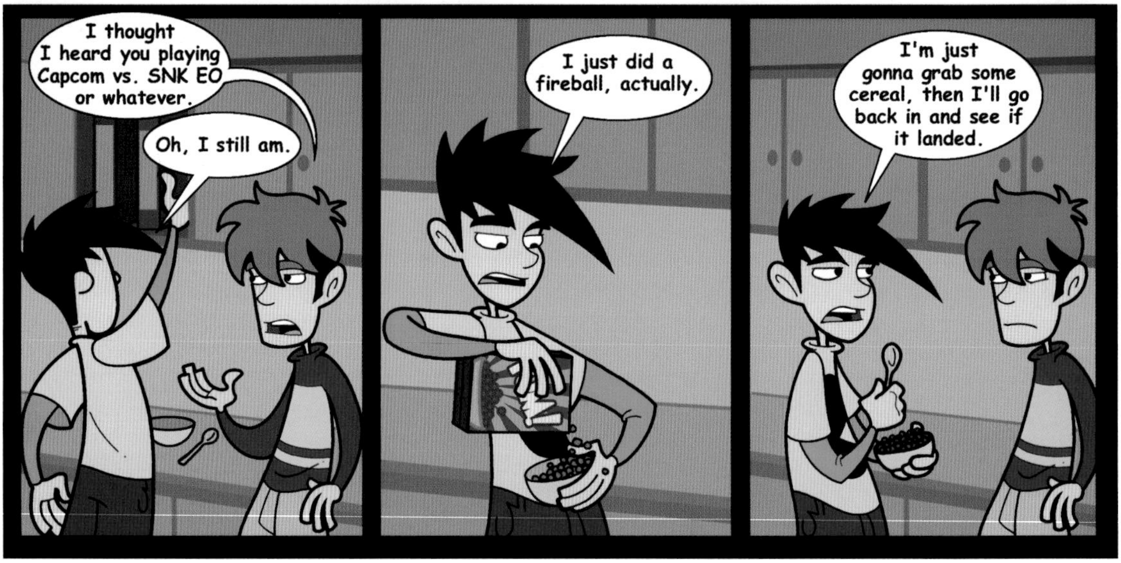
I thought I heard you playing Capcom vs. SNK EO or whatever.
Oh, I still am.
I just did a fireball, actually.
I'm just gonna grab some cereal, then I'll go back in and see if it landed.

CRESCENT FRESH

February 12, 2003 Asheron's Call 2 was the first of the really big-name MMOs to go under, so when the simulated universe ceased to exist, his subscription was probably canceled by default. You know. *Probably.*

WELCOME BACK TO EXAGGERATION THEATRE

February 14, 2003 I've heard people say that it depends on the connection, or that one must pause briefly before beginning the match, or that somehow *constellations* are involved, but I've never seen an online match in any Capcom fighter run respectably. None of the strange message board rituals I have heard extolled have made the slightest bit of difference. No latency gods have ever been appeased by my *burnt offerings*.

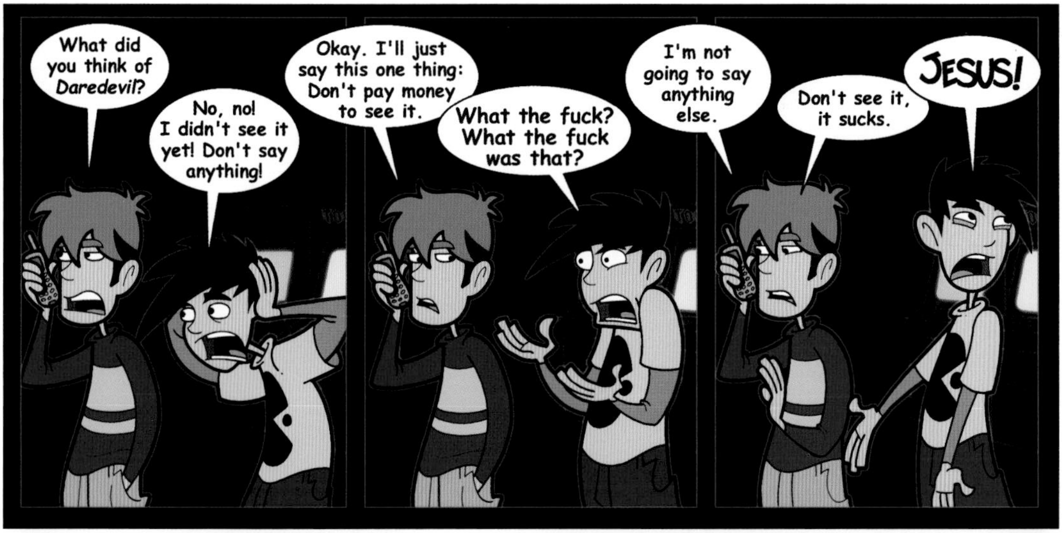
What did you think of *Daredevil*?
No, no! I didn't see it yet! Don't say anything!
Okay. I'll just say this one thing: Don't pay money to see it.
What the fuck? What the fuck was that?
I'm not going to say anything else.
Don't see it, it sucks.
JESUS!

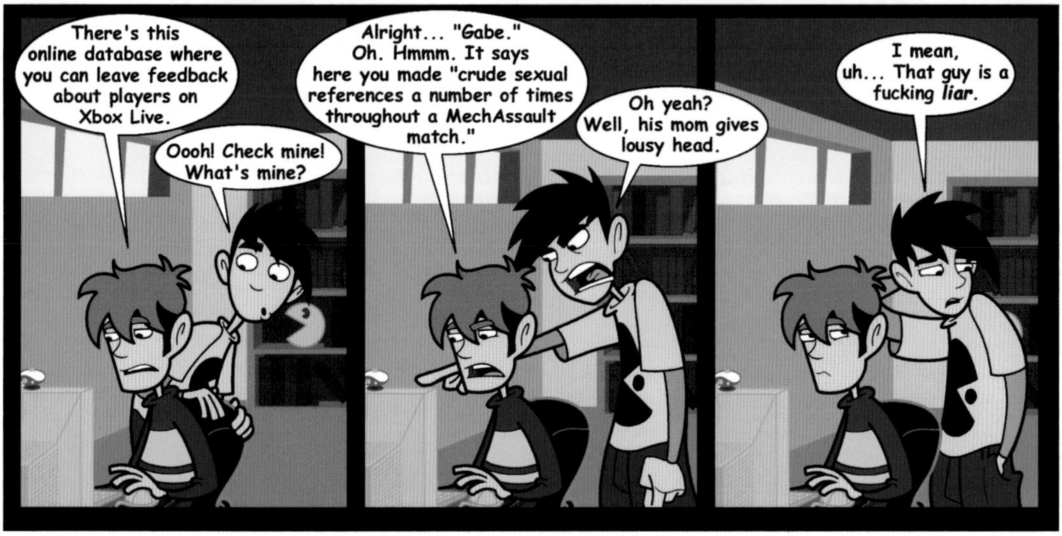
There's this online database where you can leave feedback about players on Xbox Live.
Oooh! Check mine! What's mine?
Alright... "Gabe." Oh. Hmmm. It says here you made "crude sexual references a number of times throughout a MechAssault match."
Oh yeah? Well, his mom gives lousy head.
I mean, uh... That guy is a fucking *liar*.

THPOILERTH

February 17, 2003 I was sort of just messing with Gabe in this strip, because at the time we both (basically) liked the film. I was on a plane a few months after this strip went up, and I was mildly excited to see that *Daredevil* was playing on my flight. Let me tell you that the movie did not sit well the second time around. The flight was relatively smooth, but I still had an opportunity to make use of the *motion discomfort bag*.

THE REAL GABRIEL

February 19, 2003 I would love to say that this was a completely fictional scenario, but it wasn't. There were a couple of sites like this—places that tried to build a sense of community—back when the built-in tools weren't as robust. In any event, he'd made a name for himself online with his creative (and occasionally insightful) verbal javelins. It may be that I am just used to the way he plays, but competition does tend to bring out The Other Gabe—the swingin', two-fisted son of a bitch that his opponents have come to know.

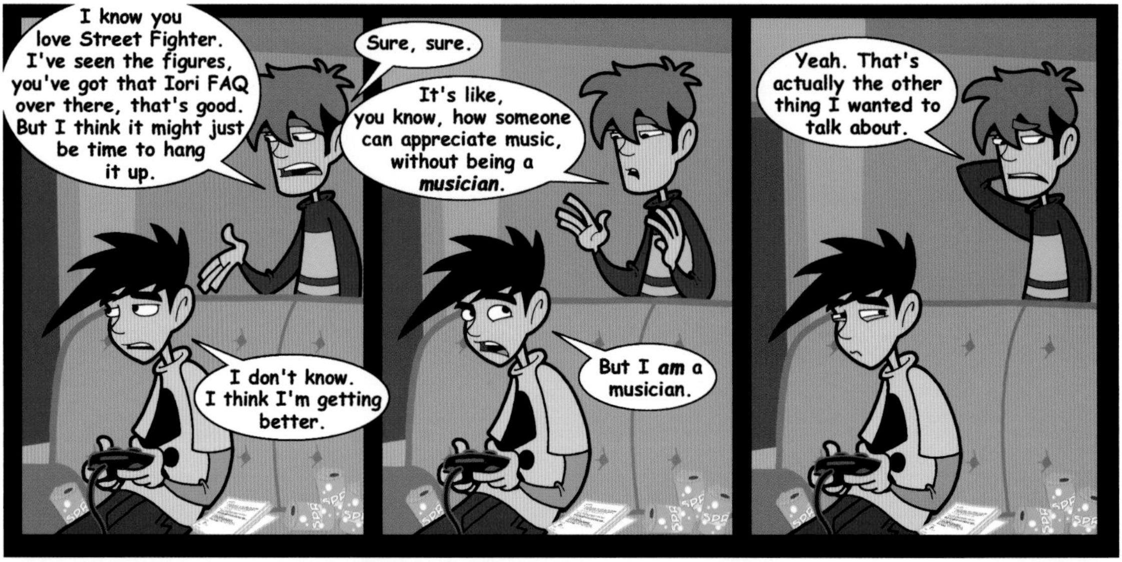
I know you love Street Fighter. I've seen the figures, you've got that Iori FAQ over there, that's good. But I think it might just be time to hang it up.
I don't know. I think I'm getting better.
Sure, sure.
It's like, you know, how someone can appreciate music, without being a *musician*.
But I *am* a musician.
Yeah. That's actually the other thing I wanted to talk about.

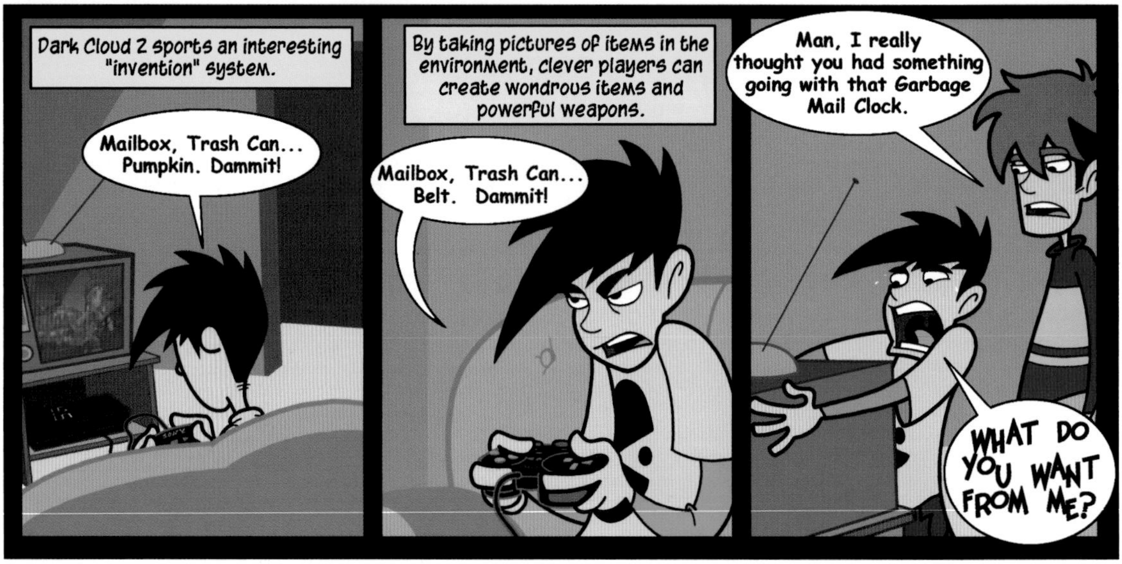
Dark Cloud 2 sports an interesting "invention" system.
Mailbox, Trash Can... Pumpkin. Dammit!
By taking pictures of items in the environment, clever players can create wondrous items and powerful weapons.
Mailbox, Trash Can... Belt. Dammit!
Man, I really thought you had something going with that Garbage Mail Clock.
WHAT DO YOU WANT FROM ME?

HE IS WHAT WE CALL HOPELESS

February 21, 2003 I do it sometimes, but it's rare for the most part—printing out one of those huge online FAQs and banging on the controller until I've mastered some rare maneuver. I usually approach games in a more organic fashion, *accruing* mastery rather than explicitly building it, which may be why I keep getting my ass kicked.

THE MOTHER OF NECESSITY

February 24, 2003 My problem with systems like this camera-based invention thing is that they quickly become the entire focus of a game for me. If I had gotten into this game as deeply as he did—and I may well have, if I hadn't been moving when it came out—you may be sure that I would *still* be coaxing Garbage and Clock into a more intimate union.

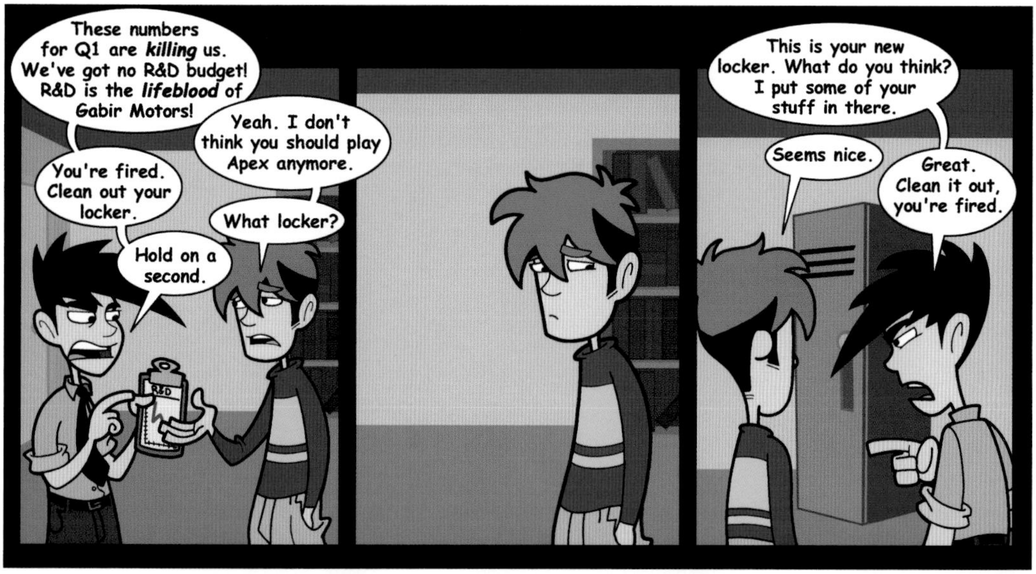
These numbers for Q1 are *killing* us. We've got no R&D budget! R&D is the *lifeblood* of Gabir Motors!
Yeah. I don't think you should play Apex anymore.
You're fired. Clean out your locker.
What locker?
Hold on a second.
R&D
This is your new locker. What do you think? I put some of your stuff in there.
Seems nice.
Great. Clean it out, you're fired.

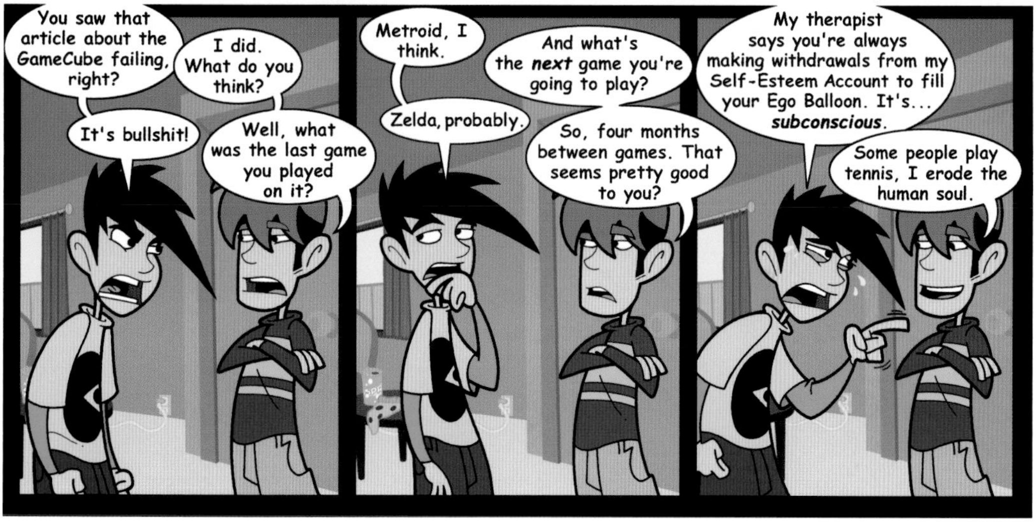
You saw that article about the GameCube failing, right?
I did. What do you think?
It's bullshit!
Well, what was the last game you played on it?
Metroid, I think.
And what's the *next* game you're going to play?
Zelda, probably.
So, four months between games. That seems pretty good to you?
My therapist says you're always making withdrawals from my Self-Esteem Account to fill your Ego Balloon. It's... *subconscious*.
Some people play tennis, I erode the human soul.

THE NAME OF THE STRIP

February 26, 2003 Apex was pretty tough to find, but if you managed to come across it there was something interesting there, which even the middling reviews had to admit. A driving game with some sort of adventure/management bits bolted on, you could choose what cars your newly formed "company" would develop, and their performance in races would lead to greater sales, which were then plowed back into the company . . . I'd love to see the concept revisited.

THE PREDICAMENT

February 28, 2003 And here we are again, with the Wii. I'd love to see it kindle the true enthusiast and the new player alike, as its sibling the DS has done, but whether or not that will ever happen is the sort of thing no man can know. I bought the system knowing full well that many of its brightest moments were going to be first-party titles resulting from patient internal development. I'd just love to see this weird little machine (and the bold ideas behind it) flourish.

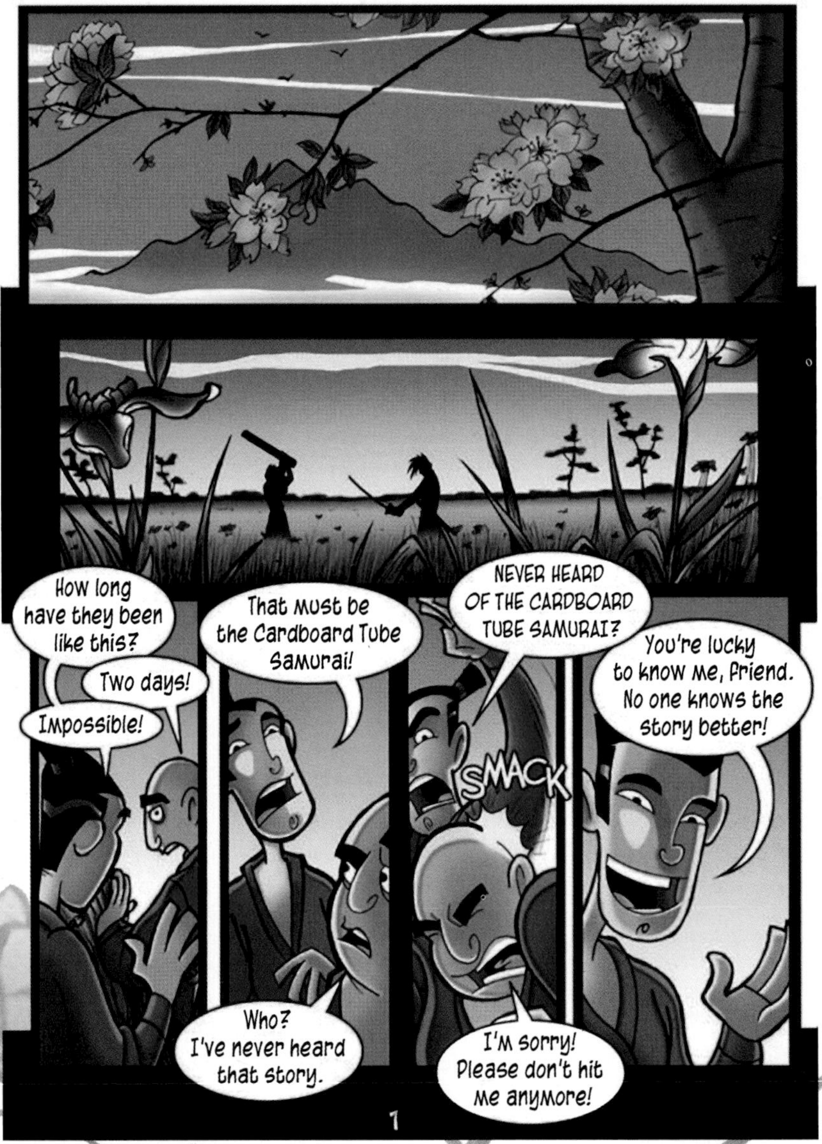
How long have they been like this?
Two days!
Impossible!
That must be the Cardboard Tube Samurai!
Who? I've never heard that story.
NEVER HEARD OF THE CARDBOARD TUBE SAMURAI?
SMACK
I'm sorry! Please don't hit me anymore!
You're lucky to know me, friend. No one knows the story better!
7

CARDBOARD AND STEEL

March 3–14, 2003 The deeper you and I get into this year, the more strange materials we find. Look at this, now . . . On *Penny Arcade*, an online comic where one expects to find three-panel excursions into electronic gaming culture, people were presented with six page-long episodes of some kind of mock samurai epic. Nowadays, the tone and narrative of the Cardboard Tube Samurai's stories are both deadly serious. This one has some slapstick silliness, though, and literally involves a stolen *pig*.

These days, we try not to push him on readers more than once a year—we know how far out of our charter things like this are. We like making comics for a living, and we recognize that you are the ones who let us do so.

But I look forward to those strips all year.

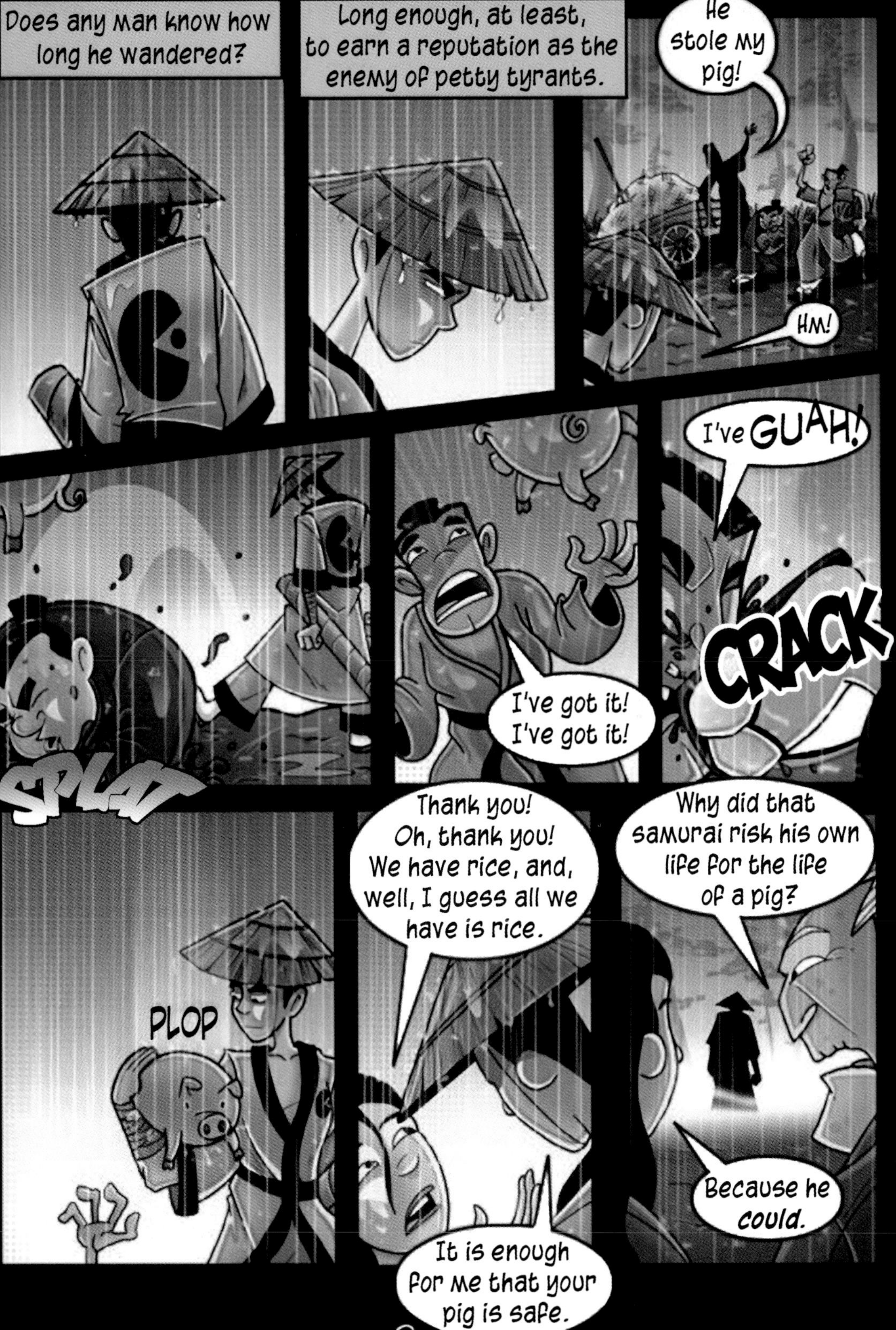
Does any man know how long he wandered?
Long enough, at least, to earn a reputation as the enemy of petty tyrants.
He stole my pig!
HM!
SPLAT
I've got it! I've got it!
I've GUAH!
CRACK
PLOP
Thank you! Oh, thank you! We have rice, and, well, I guess all we have is rice.
It is enough for me that your pig is safe.
Why did that samurai risk his own life for the life of a pig?
Because he could.

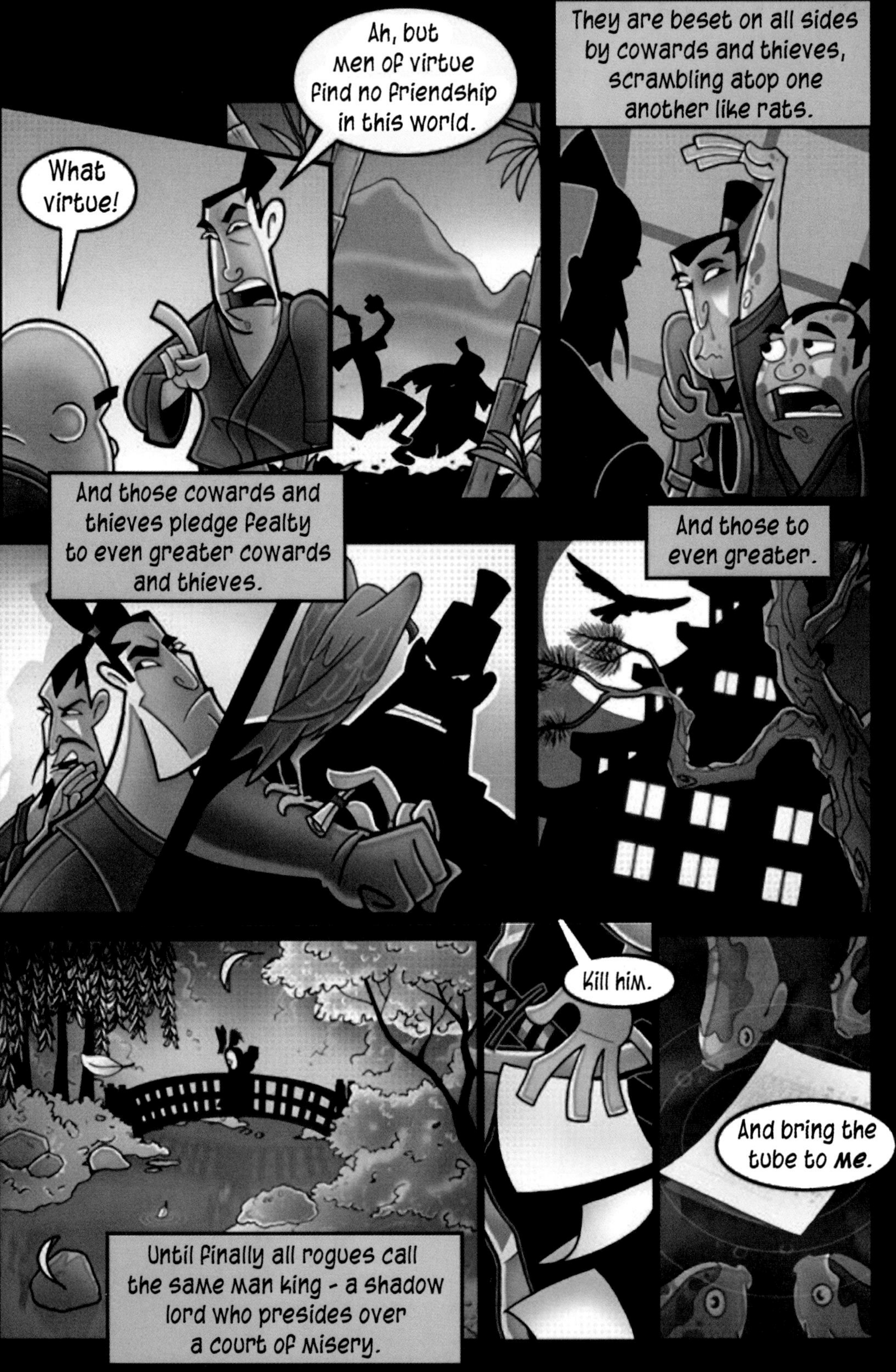
What virtue!
Ah, but men of virtue find no friendship in this world.
They are beset on all sides by cowards and thieves, scrambling atop one another like rats.
And those cowards and thieves pledge fealty to even greater cowards and thieves.
And those to even greater.
Until finally all rogues call the same man king - a shadow lord who presides over a court of misery.
Kill him.
And bring the tube to *me*.

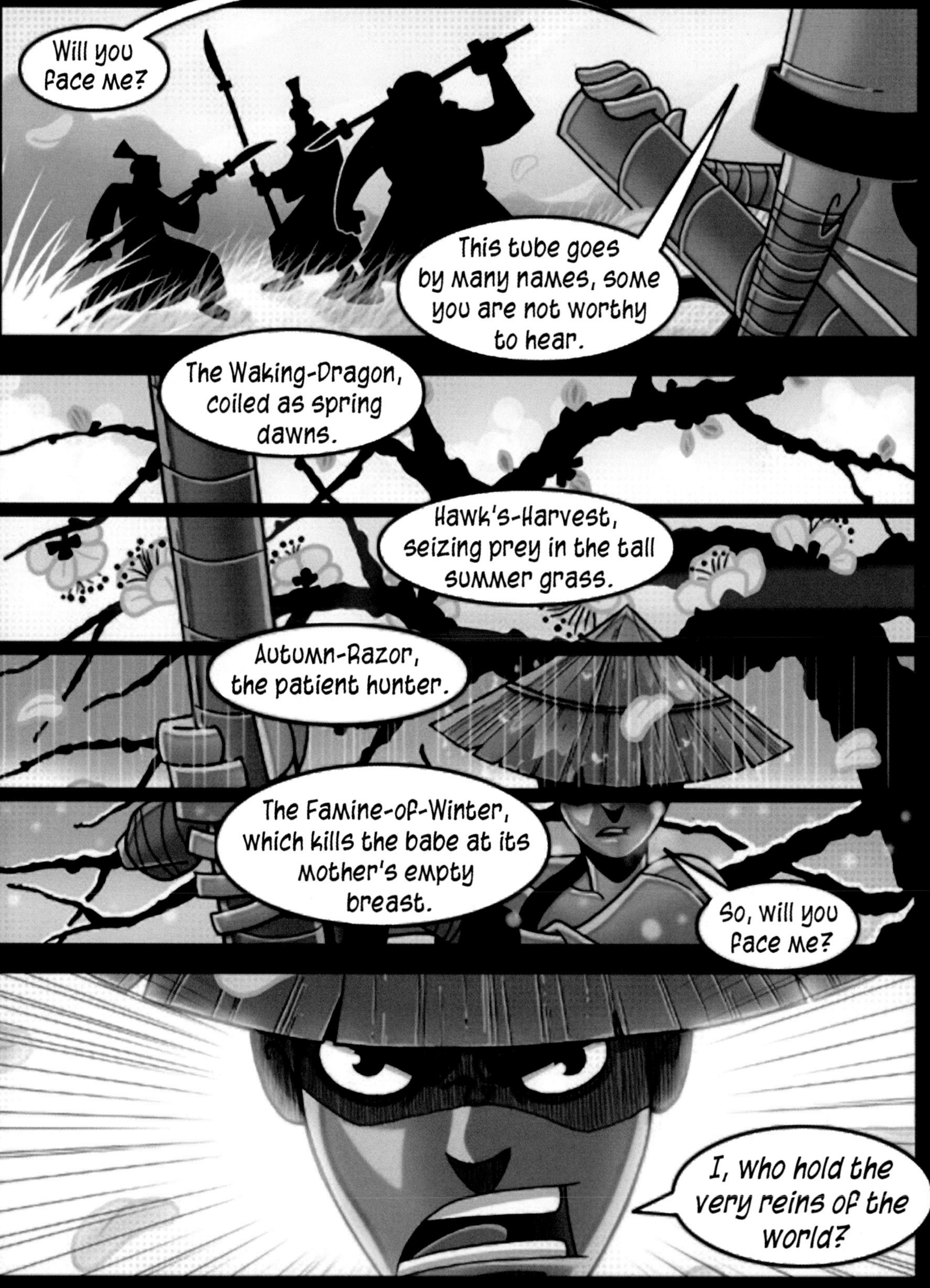
Will you face me?
This tube goes by many names, some you are not worthy to hear.
The Waking-Dragon, coiled as spring dawns.
Hawk's-Harvest, seizing prey in the tall summer grass.
Autumn-Razor, the patient hunter.
The Famine-of-Winter, which kills the babe at its mother's empty breast.
So, will you face me?
I, who hold the very reins of the world?

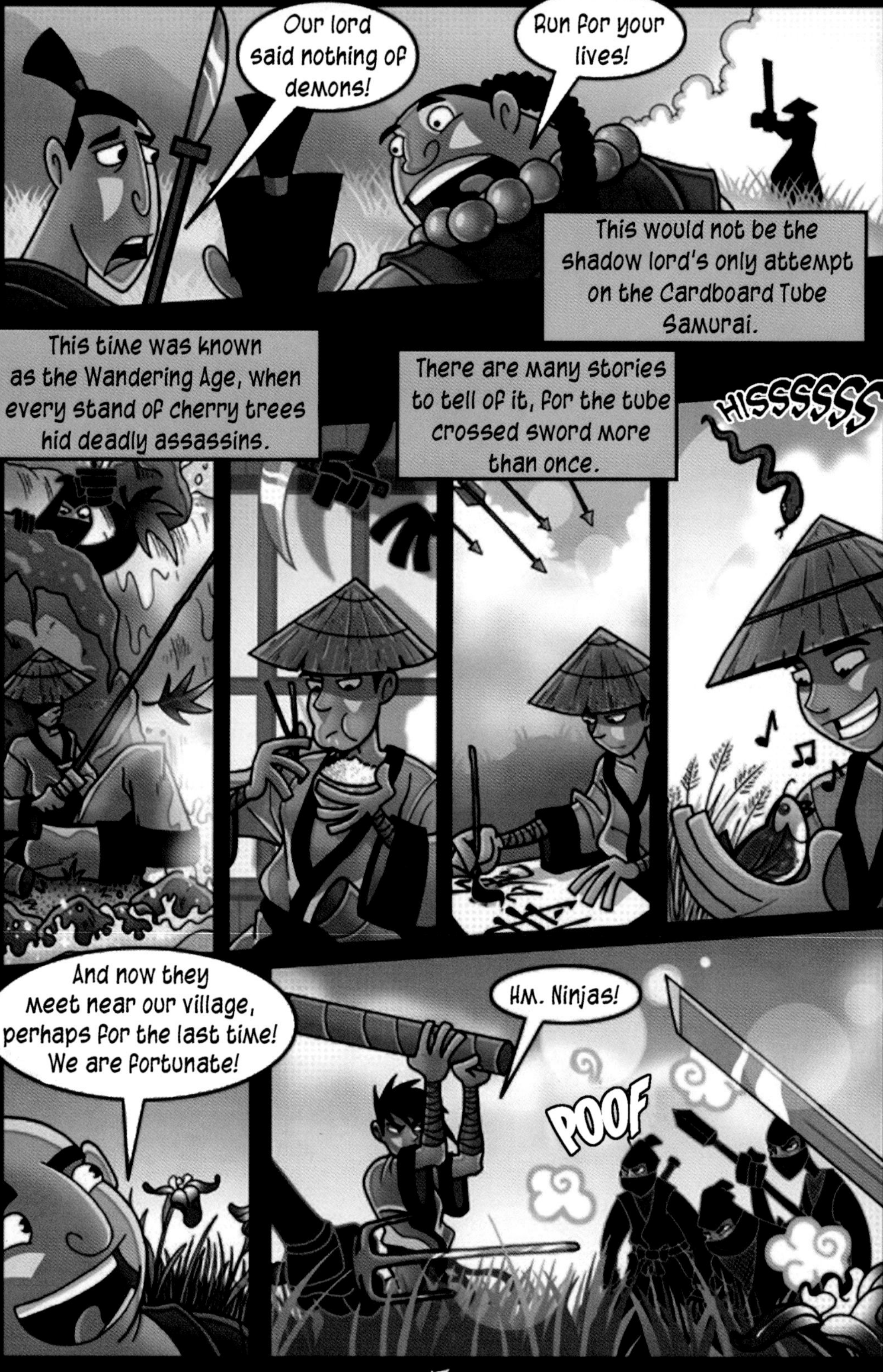
Our lord said nothing of demons!
Run for your lives!
This would not be the shadow lord's only attempt on the Cardboard Tube Samurai.
This time was known as the Wandering Age, when every stand of cherry trees hid deadly assassins.
There are many stories to tell of it, for the tube crossed sword more than once.
HISSSSSS
And now they meet near our village, perhaps for the last time! We are fortunate!
HM. Ninjas!
POOF

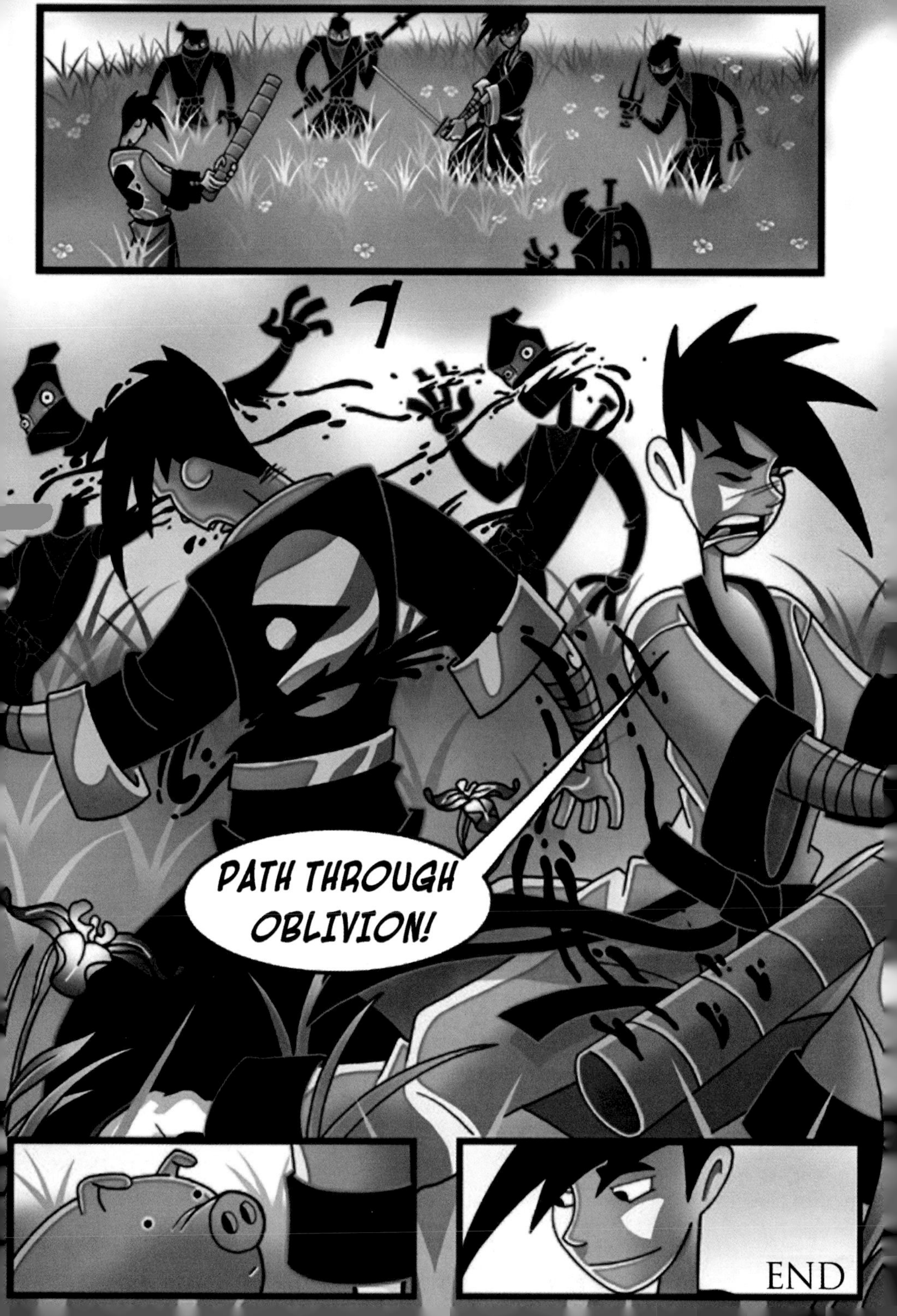
PATH THROUGH OBLIVION!
END

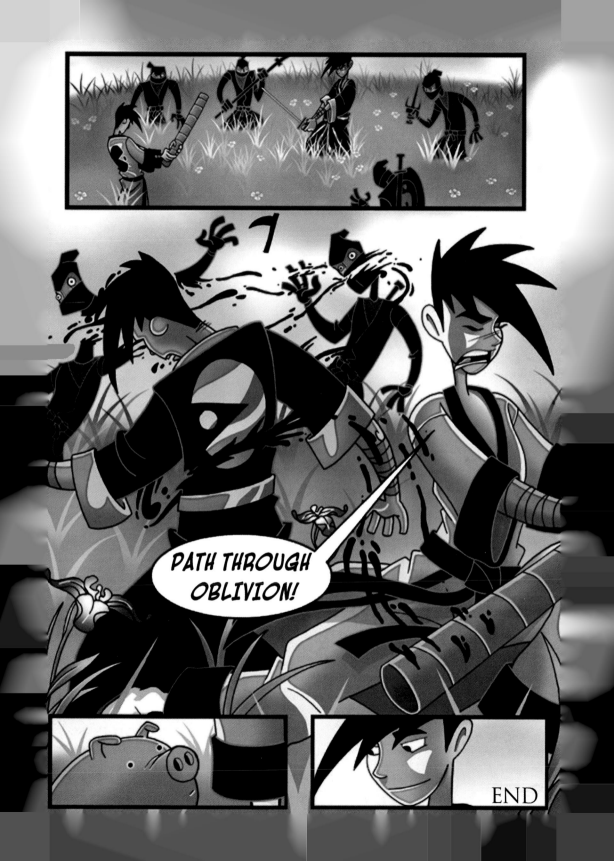

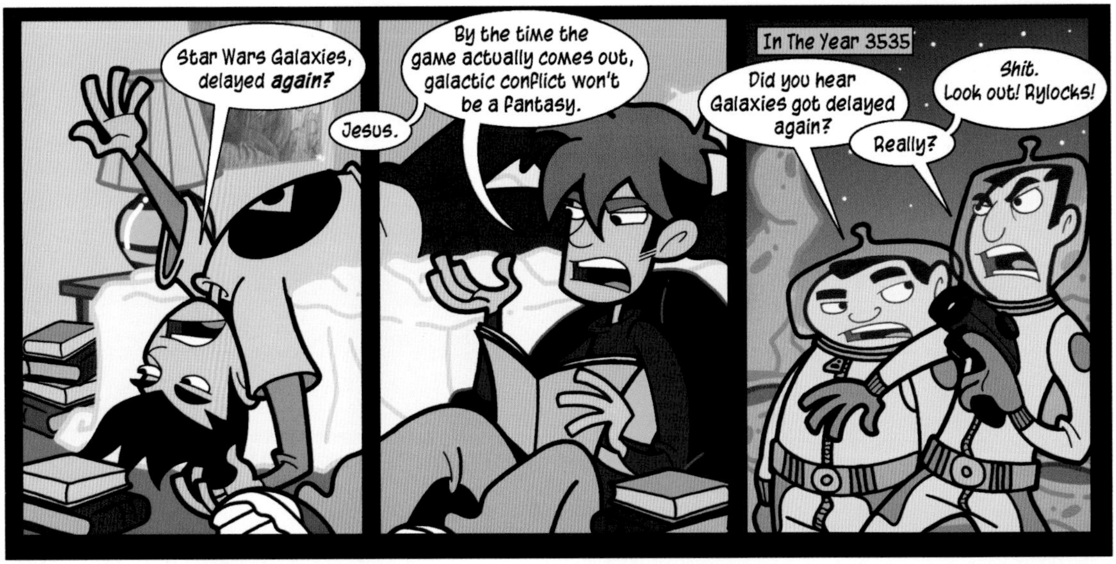
Star Wars Galaxies, delayed *again?*
By the time the game actually comes out, galactic conflict won't be a fantasy.
Jesus.
In The Year 3535
Did you hear Galaxies got delayed again?
Really?
Shit. Look out! Rylocks!

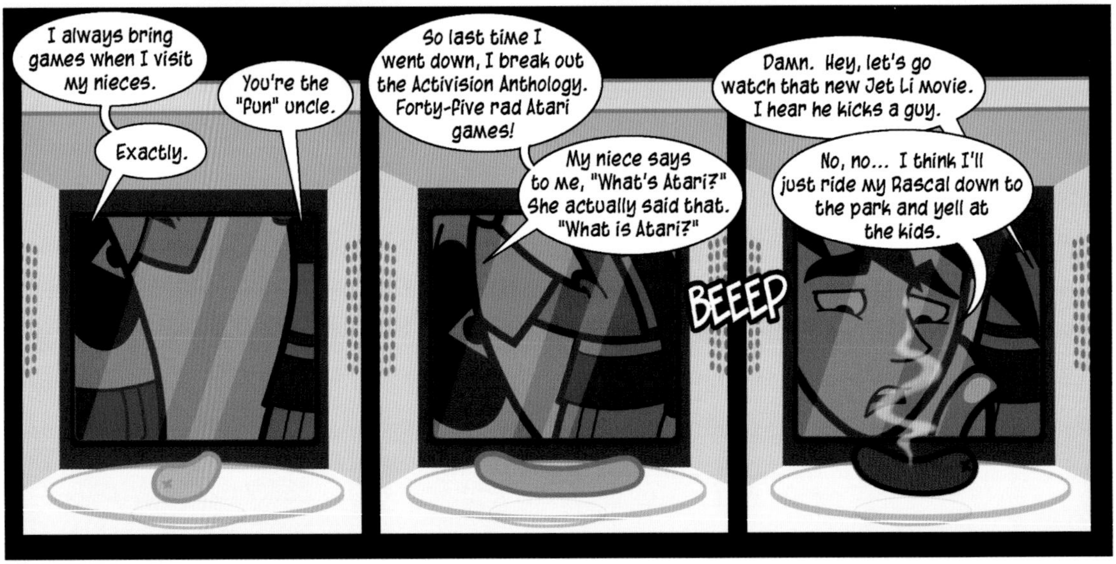
I always bring games when I visit my nieces.
You're the "fun" uncle.
Exactly.
So last time I went down, I break out the Activision Anthology. Forty-five rad Atari games!
My niece says to me, "What's Atari?" She actually said that. "What is Atari?"
BEEEP
Damn. Hey, let's go watch that new Jet Li movie. I hear he kicks a guy.
No, no... I think I'll just ride my Rascal down to the park and yell at the kids.

A GENUINE APPRAISAL

March 17, 2003 It's been such a long time since I cared about Galaxies that I had forgotten just how completely we were seized by the idea of an MMO set in the Star Wars universe. It's been redesigned from the ground up something like three times now, so apparently it wasn't delayed long *enough*.

FRANKLY

March 18, 2003 There are people who read *Penny Arcade* whose first system was the Playstation. The *Sony* Playstation, not some other, older type of Playstation. I'm not saying that to impugn their gaming credentials or anything—I'm simply saying that we are Goddamn *old*. Gabe's first system had woodgrain on it if that tells you anything, and my first system was the Odyssey[2]—a machine that was delivered to retail in 1978. Now if you'll excuse me, I need to crawl back into my sarcophagus and regenerate.

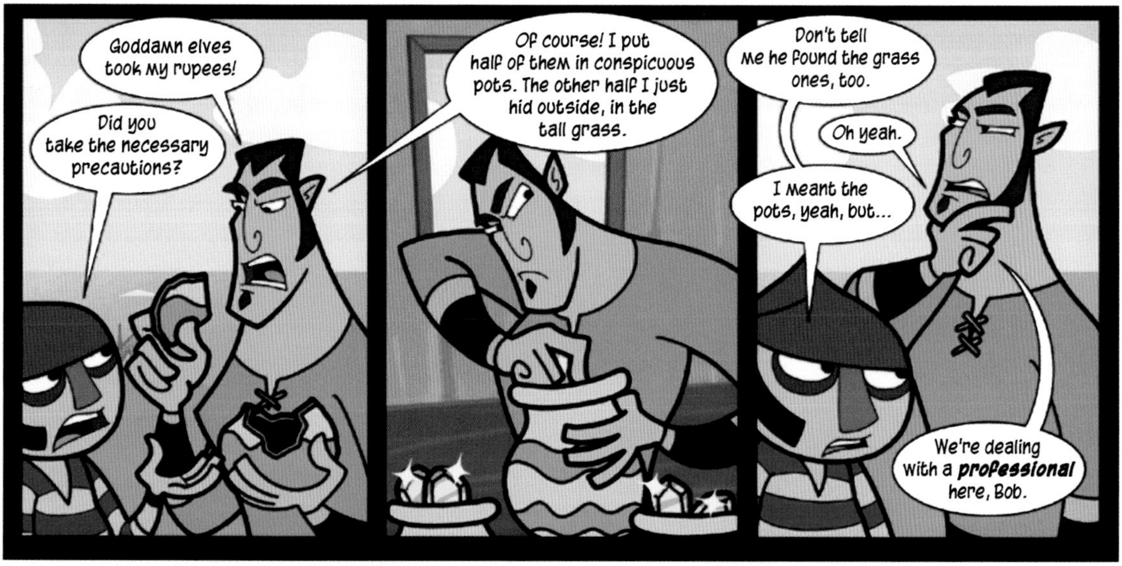
Goddamn elves took my rupees!
Did you take the necessary precautions?
Of course! I put half of them in conspicuous pots. The other half I just hid outside, in the tall grass.
Don't tell me he found the grass ones, too.
Oh yeah.
I meant the pots, yeah, but...
We're dealing with a professional here, Bob.

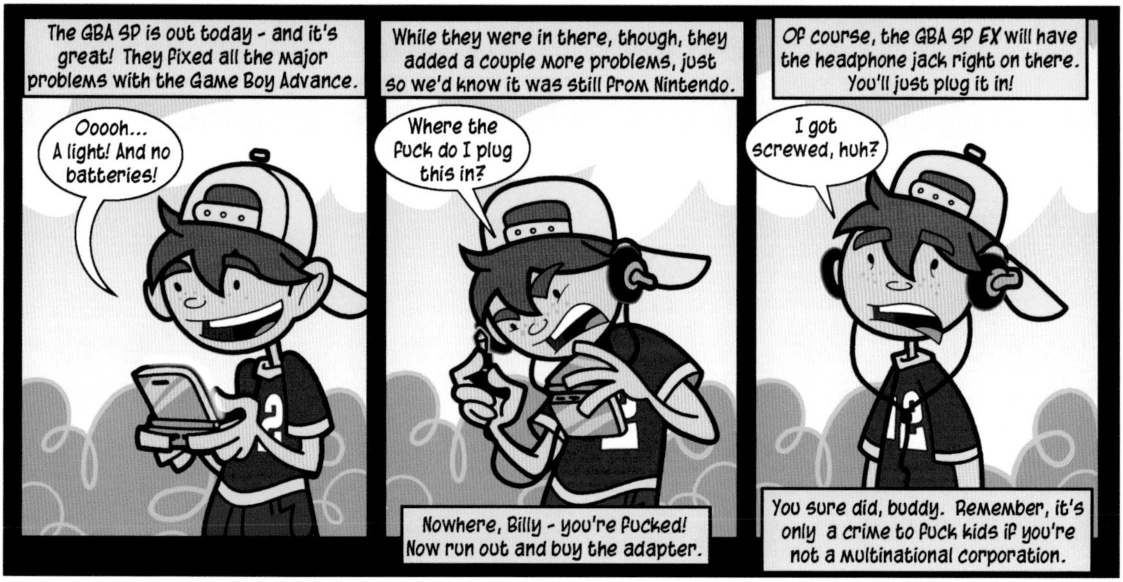
The GBA SP is out today - and it's great! They fixed all the major problems with the Game Boy Advance.
Ooooh... A light! And no batteries!
While they were in there, though, they added a couple more problems, just so we'd know it was still from Nintendo.
Where the fuck do I plug this in?
Nowhere, Billy - you're fucked! Now run out and buy the adapter.
Of course, the GBA SP EX will have the headphone jack right on there. You'll just plug it in!
I got screwed, huh?
You sure did, buddy. Remember, it's only a crime to fuck kids if you're not a multinational corporation.

WHY ELVES GOTS TO BE LIKE THAT

March 21, 2003 I recognize that, by now, poor money management is just a Zelda *thing*—many games and many years having made it a tradition. But you would imagine that, after many years of these abuses, the locals would begin to tire of elven bullshit, and would start protecting their rupee hoards with *crude traps* or looking into the premiums on elf insurance.

:(

March 24, 2003 The headphone jack was quite an omission, but even without it we got a lot of use out of this version of the hardware. We traveled to conventions sometimes, a couple per year, and we were never without that equipment. Our friend Porkfry dragged his everywhere, like a beloved stuffed animal—he'd pull it out between rounds of Battlefield and simply drift away.

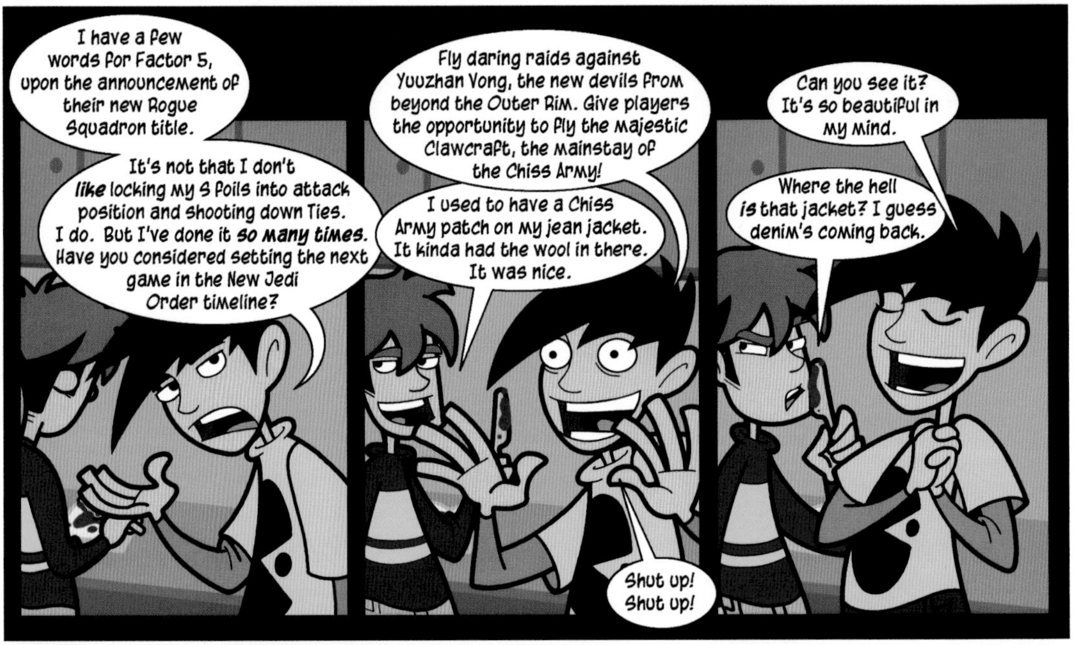
I have a few words for Factor 5, upon the announcement of their new Rogue Squadron title.
It's not that I don't *like* locking my S foils into attack position and shooting down Ties. I do. But I've done it **so many times.** Have you considered setting the next game in the New Jedi Order timeline?
Fly daring raids against Yuuzhan Vong, the new devils from beyond the Outer Rim. Give players the opportunity to fly the majestic Clawcraft, the mainstay of the Chiss Army!
I used to have a Chiss Army patch on my jean jacket. It kinda had the wool in there. It was nice.
Shut up! Shut up!
Can you see it? It's so beautiful in my mind.
Where the hell *is* that jacket? I guess denim's coming back.

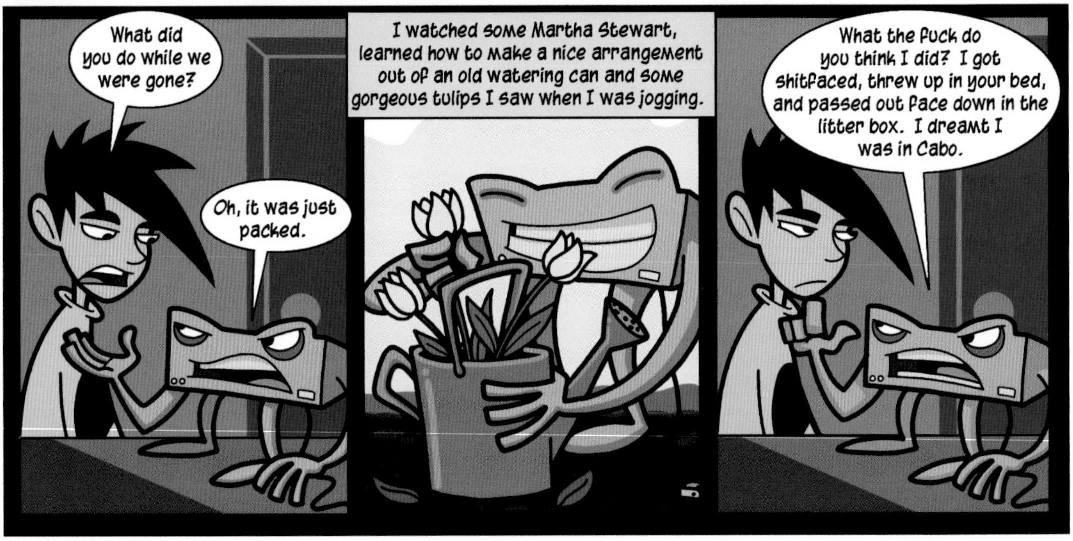
What did you do while we were gone?
Oh, it was just packed.
I watched some Martha Stewart, learned how to make a nice arrangement out of an old watering can and some gorgeous tulips I saw when I was jogging.
What the fuck do you think I did? I got shitfaced, threw up in your bed, and passed out face down in the litter box. I dreamt I was in Cabo.

DEAR FACTOR 5

March 26, 2003 I think it's fair to say that Factor 5 got sick of it too, after a while—after cutting their ties with LucasArts, you didn't hear much from them. Then, when the PS3 launch started to heat up, we got wind of Lair. Now, instead of flying a *spaceship* around and shooting stuff, you're flying *a dragon* around and shooting stuff. I assume you still travel to Hoth at some point.

LOVELY

April 2, 2003 I don't actually know where or even what a Cabo is, but Gabriel assured me that it was (in some way) sand related. It sounds sort of marsupial, doesn't it? Yes. I can picture an adult Cabo gazing out from a tree, while an adorable Cablet peeks out from the bulging pouch.

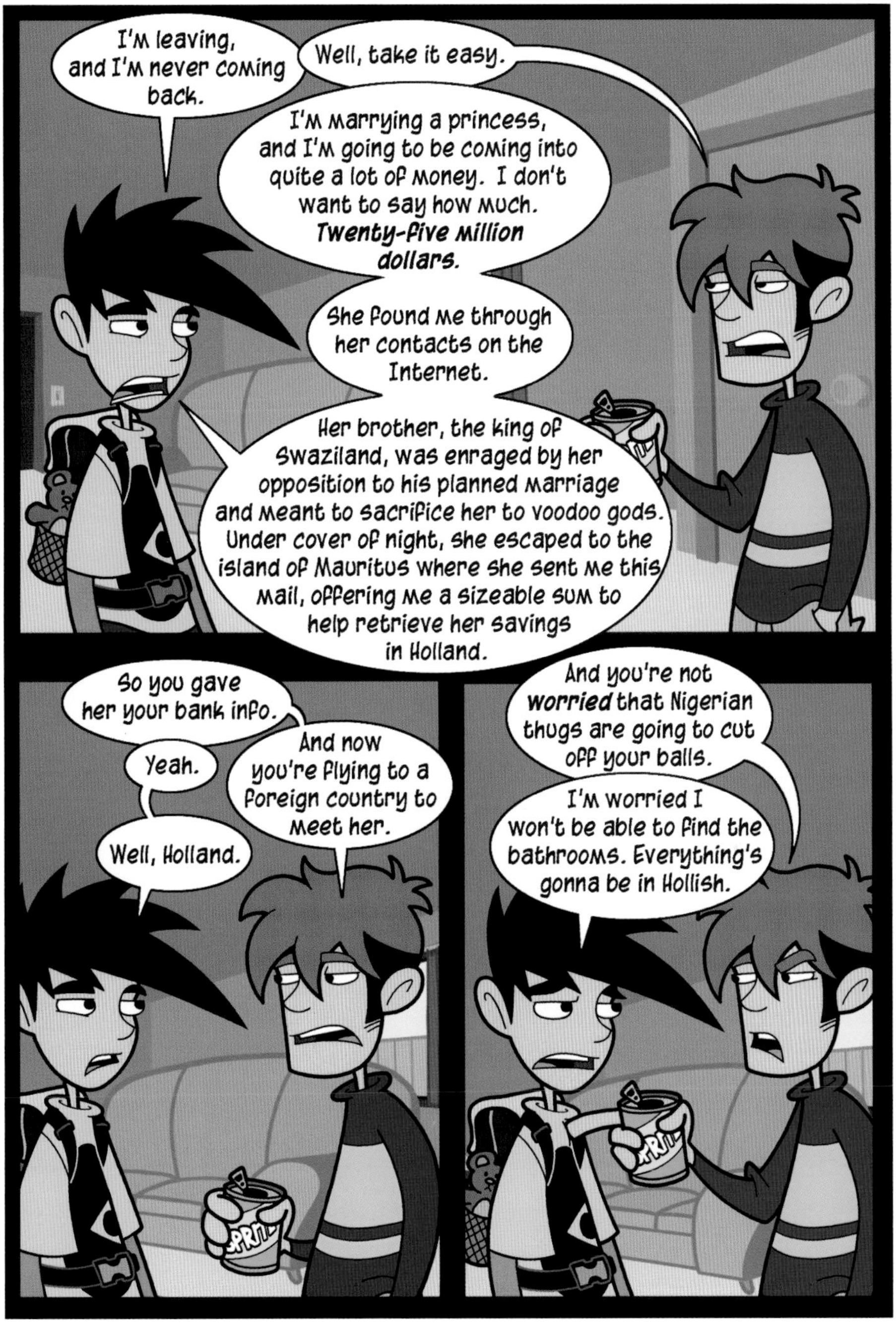
I'm leaving, and I'm never coming back.
Well, take it easy.
I'm marrying a princess, and I'm going to be coming into quite a lot of money. I don't want to say how much. **Twenty-five million dollars.**
She found me through her contacts on the Internet.
Her brother, the king of Swaziland, was enraged by her opposition to his planned marriage and meant to sacrifice her to voodoo gods. Under cover of night, she escaped to the island of Mauritus where she sent me this mail, offering me a sizeable sum to help retrieve her savings in Holland.
So you gave her your bank info.
Yeah.
Well, Holland.
And now you're flying to a foreign country to meet her.
And you're not ***worried*** that Nigerian thugs are going to cut off your balls.
I'm worried I won't be able to find the bathrooms. Everything's gonna be in Hollish.

I'M SURE IT WILL BE FINE

March 28, 2003 The "Tycho" account at Penny Arcade has been around since '99 or so, making it one of the most ancient e-mail addresses on Earth. It is (either as a natural result of the passing of time or thanks to active treachery on the part of my enemies) currently subscribed to every mailing list in existence, including (and this is a treat!) several in Afrikaans. It receives almost two hundred e-mails, daily, from Nigeria *alone*.

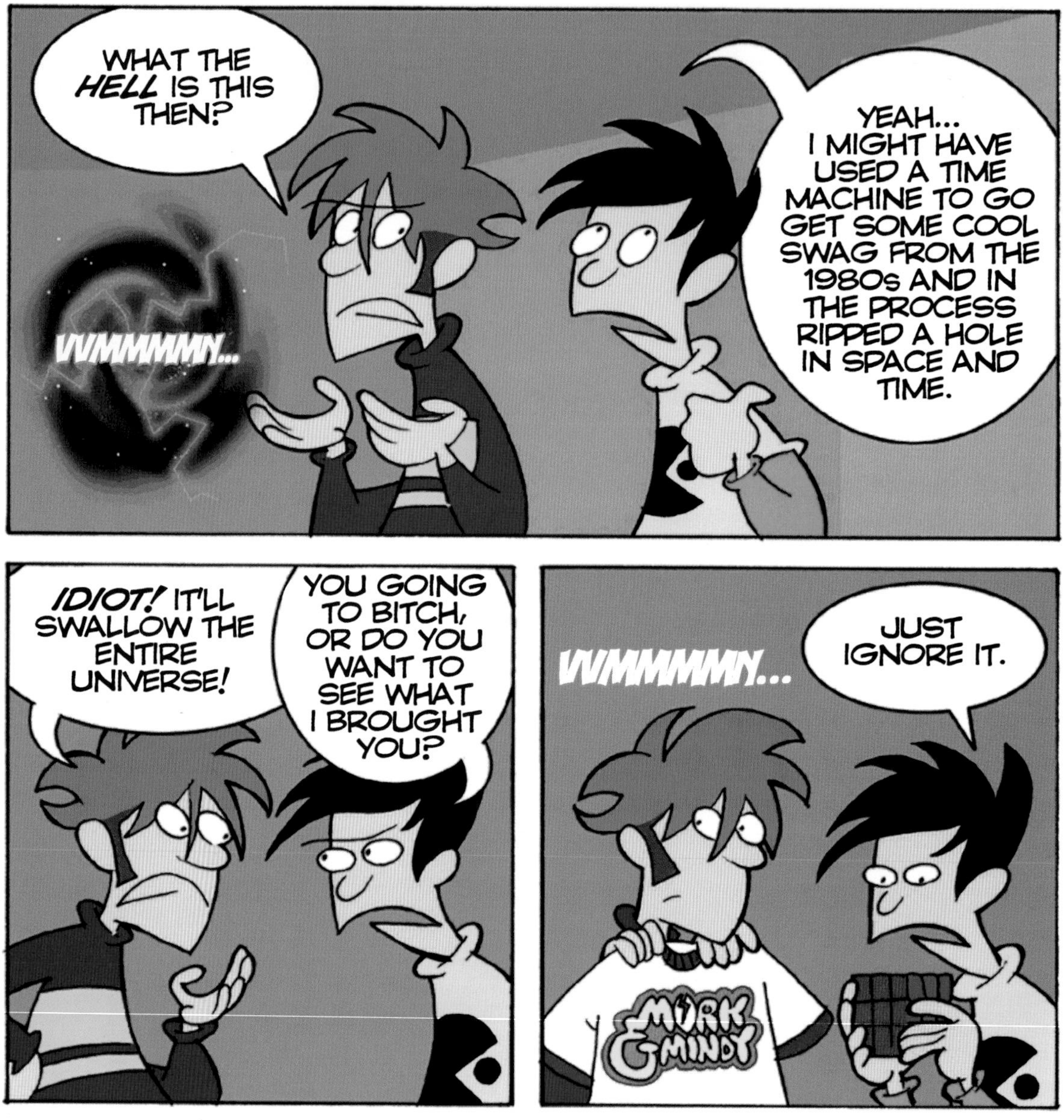
WHAT THE *HELL* IS THIS THEN?
YEAH... I MIGHT HAVE USED A TIME MACHINE TO GO GET SOME COOL SWAG FROM THE 1980s AND IN THE PROCESS RIPPED A HOLE IN SPACE AND TIME.
VVMMMMN...
IDIOT! IT'LL SWALLOW THE ENTIRE UNIVERSE!
YOU GOING TO BITCH, OR DO YOU WANT TO SEE WHAT I BROUGHT YOU?
VVMMMMMN...
JUST IGNORE IT.
MORK & MINDY

THANK YOU, SCOTT

March 31, 2003 I believe I might have referred to Scott Kurtz as either a) Steve Kuntz, which is *not* his name, or b) a "slime-encrusted human nightmare," in our first book. He is neither, though there are often times when we must enter into ritual combat to resolve a grievance. He is still the only other entity we have allowed to upload strips to our server, a powerful responsibility he has managed with aplomb. Here is the second of those two.

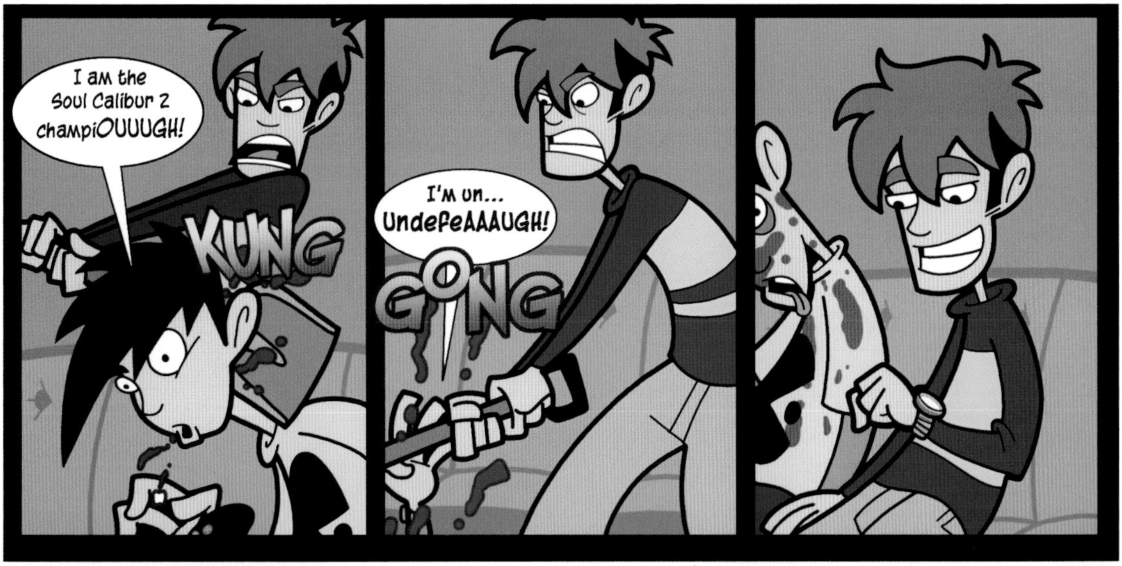
I am the Soul Calibur 2 champiOUUUGH!
KUNG
I'm un... undefeAAAUGH!
GONG

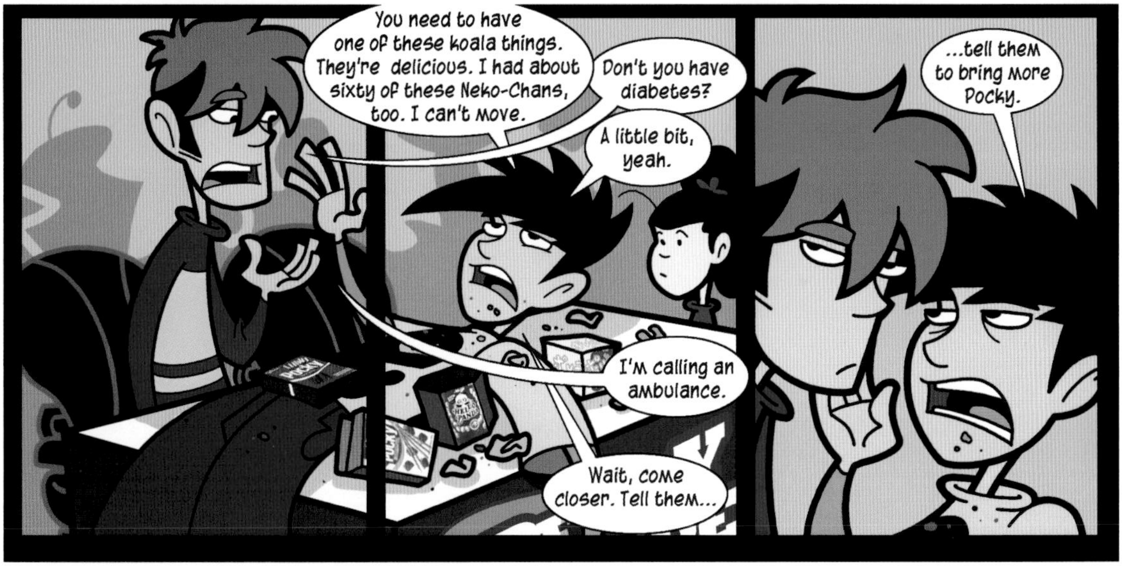
You need to have one of these koala things. They're delicious. I had about sixty of these Neko-Chans, too. I can't move.
Don't you have diabetes?
A little bit, yeah.
I'm calling an ambulance.
Wait, come closer. Tell them...
...tell them to bring more Pocky.

FAN FAVORITES, VOL. 2

April 4, 2003 Ah yes, the *watch*. We often use "Gabe" and "Tycho" to tell a story, even if the events we're talking about happened to other people. The Soul Calibur rivalry between Robert and Gabriel is the sort of thing that, in another age, would have been immortalized as an opera—and we wanted to capture it. Lost rounds often ended in—and I am not making this up—*choking*.

HELLO PANDA

April 7, 2003 When we were setting up our booth for SakuraCon, the family setting up shop next to us had a bored little girl who Kara, Gabe, Robert, and I basically adopted. This was a long time ago. We see them every year now, often several times a year—they've even come by the office to help with our Feng Shui, which I guess is actually pronounced *Foong Soy*.

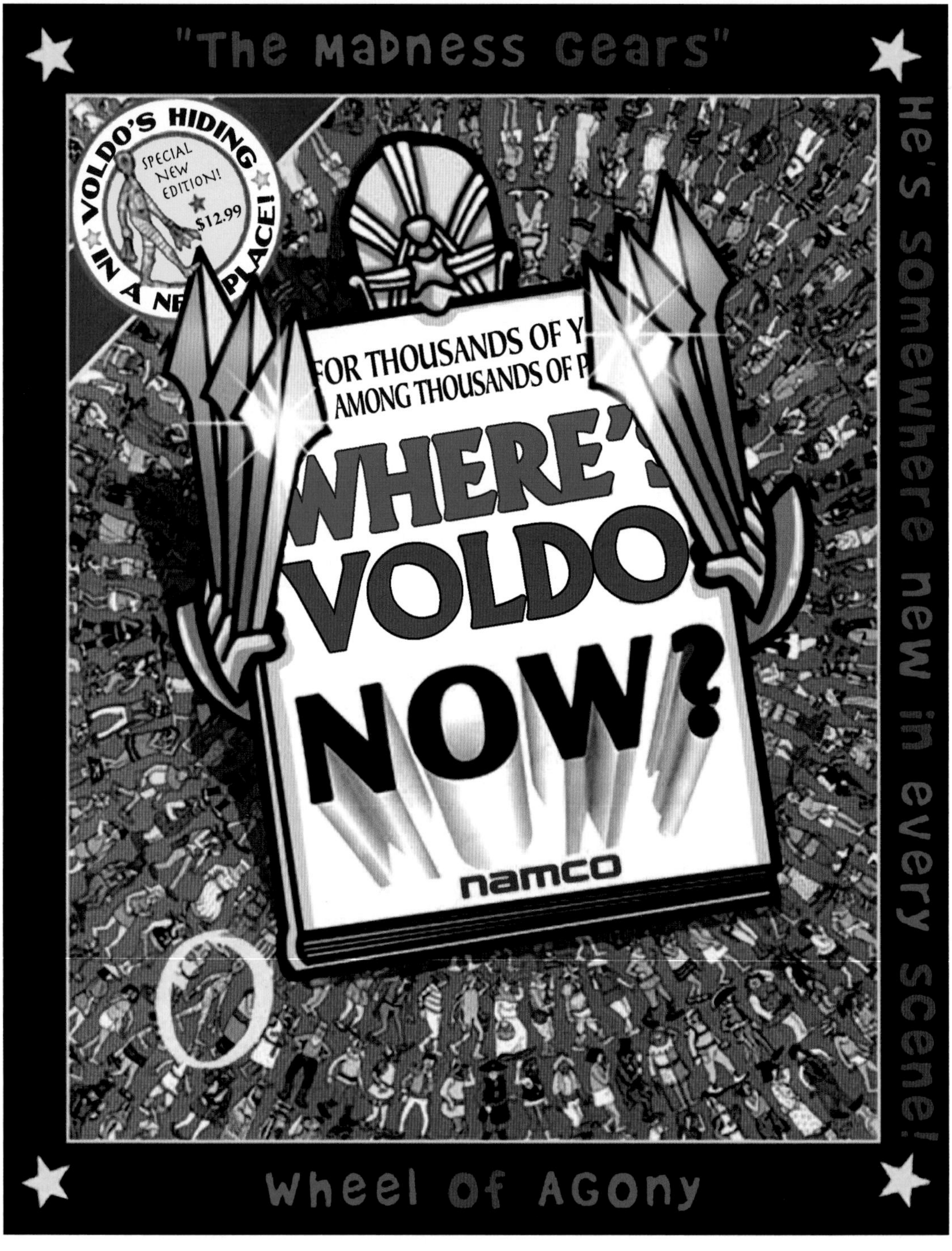
"The MaDness Gears"
He's somewhere new in every scene!
VOLDO'S HIDING IN A NEW PLACE!
SPECIAL NEW EDITION!
$12.99
FOR THOUSANDS OF Y
AMONG THOUSANDS OF P
WHERE'S VOLDO NOW?
namco
Wheel of AGOny

OH, THERE HE IS

April 9, 2003 I don't know. There's those *Where's Waldo* books, and we'd been playing a lot of Soul Calibur, and there's a guy in Soul Calibur whose name *sounds* like Voldo . . . We are but men! Every day can't be Christmas!

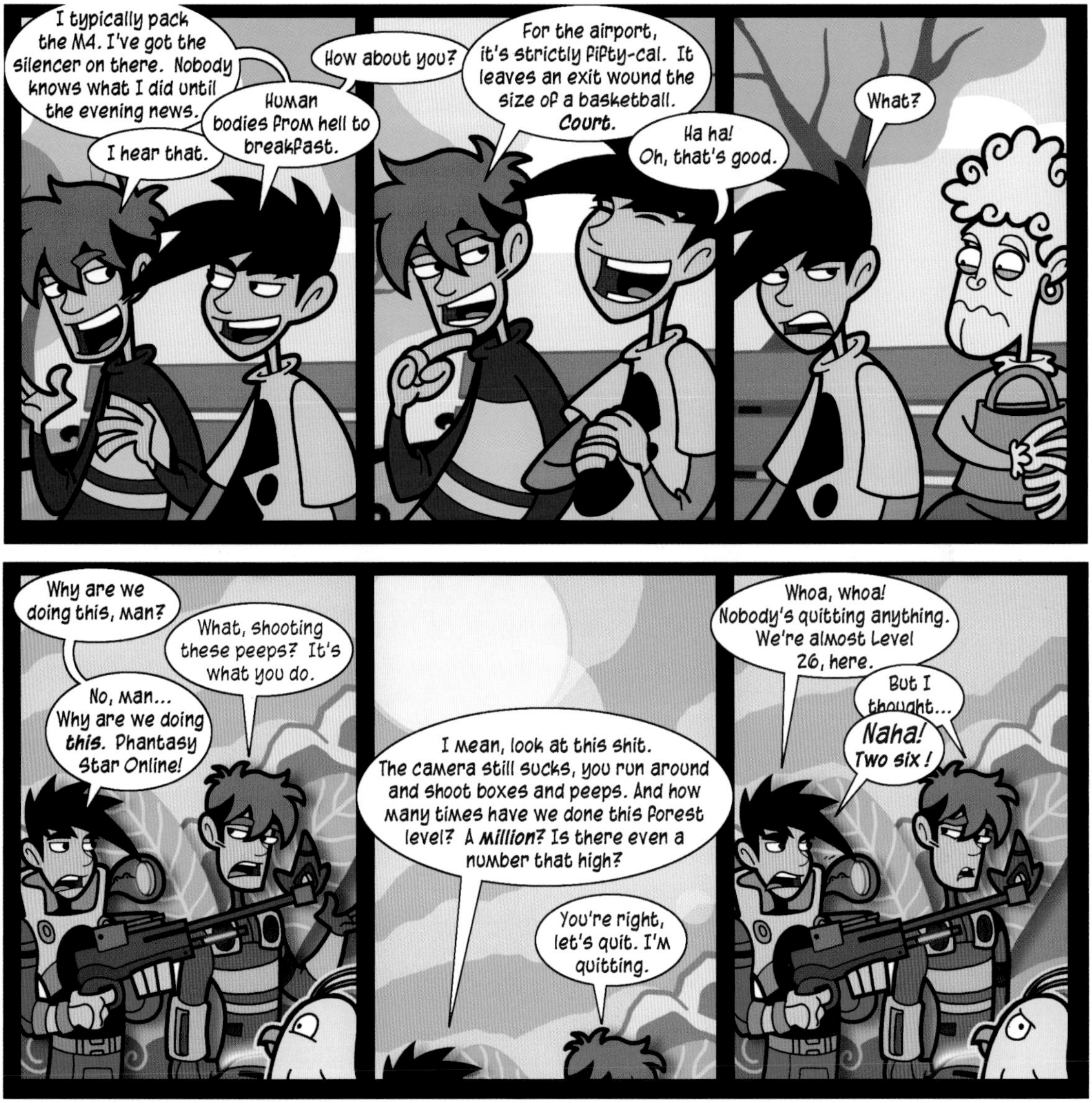
I typically pack the M4. I've got the silencer on there. Nobody knows what I did until the evening news.
I hear that.
Human bodies from hell to breakfast.
How about you?
For the airport, it's strictly fifty-cal. It leaves an exit wound the size of a basketball. Court.
Ha ha! Oh, that's good.
What?
Why are we doing this, man?
What, shooting these peeps? It's what you do.
No, man... Why are we doing this. Phantasy Star Online!
I mean, look at this shit. The camera still sucks, you run around and shoot boxes and peeps. And how many times have we done this forest level? A million? Is there even a number that high?
You're right, let's quit. I'm quitting.
Whoa, whoa! Nobody's quitting anything. We're almost Level 26, here.
But I thought...
Naha! Two six!

HAS THIS EVER HAPPENED TO YOO

April 11, 2003 This just happened again, I mean, like *last week*, only we were eating teriyaki and the people listening to us were four cops. Once we noticed our audience, we began to talk about how much we like to *pet dogs* and how ice cream is, in fact, *so good*.

SECOND VERSE, SAME AS THE FIRST

April 16, 2003 You know, in all those years playing the first Phantasy Star Online I always (ahem) "phantasized" about what the sequel would be like. Now it's out, and I've never even touched it. The Sega moniker these days always makes me a little uneasy, and I've just never been able to stomach the idea of paying a monthly fee for an action game, even an action game where you have *stats*.

R.I.P. 4-14-2003

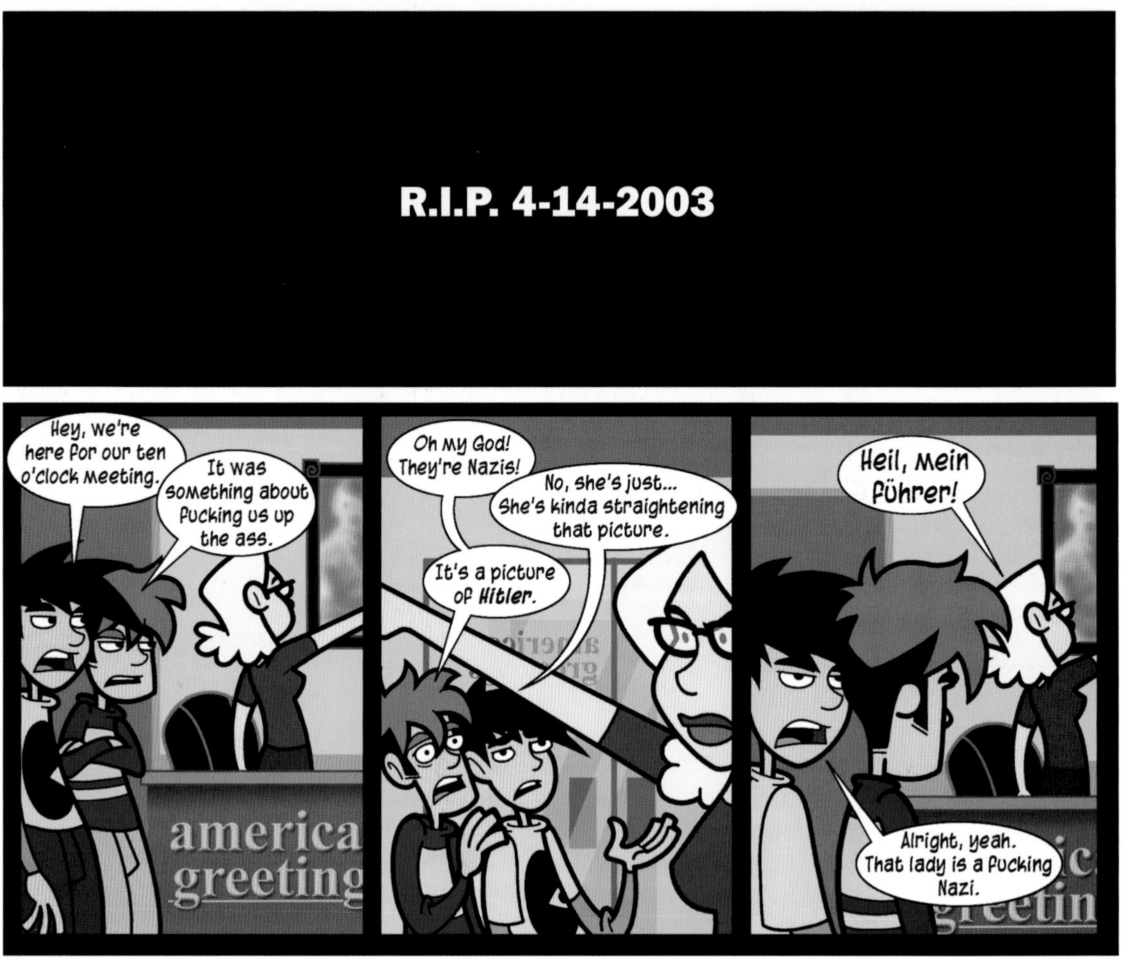
Hey, we're here for our ten o'clock meeting.
It was something about fucking us up the ass.
Oh my God! They're Nazis!
No, she's just... She's kinda straightening that picture.
It's a picture of *Hitler*.
Heil, mein Führer!
Alright, yeah. That lady is a fucking Nazi.

TART AS A DOUBLE ENTENDRE

April 14, 2003 This is the part of the book where the comic of Strawberry Shortcake in lingerie would have gone, but American Greetings isn't an especially American company, and also the greetings they sent us were just Cease and Desist letters from their lawyer. This strip isn't especially hard to find online.

READ IT BEFORE THEY TAKE LEGAL ACTION

April 27, 2003 We had gotten in trouble with our Strawberry Shortcake comic because—at least, this is what the lawyers said—we were using one group's property (Strawberry Shortcake) to make fun of another (American McGee's Alice). So we decided to go with something more direct.

I told an odd story when the Strawberry Shortcake comic was posted, not *about* the comic, just . . . I'm not sure exactly what it is about. I've always liked it, though, and I thought we may as well include it. Enjoy!

Safety Monkey has a friend named Wally, who I often refer to as Wallingford, or by his handle, Xarion. They're friends to this day because of Meridian 59, which they played years ago, and he used to visit from Wisconsin from time to time. He has no accent to speak of, except when he says "cat," which comes out like "kyat." In any event, he doesn't need to visit anymore because he lives here. This story is from when he didn't.

On a whim, he and two friends drove from Wisconsin to Seattle at a straight shot, and that seemed like something worth celebrating. If you are a young person, I recommend that you celebrate a trek like that with wholesome milk. We did not. We celebrated with liquor, which is like milk, except that it issues forth from the devil's cold teat. Being bartenders, Xarion and his cohorts crafted beverages whose names are not known to men. He even invented a drink for me, which was exceedingly vile and was constructed thusly: two shots of vodka, grenadine, and Alka Seltzer. I'm not actually sure if he likes me very much.

That was the second place we went. The first place was Sushi Chiso, where I had sea urchin. They had two kinds of sea urchin there—cheap and very expensive—and I am glad I got the cheap one because I threw up in my mouth. It tasted like a combination of sand, peanut butter, and bile, and apparently my stomach couldn't wait to start digesting it.

By the time we made it to the fourth such establishment, my friend Gone had mentioned something called a Cowboy Killer more than once. I don't have any particular interest in cowboys, but the killing seemed interesting. However, he would not discuss the specifics of it, murmuring something about red and blue pills and how I couldn't be told what the Matrix was. I was like, *whatever*. A couple of the other guys almost got into a fight over something in the *Dungeon Master's Guide*, so we were none of us feeling any pain. Yet.

Xarion's friend wanted to know if my man Nihil and I were ready to do Cowboy Killers. I had tried to go to the bathroom just before this, but a loop from my fleece jacket had gotten caught on the pinball machine. I couldn't move, and I had chalked it up to "force fields." This is the state of mind I was in when a shot of tequila, two lemon wedges, and a rubber band were placed before me.

I looked at them for a moment.

I couldn't imagine any way to combine these things that would not hurt. Bob Wisconsin (I can't remember his name) began to speak:

"Place the rubber band around your head, then squeeze the lemons into your eyes. Fumble around like a sightless kitten until you find your shot of tequila, at which point you will drink it and snap the rubber band."

Do I need to put some kind of disclaimer on here? What I was about to do is not glamorous. Please don't do this. It sucks.

As I squeezed the lemons into my eyes, new genres of pain were revealed. I reached out in agony for my liquor, which seemed distant. I ran into Nihil and nearly fell, but came up with the tequila, and did my duty by it. I felt like an Olympian, such was my dedication to this act. I snapped the rubber band, and it was like being hit with a hammer. My cruel tormentor claimed I had not snapped it with enough vigor, which seems strange to me as my mind still echoes with that blow, as the music hall recalls the strains of the master's violin. I pulled it out to nearly twice its length—I wasn't going to do this again—and it came back like a gunshot, knocking my head back and leaving a welt I would see the next day.

So do not, do *not*, under any circumstances become curious as to the nature of Cowboy Killers. They are administered by psychotic people from Wisconsin who are nourished by human suffering.

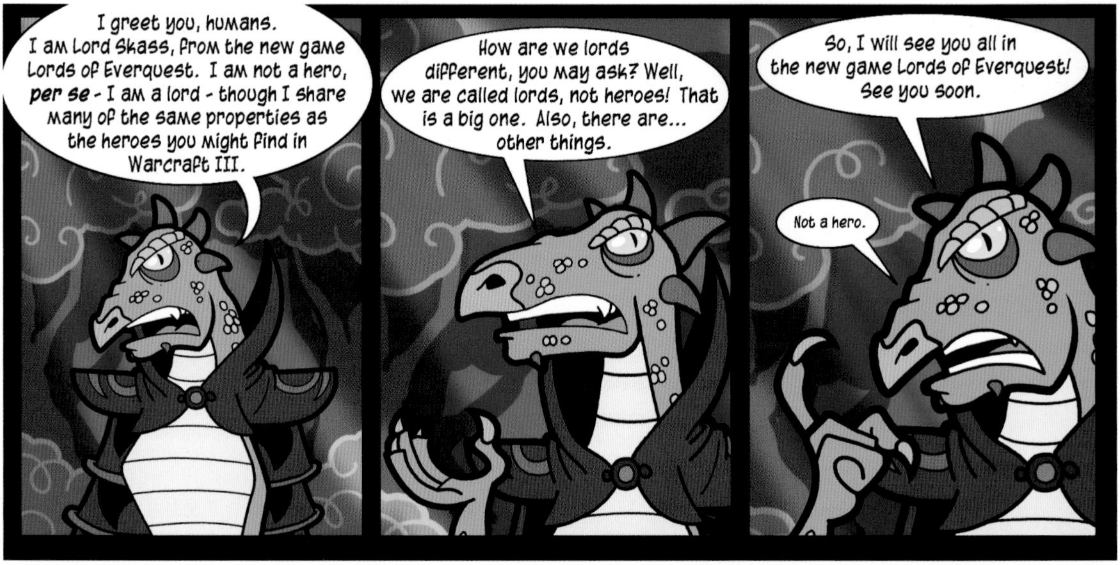
I greet you, humans. I am Lord Skass, from the new game Lords of Everquest. I am not a hero, *per se* - I am a lord - though I share many of the same properties as the heroes you might find in Warcraft III.
How are we lords different, you may ask? Well, we are called lords, not heroes! That is a big one. Also, there are... other things.
So, I will see you all in the new game Lords of Everquest! See you soon.
Not a hero.

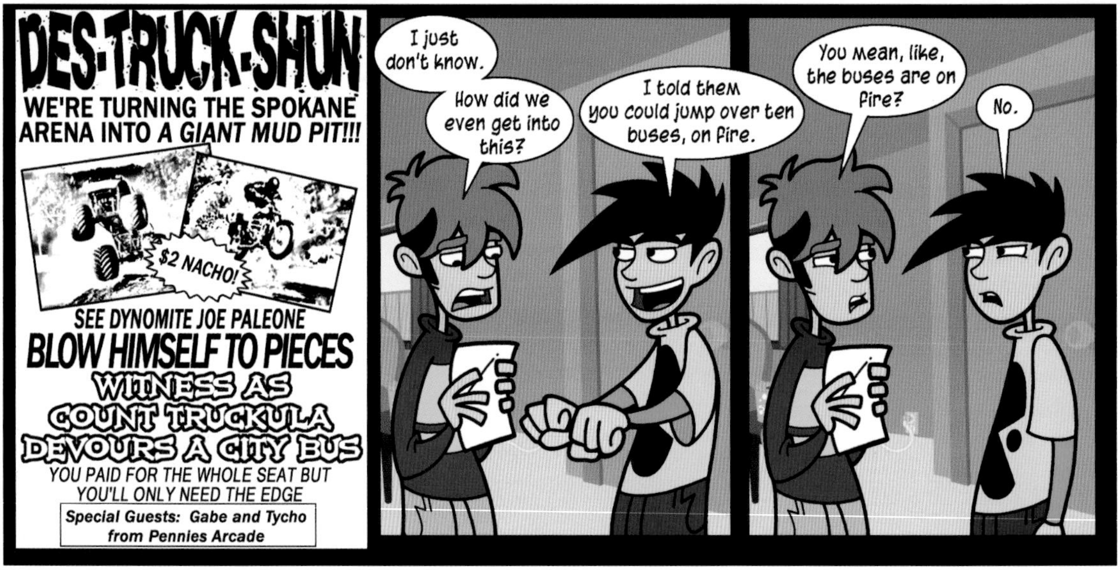
DES-TRUCK-SHUN
WE'RE TURNING THE SPOKANE ARENA INTO A *GIANT MUD PIT!!!*
$2 NACHO!
SEE DYNOMITE JOE PALEONE
BLOW HIMSELF TO PIECES
WITNESS AS COUNT TRUCKULA DEVOURS A CITY BUS
YOU PAID FOR THE WHOLE SEAT BUT YOU'LL ONLY NEED THE EDGE
Special Guests: Gabe and Tycho from Pennies Arcade
I just don't know.
How did we even get into this?
I told them you could jump over ten buses, on fire.
You mean, like, the buses are on fire?
No.

GREETINGSSSSS

April 18, 2003 I like Lord Skass! For lizard royalty, he's surprisingly down-to-earth.

ONE DAY ONLY

April 21, 2003 SakuraCon was a little tense and harrowing at first, partly because—even though we were explicitly invited—we still felt a little like we were crashing someone's party. Certainly, there was also some hostility on the part of attendees, who *also* felt like we were crashing their party. Now, with four of them under our belt, it's kind of exciting. It feels kind of like an *expedition*. But back then, this comic was us trying to imagine an event we would feel even *less* comfortable at.

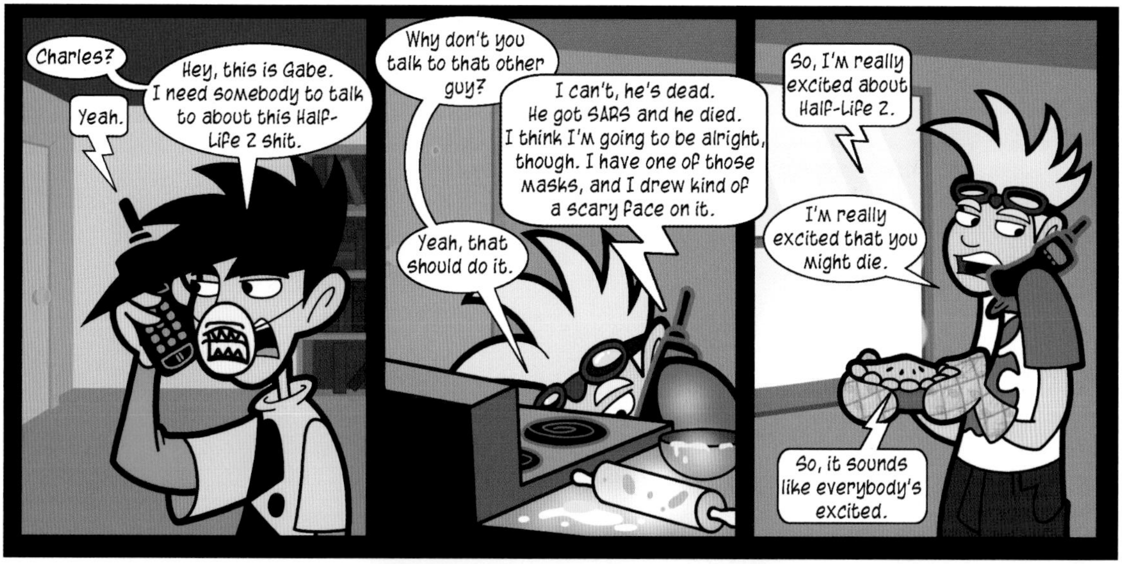

Charles?
Yeah.
Hey, this is Gabe. I need somebody to talk to about this Half-Life 2 shit.
Why don't you talk to that other guy?
I can't, he's dead. He got SARS and he died. I think I'm going to be alright, though. I have one of those masks, and I drew kind of a scary face on it.
Yeah, that should do it.
So, I'm really excited about Half-Life 2.
I'm really excited that you might die.
So, it sounds like everybody's excited.

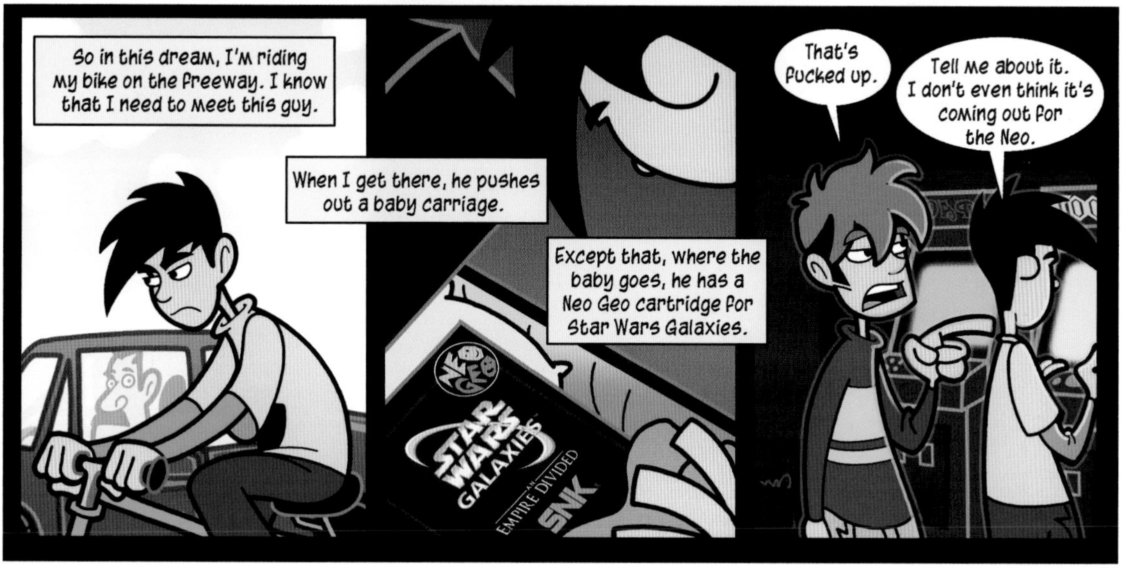

So in this dream, I'm riding my bike on the freeway. I know that I need to meet this guy.
When I get there, he pushes out a baby carriage.
Except that, where the baby goes, he has a Neo Geo cartridge for Star Wars Galaxies.
NEO GEO
STAR WARS GALAXIES
AN EMPIRE DIVIDED
SNK
That's fucked up.
Tell me about it. I don't even think it's coming out for the Neo.

CHARLESTON CHEW

April 23, 2003 The "Half-Life 2 shit" was the lifting of the NDA, which at the time seemed very important—we didn't know then that the game wouldn't see release for another year and a half. The bit about SARS isn't *completely* random—Robert had just contracted it in Hong Kong, and he proceeded to sweat and shake for a month. Our archive is studded with weird, coded entries like this.

MEANWHILE, IN THE SUBCONSCIOUS

April 25, 2003 For younger readers—those who may be confused by the freaky neon realm Gabe and Tycho inhabit in the last panel—do not be frightened! It is only an *arcade*. Our people once worshiped in these gaudy temples, offering up quarters to cruel gods.

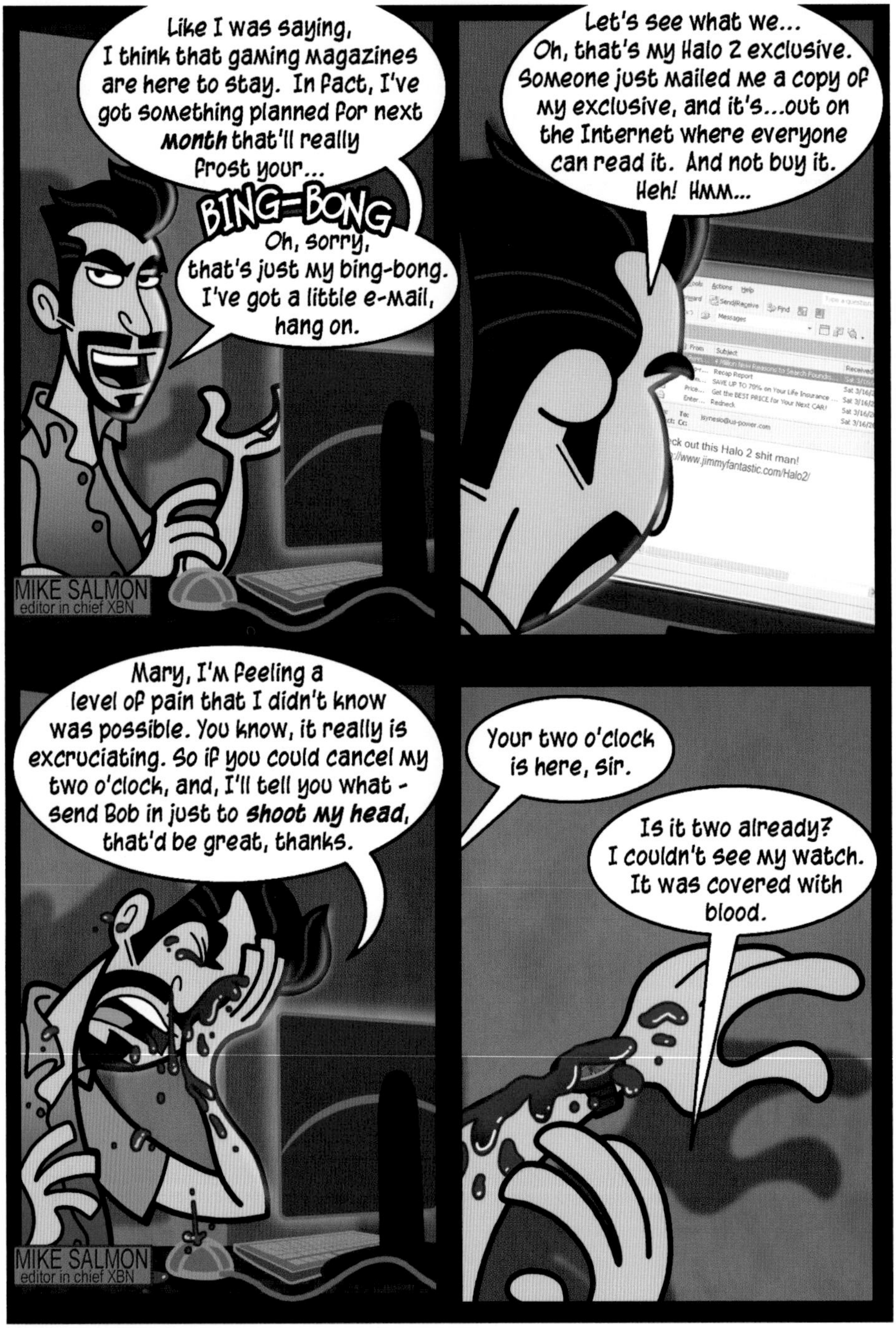
Like I was saying, I think that gaming magazines are here to stay. In fact, I've got something planned for next month that'll really frost your...
BING-BONG
Oh, sorry, that's just my bing-bong. I've got a little e-mail, hang on.
MIKE SALMON editor in chief XBN
Let's see what we... Oh, that's my Halo 2 exclusive. Someone just mailed me a copy of my exclusive, and it's...out on the Internet where everyone can read it. And not buy it. Heh! HMM...
Mary, I'm feeling a level of pain that I didn't know was possible. You know, it really is excruciating. So if you could cancel my two o'clock, and, I'll tell you what - send Bob in just to shoot my head, that'd be great, thanks.
MIKE SALMON editor in chief XBN
Your two o'clock is here, sir.
Is it two already? I couldn't see my watch. It was covered with blood.

OCCUPATIONAL HAZARD

April 30, 2003 I feel nothing but compassion for the hard working editor pictured here, who represents all print editors everywhere, for every physical publication. They're bailing with a (proverbial) sieve. One can readily picture them riding a brontosaurus to work, or chowing on some huge ribs like in the *Flintstones* intro.

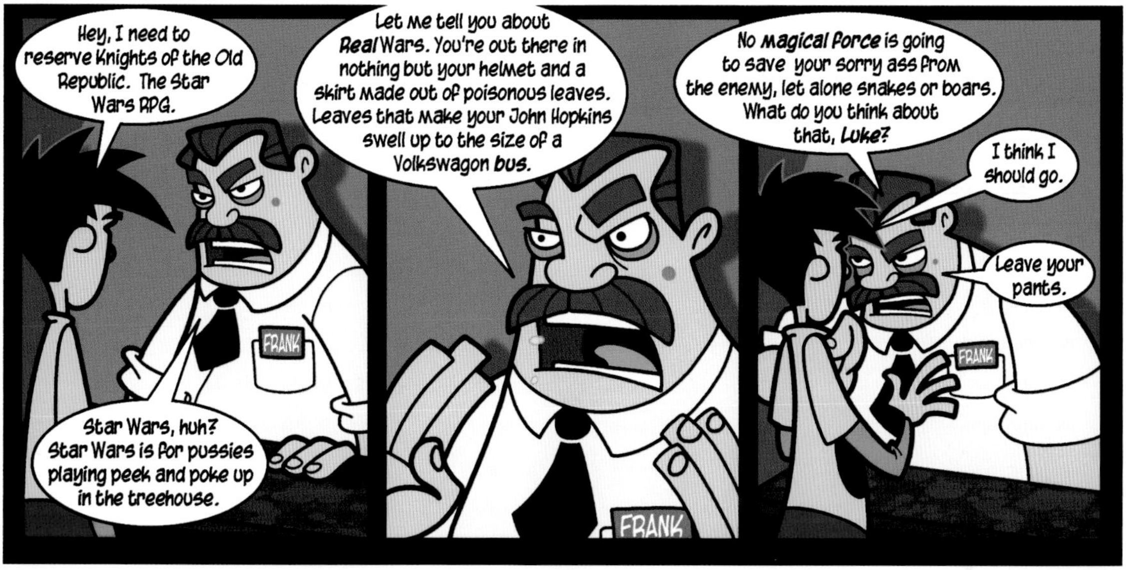
Hey, I need to reserve Knights of the Old Republic. The Star Wars RPG.
Star Wars, huh? Star Wars is for pussies playing peek and poke up in the treehouse.
FRANK
Let me tell you about *Real* Wars. You're out there in nothing but your helmet and a skirt made out of poisonous leaves. Leaves that make your John Hopkins swell up to the size of a Volkswagon *bus.*
FRANK
No *Magical Force* is going to save your sorry ass from the enemy, let alone snakes or boars. What do you think about that, *Luke?*
I think I should go.
Leave your pants.
FRANK

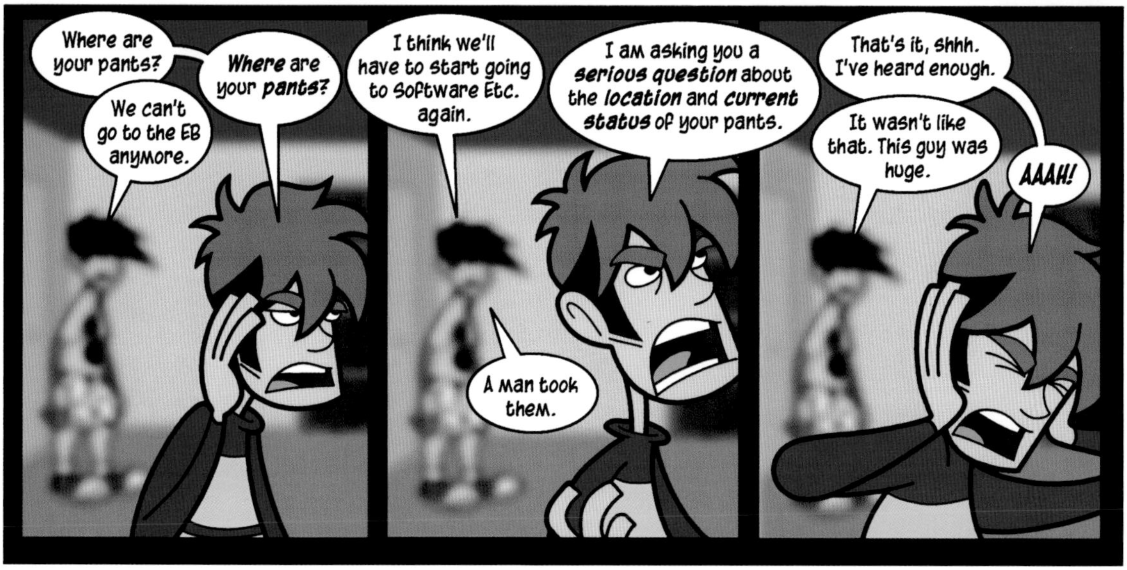
Where are your pants?
Where are your *pants?*
We can't go to the EB anymore.
I think we'll have to start going to Software Etc. again.
I am asking you a *serious question* about the *location* and *current status* of your pants.
A man took them.
That's it, shhh. I've heard enough.
It wasn't like that. This guy was huge.
AAAH!

A HUMOROUS ANECDOTE

May 2, 2003 We are not actually sure what it would mean to peek, let alone *poke*, in a treehouse or any other place. We leave these rich possibilities to our capable readers.

THE SPECTRE OF CONTINUITY

May 5, 2003 It might be hard to believe, but I think that we originally planned to execute some intense, extended narrative about these lost pants. I guess Gabe was going to get them back? Eventually? Or something? There ain't a lot of meat on them bones.

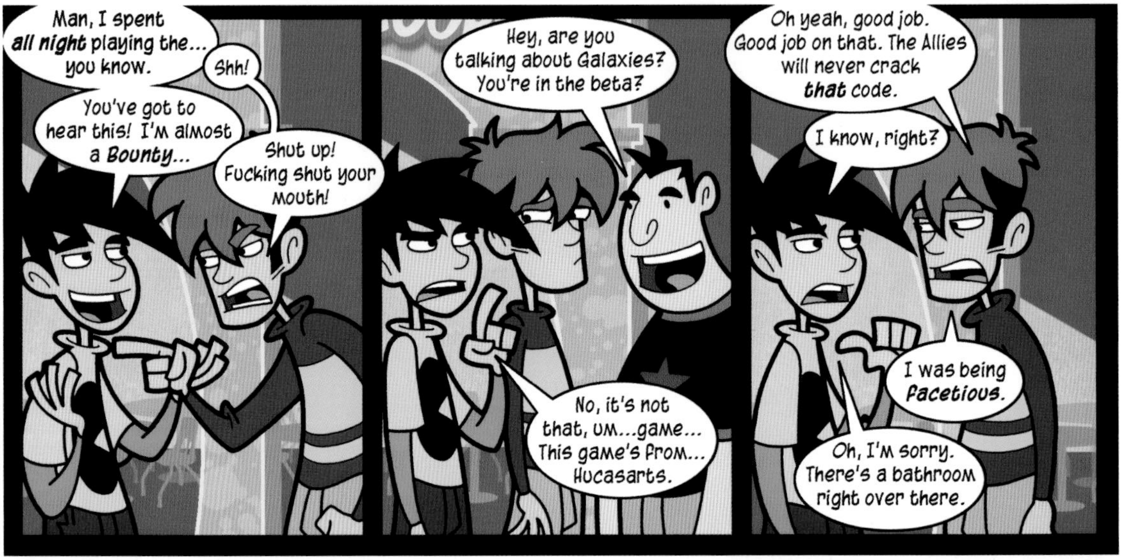
Man, I spent **all night** playing the... you know.
Shh!
You've got to hear this! I'm almost a *Bounty*...
Shut up! Fucking shut your mouth!
Hey, are you talking about Galaxies? You're in the beta?
No, it's not that, um...game... This game's from... Hucasarts.
Oh yeah, good job. Good job on that. The Allies will never crack **that** code.
I know, right?
I was being *facetious*.
Oh, I'm sorry. There's a bathroom right over there.

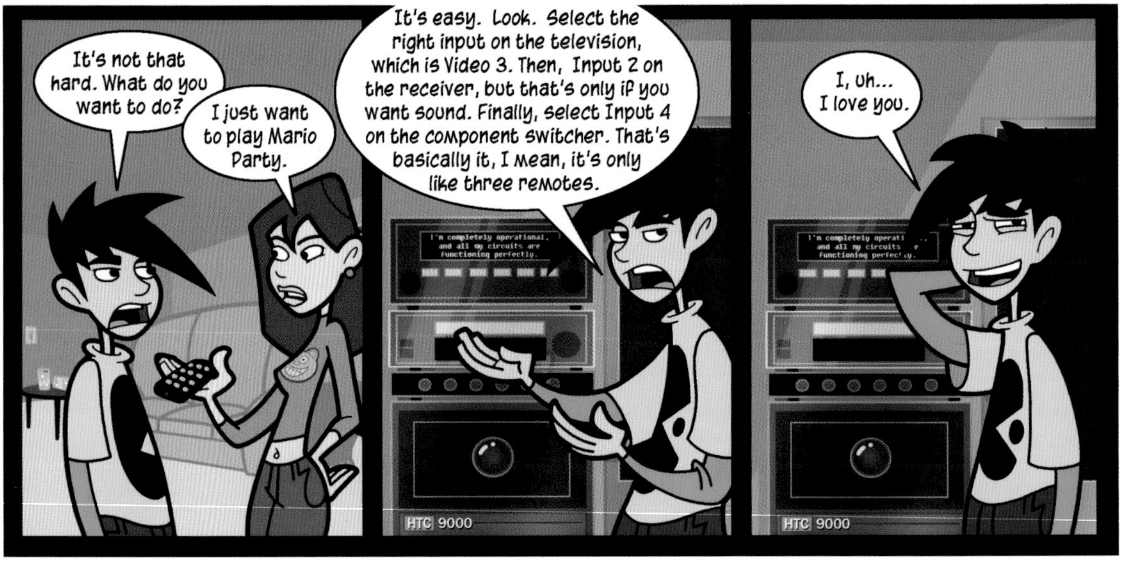
It's not that hard. What do you want to do?
I just want to play Mario Party.
It's easy. Look. Select the right input on the television, which is Video 3. Then, Input 2 on the receiver, but that's only if you want sound. Finally, select Input 4 on the component switcher. That's basically it, I mean, it's only like three remotes.
I'm completely operational, and all my circuits are functioning perfectly.
HTC 9000
I, uh... I love you.
HTC 9000

JUST ADD H

May 7, 2003 See, this was back when we still believed that this game would be impossible to screw up. Also, it was a gentler, brighter age, when we would play a beta and just *believe the best* about the state it would be in at release—eating up the good bits and tossing the rest, as though it were an electronic version of the Whitman's Sampler.

TALES FROM TRUE LIFE

May 9, 2003 Modern, *psychic* receivers know your will, and they ferry the correct signal without complaint. In the savage age of 2003, we rubbed sticks and sang songs in order to curry favor with the magnificent Channel Lords who dwell (it is said) "on high."

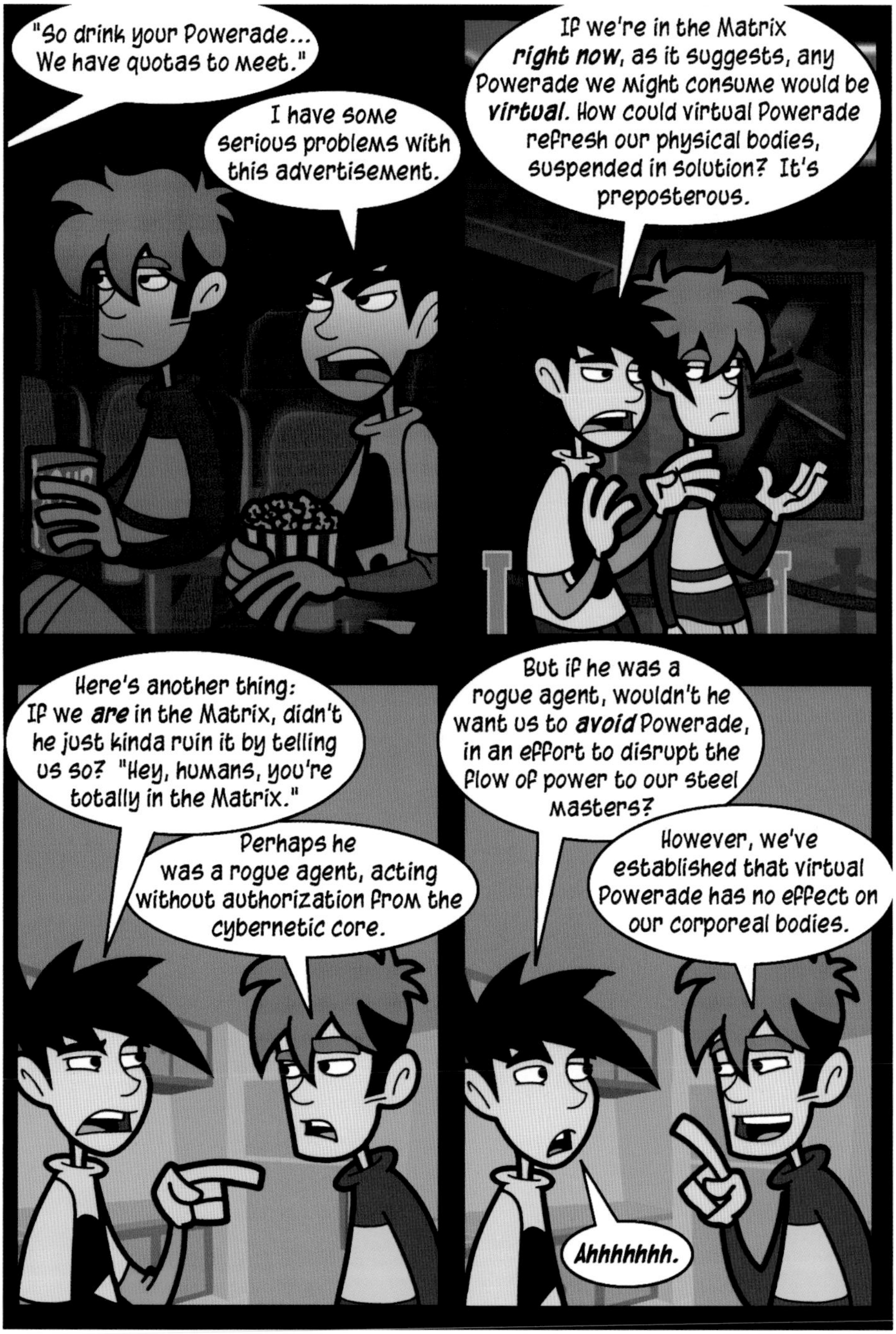
"So drink your Powerade... We have quotas to meet."
I have some serious problems with this advertisement.
If we're in the Matrix ***right now***, as it suggests, any Powerade we might consume would be ***virtual***. How could virtual Powerade refresh our physical bodies, suspended in solution? It's preposterous.
Here's another thing: If we ***are*** in the Matrix, didn't he just kinda ruin it by telling us so? "Hey, humans, you're totally in the Matrix."
Perhaps he was a rogue agent, acting without authorization from the cybernetic core.
But if he was a rogue agent, wouldn't he want us to ***avoid*** Powerade, in an effort to disrupt the flow of power to our steel masters?
However, we've established that virtual Powerade has no effect on our corporeal bodies.
Ahhhhhhh.

QUESTIONS AND CONCERNS

May 12, 2003 I already hate paying ten dollars to see a first-run feature film, but when they show me twenty minutes of inescapable commercials beforehand my hand becomes a *fist*. Remember when *The Matrix* was a "thing"? There were these Goddamn Powerade commercials they used to show that drove me to drink. More, I mean. Drove me to drink *more*. And I don't mean more Powerade.

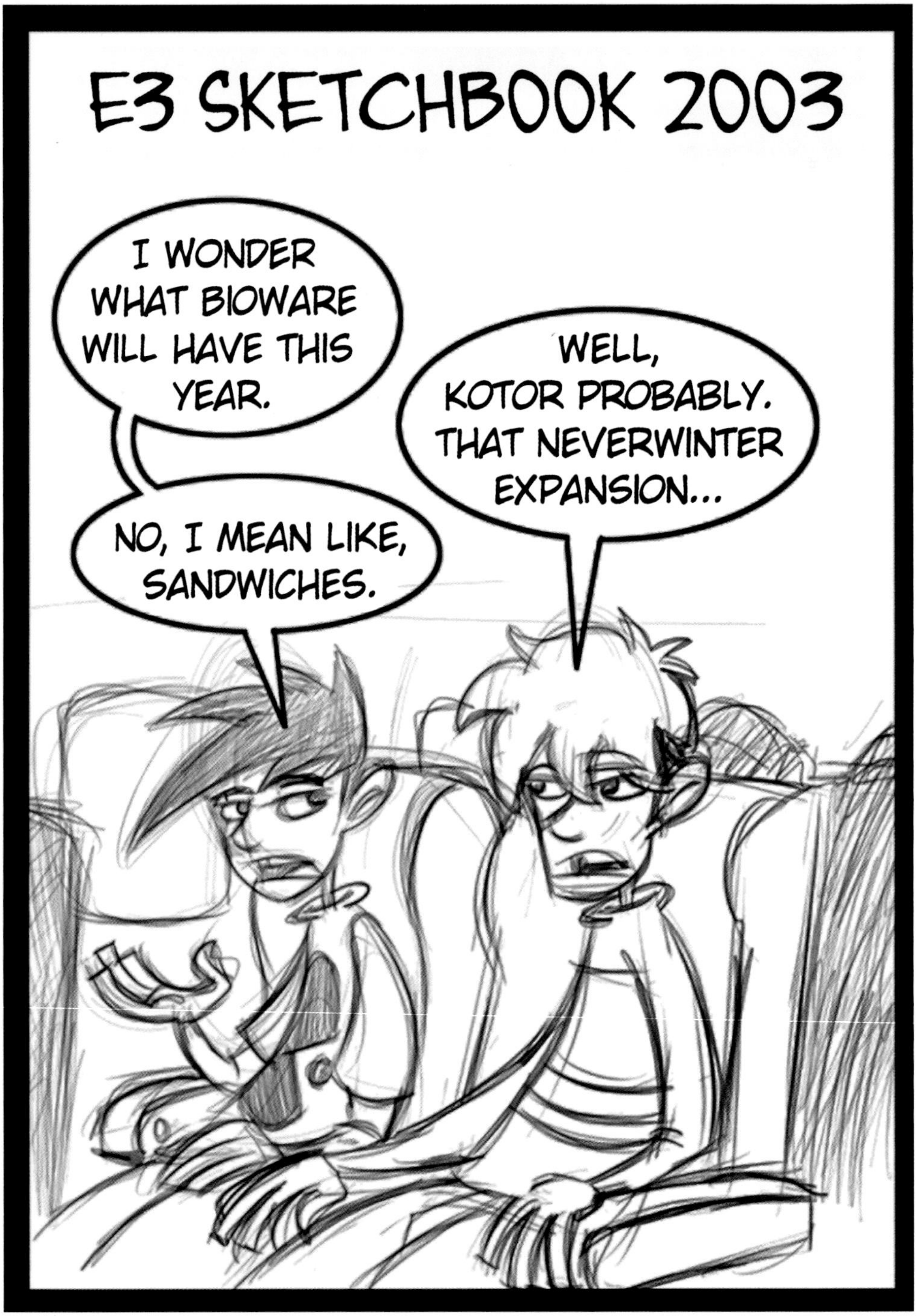
E3 SKETCHBOOK 2003
I WONDER WHAT BIOWARE WILL HAVE THIS YEAR.
WELL, KOTOR PROBABLY. THAT NEVERWINTER EXPANSION...
NO, I MEAN LIKE, SANDWICHES.

E32K3: NORTHERN BOUNTY

May 14, 2003 As you might recall from volume one, we came to see the Bioware booth as more of a larder than anything else. Certainly, we were interested in what they had to say about . . . whatever game they were working on. Swordy Game. Legend of Sword Guy at Night. It was something like that.

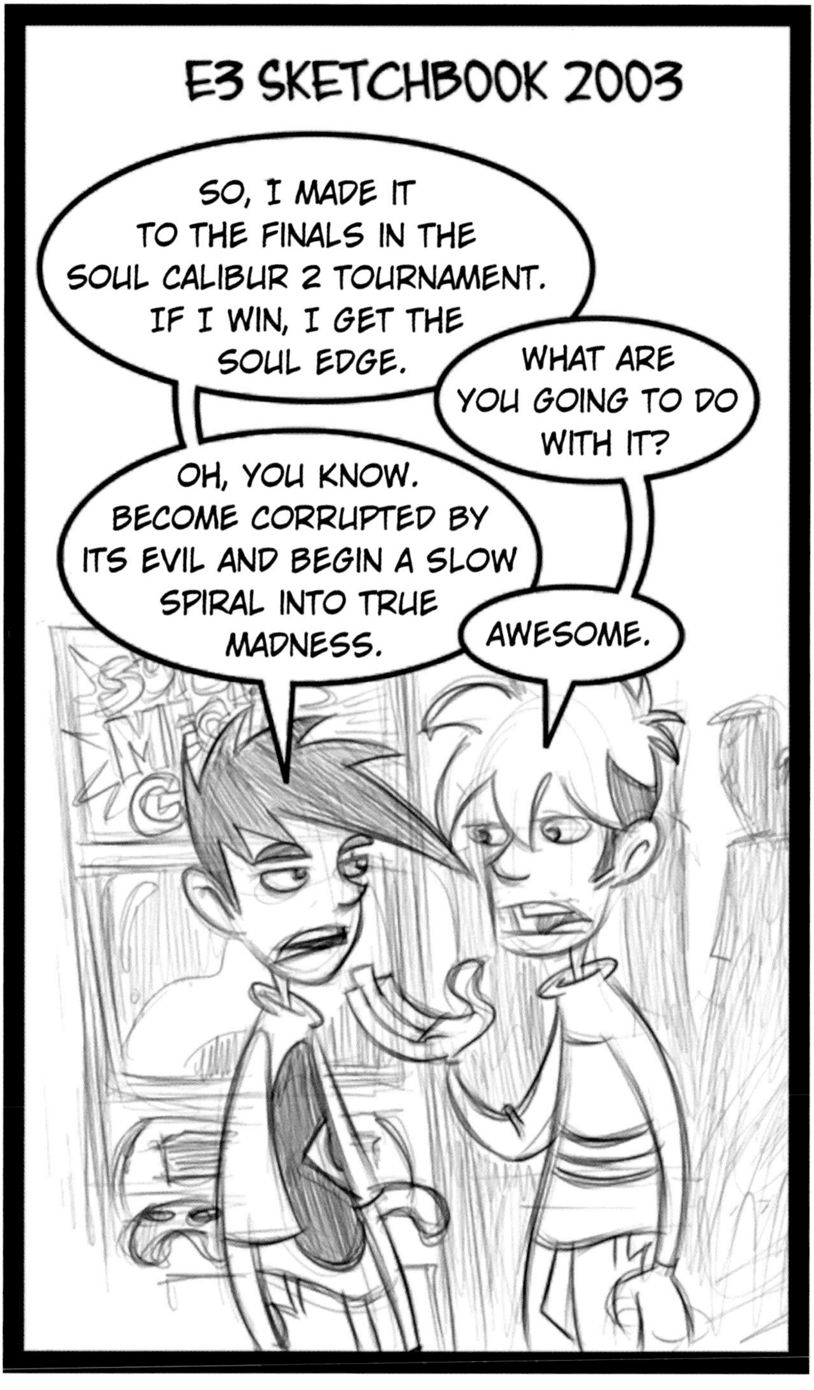
E3 SKETCHBOOK 2003
SO, I MADE IT TO THE FINALS IN THE SOUL CALIBUR 2 TOURNAMENT. IF I WIN, I GET THE SOUL EDGE.
WHAT ARE YOU GOING TO DO WITH IT?
OH, YOU KNOW. BECOME CORRUPTED BY ITS EVIL AND BEGIN A SLOW SPIRAL INTO TRUE MADNESS.
AWESOME.

E32K3: THE STAGE OF HISTORY

May 15, 2003 You've always got that guy in your group who dominates at fighters, and these days it's usually a toss-up between Gabe and Robert. This was one of the first opportunities we had to see how our best man could fare against the world's finest on The Stage of History. The verdict? *Not well.*

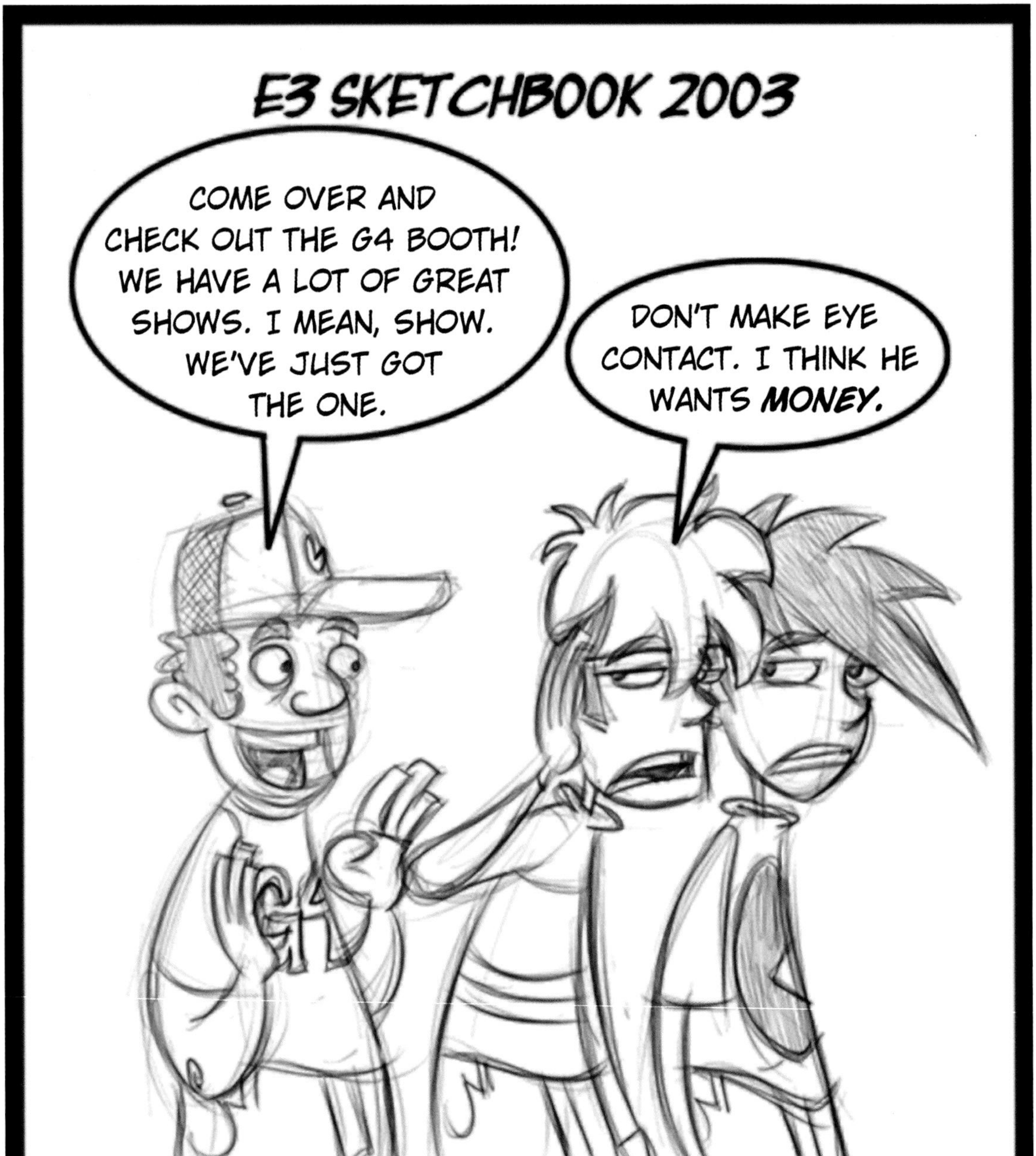
E3 SKETCHBOOK 2003
COME OVER AND CHECK OUT THE G4 BOOTH! WE HAVE A LOT OF GREAT SHOWS. I MEAN, SHOW. WE'VE JUST GOT THE ONE.
DON'T MAKE EYE CONTACT. I THINK HE WANTS ***MONEY.***

E32K3: GABE WILL TELL YOU LATER

May 16, 2003 You can bag on G4, but they always get that dopey sort of *I might cry* look that strips all the joy out of it.

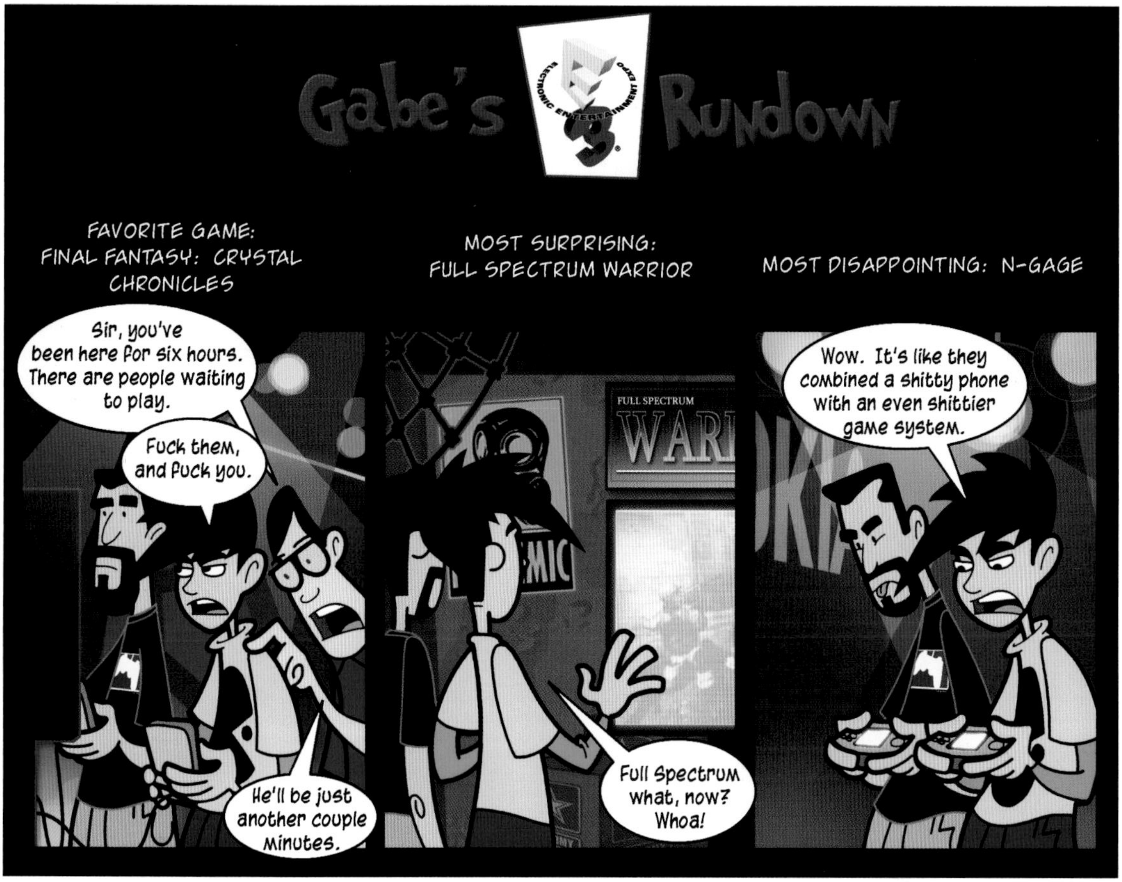
Gabe's
ELECTRONIC ENTERTAINMENT EXPO
E3
Rundown
FAVORITE GAME:
FINAL FANTASY: CRYSTAL CHRONICLES
Sir, you've been here for six hours. There are people waiting to play.
Fuck them, and fuck you.
He'll be just another couple minutes.
MOST SURPRISING:
FULL SPECTRUM WARRIOR
FULL SPECTRUM
WARI
Full Spectrum what, now? Whoa!
MOST DISAPPOINTING: N-GAGE
Wow. It's like they combined a shitty phone with an even shittier game system.

GABE'S E3 RUNDOWN

May 19, 2003 Gabe and Kiko have very similar tastes in games, so we decided that we'd split off this year. Well, *we* didn't really decide it. Gabe and Kiko decided it, when I wasn't actually *there*. The long and the short of it is that I got stuck with Pork. *Awesome*.

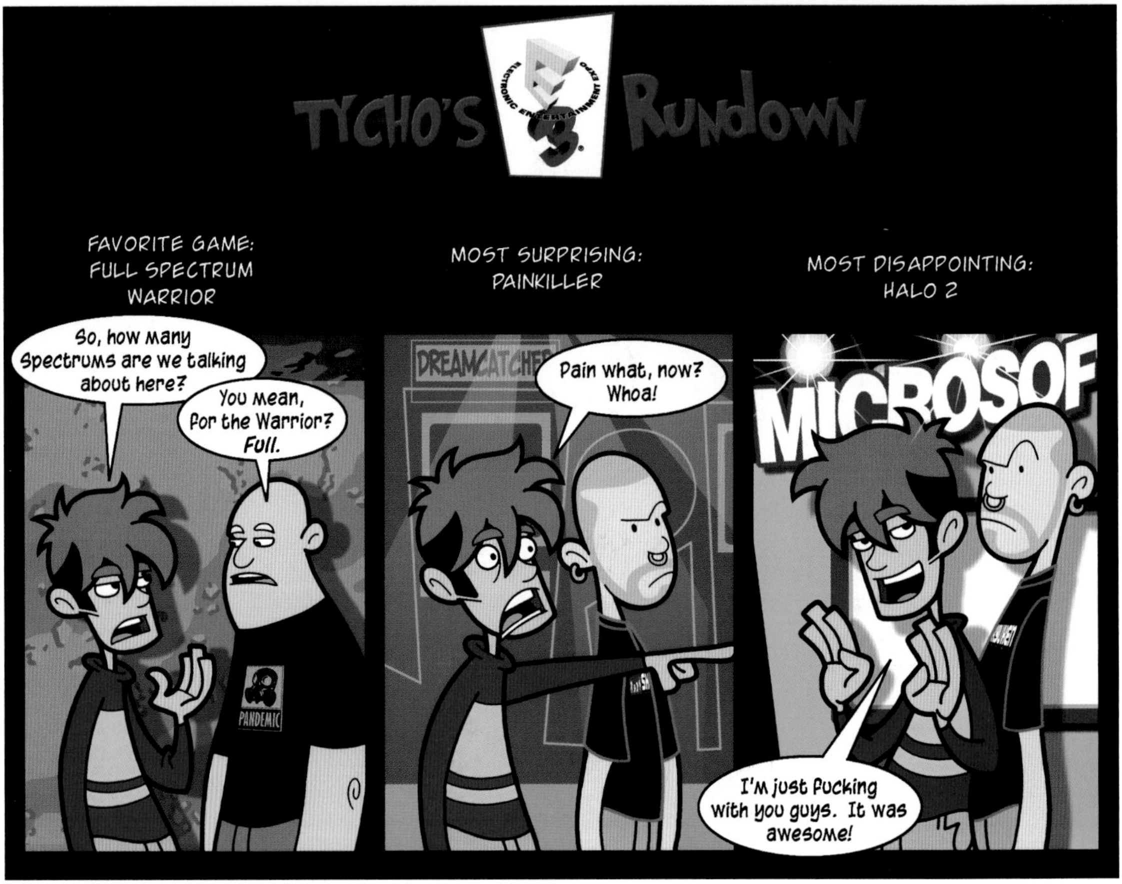
TYCHO'S E3 RUNDOWN
ELECTRONIC ENTERTAINMENT EXPO
FAVORITE GAME: FULL SPECTRUM WARRIOR
So, how many Spectrums are we talking about here?
You mean, for the Warrior? Full.
PANDEMIC
MOST SURPRISING: PAINKILLER
DREAMCATCHER
Pain what, now? Whoa!
MOST DISAPPOINTING: HALO 2
MICROSOF
I'm just fucking with you guys. It was awesome!

TYCHO'S E3 RUNDOWN

May 21, 2003 I love Pork. I mean that in general terms. And we're actually a very good E3 team. But if you have ever seen him in the night, when the ADHD medication starts to wear off, then you know about that magical period known as *Pork After Hours*. He doesn't become another person so much as he becomes an intense, almost incandescent version of himself. I think you could put him in a huge hamster wheel and generate electricity.

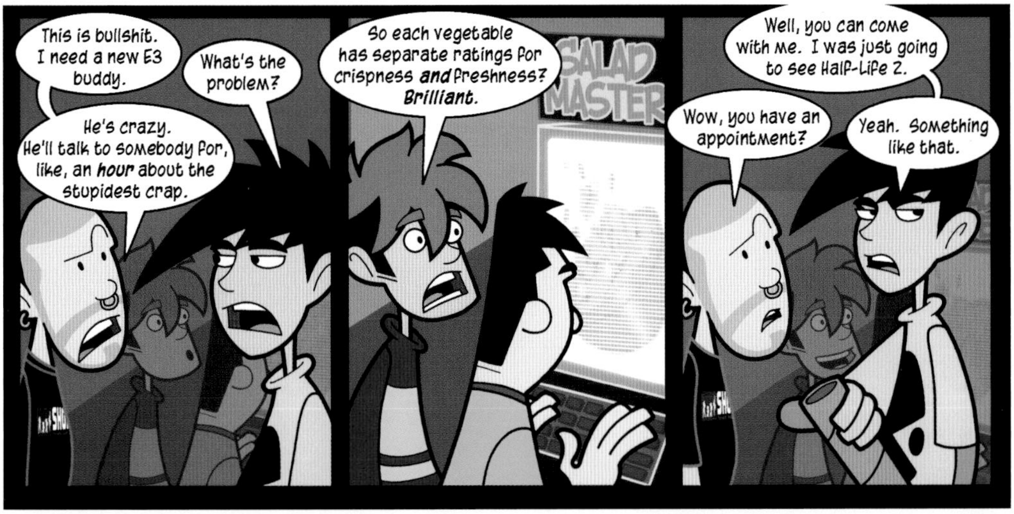
This is bullshit. I need a new E3 buddy.
What's the problem?
He's crazy. He'll talk to somebody for, like, an *hour* about the stupidest crap.
So each vegetable has separate ratings for crispness *and* freshness? *Brilliant.*
SALAD MASTER
Well, you can come with me. I was just going to see Half-Life 2.
Wow, you have an appointment?
Yeah. Something like that.

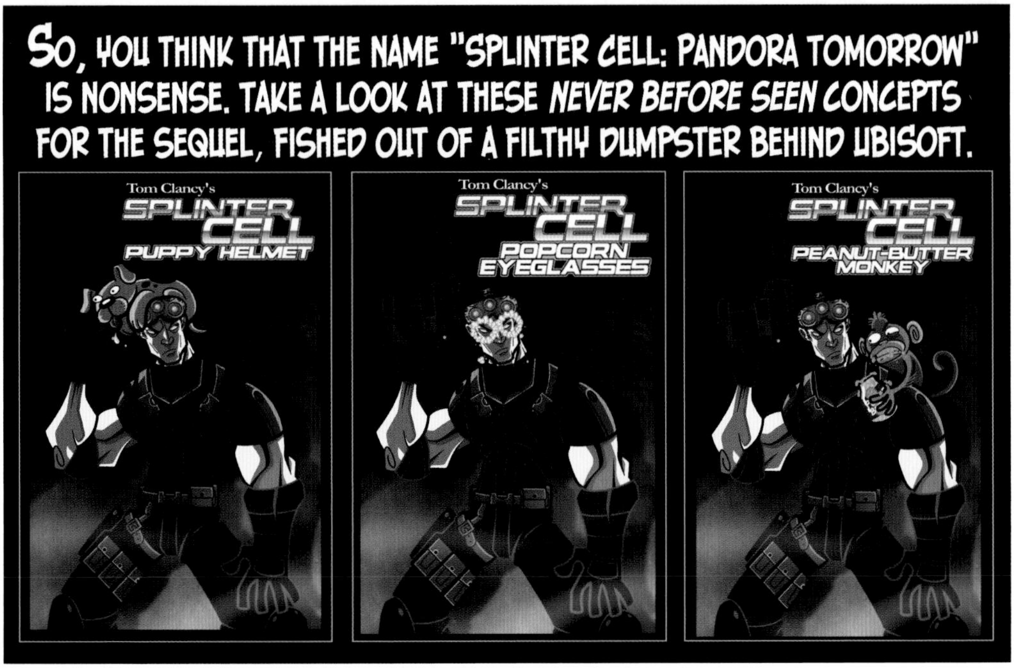
SO, YOU THINK THAT THE NAME "SPLINTER CELL: PANDORA TOMORROW" IS NONSENSE. TAKE A LOOK AT THESE *NEVER BEFORE SEEN CONCEPTS* FOR THE SEQUEL, FISHED OUT OF A FILTHY DUMPSTER BEHIND UBISOFT.
Tom Clancy's SPLINTER CELL PUPPY HELMET
Tom Clancy's SPLINTER CELL POPCORN EYEGLASSES
Tom Clancy's SPLINTER CELL PEANUT-BUTTER MONKEY

THE BUDDY SYSTEM

May 23, 2003 At any rate, *this* is why Gabriel refuses to be my E3 buddy. The game Salad Master refers to is called Culdcept, which is one of my favorite games of all time. It plays almost exactly like Monopoly, except replace the real estate moguls with *sorcerers*, and replace the real estate with *elementally attuned tiles*. Oh! And instead of hotels, there are *demons*. So that's a big change.

SPLINTER CELL: ADJECTIVE NOUN

May 26, 2003 Once you know that it's a code phrase, the name makes sense and is actually kind of cool. But people don't come to *Penny Arcade* for reasoned analysis! They come to see aging superspies who wear dogs and hang out with monkeys.

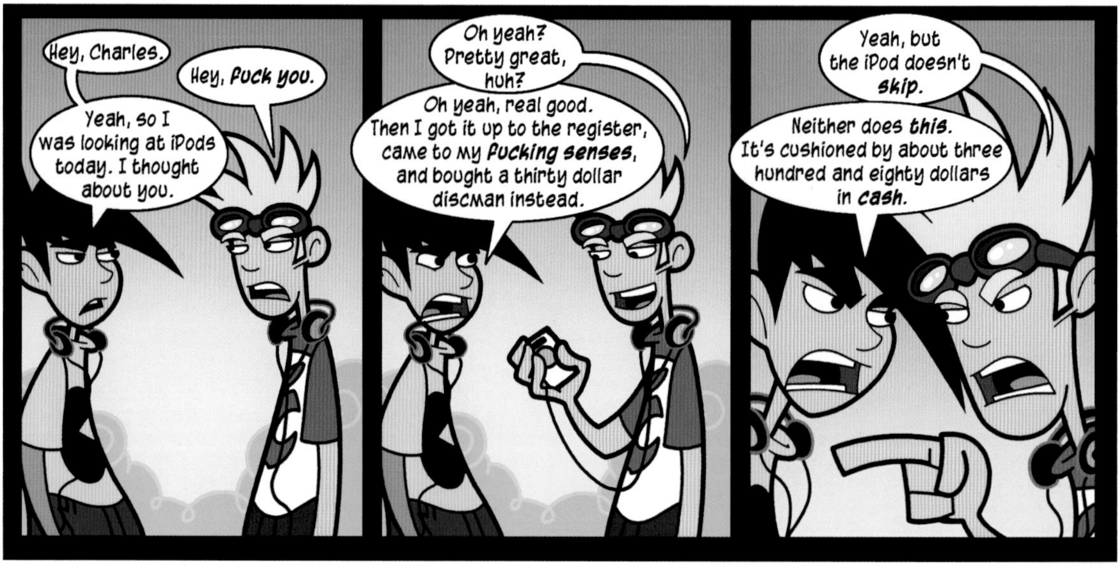
Hey, Charles.
Hey, fuck you.
Yeah, so I was looking at iPods today. I thought about you.
Oh yeah? Pretty great, huh?
Oh yeah, real good. Then I got it up to the register, came to my fucking senses, and bought a thirty dollar discman instead.
Yeah, but the iPod doesn't skip.
Neither does this. It's cushioned by about three hundred and eighty dollars in cash.

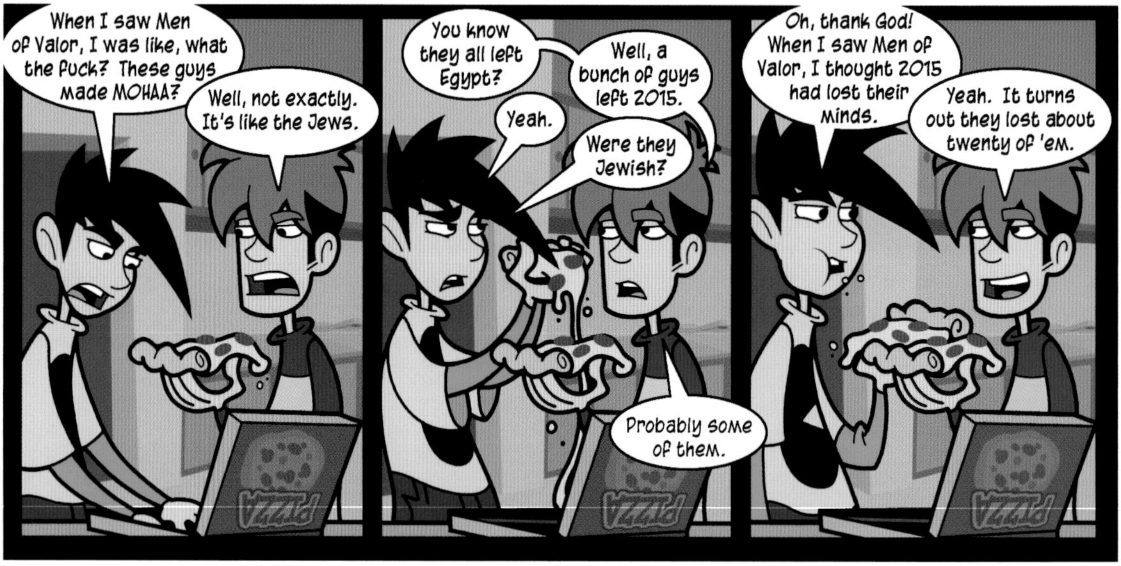
When I saw Men of Valor, I was like, what the fuck? These guys made MOHAA?
Well, not exactly. It's like the Jews.
You know they all left Egypt?
Well, a bunch of guys left 2015.
Yeah.
Were they Jewish?
Probably some of them.
Oh, thank God! When I saw Men of Valor, I thought 2015 had lost their minds.
Yeah. It turns out they lost about twenty of 'em.

A PENNY SAVED

May 28, 2003 Fast-forward to the Year of Our Lord two-thousand and *three*, and I think Gabe owns *two* iPods. He also owns two Macs. He makes movies with iDVD and shares photos with family and friends using the online tools provided by his .Mac service. I'm not trying to make any particular point. I'm just putting the information out there.

MINUS THE PLAGUES

May 30, 2003 Those people leaving actually marked the birth of Infinity Ward, creator of the Call of Duty franchise that has been so good to Activision.

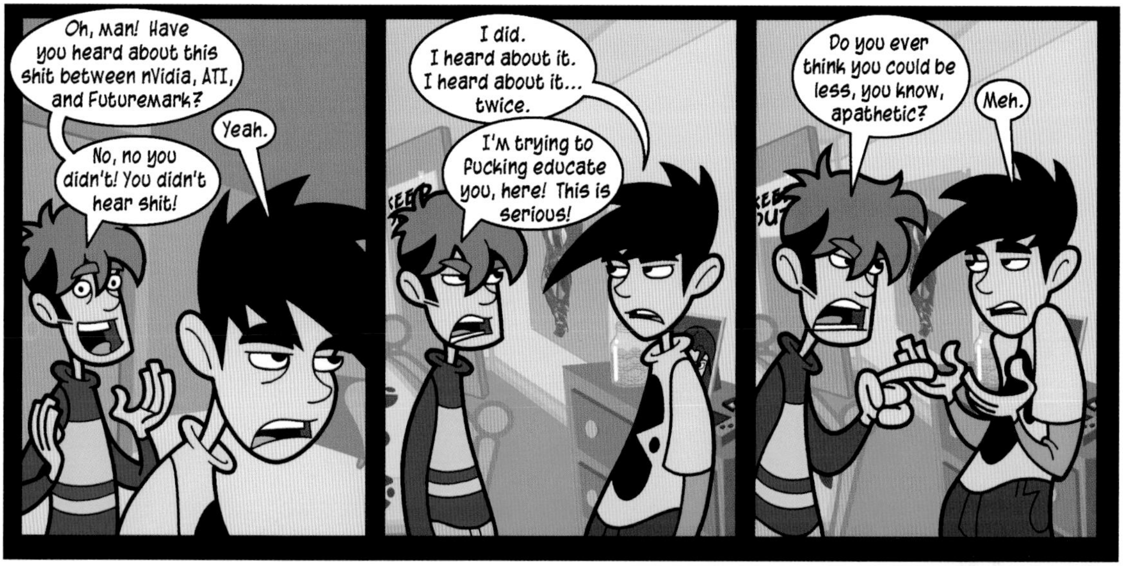
Oh, man! Have you heard about this shit between nVidia, ATI, and Futuremark?
Yeah.
No, no you didn't! You didn't hear shit!
I did. I heard about it. I heard about it... twice.
I'm trying to fucking educate you, here! This is serious!
Do you ever think you could be less, you know, apathetic?
Meh.

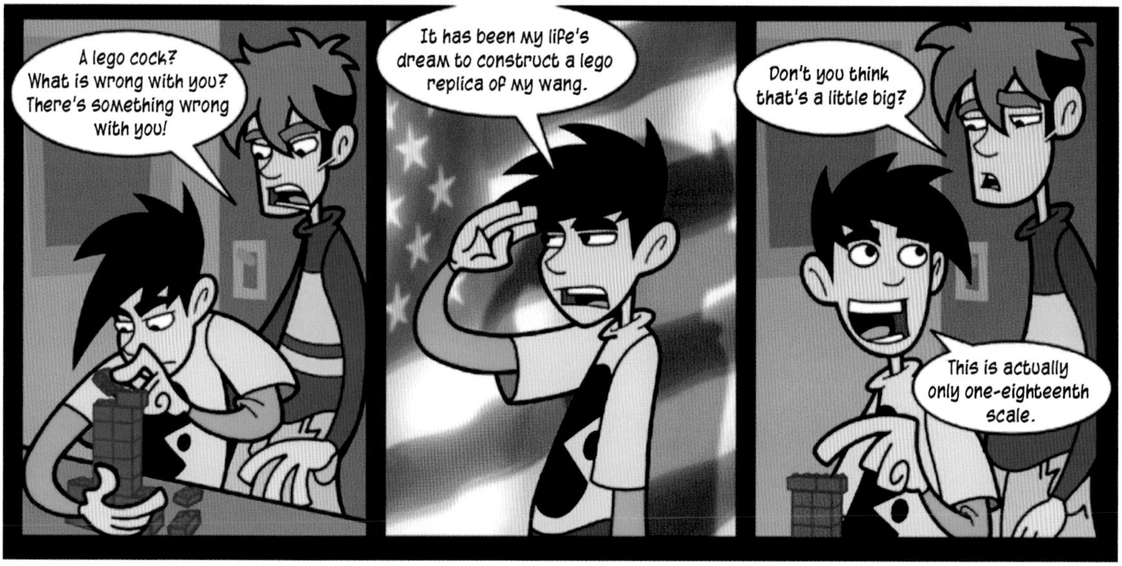
A lego cock? What is wrong with you? There's something wrong with you!
It has been my life's dream to construct a lego replica of my wang.
Don't you think that's a little big?
This is actually only one-eighteenth scale.

I JUST DON'T CARE

June 2, 2003 My ongoing campaign to give the events of his world some Goddamn context is never actually rebuffed. My reasoned evaluations just break *over* and *around* him, and he is absolutely unmoved, like a monument on a marble pedestal. I've never known someone so absolutely committed to indifference in my entire life.

I'M GONNA NEED MORE LEGOS

June 13, 2003 I have a word of advice for those of you who may approach us at this or that convention. You would do well to heed my words. People often tell my cohort to "draw whatever he wants to," and this is something that you *must* not (under *any* circumstances) do. Never suggest that he may draw "whatever he wants to," unless you want him to draw you a picture of an *erect phallus*.

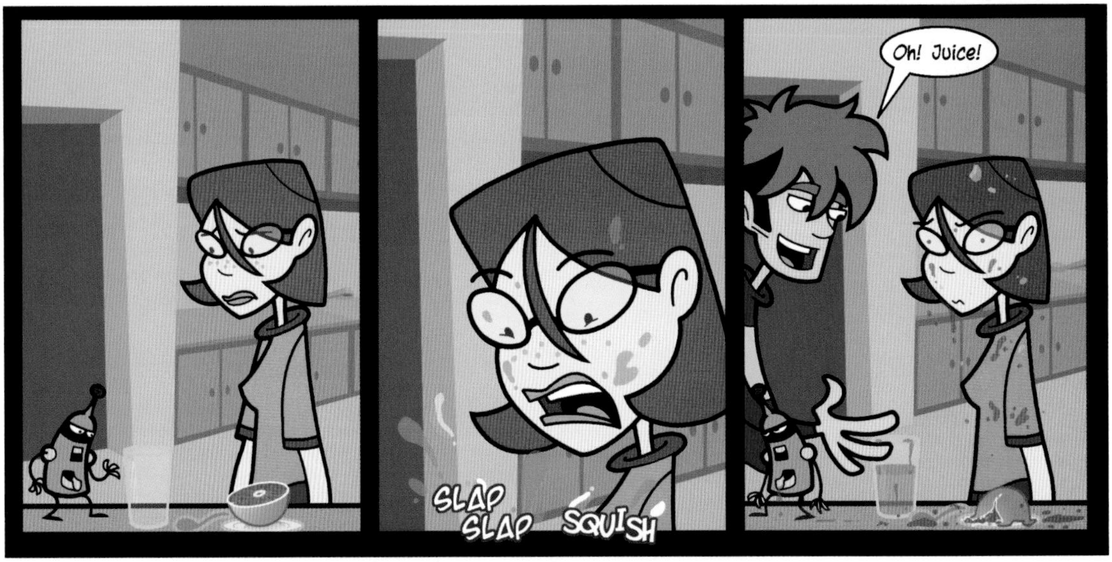
SLAP
SLAP
SQUISH
Oh! Juice!

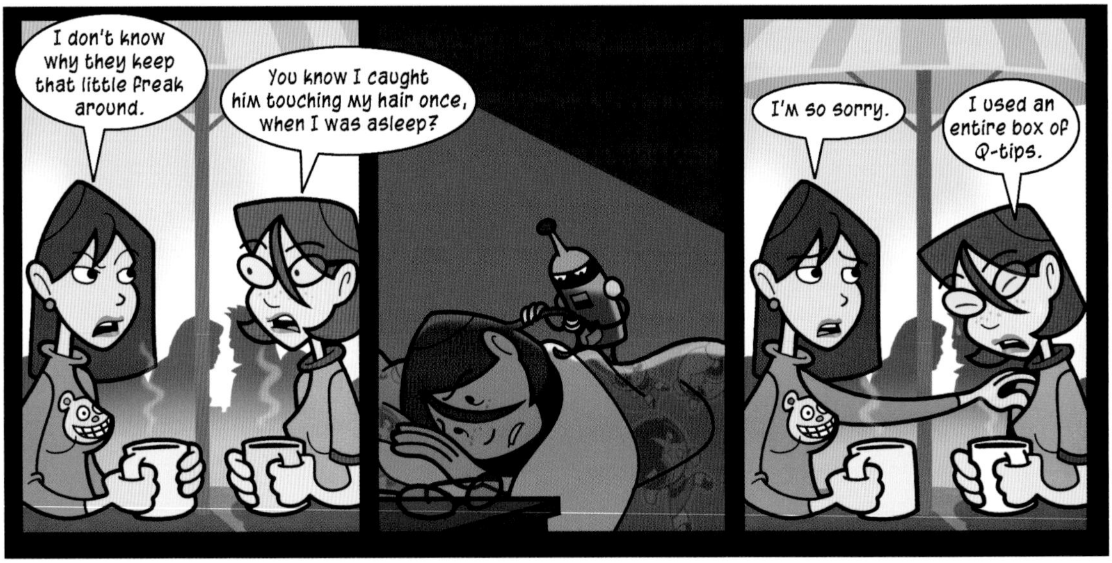
I don't know why they keep that little freak around.
You know I caught him touching my hair once, when I was asleep?
I'm so sorry.
I used an entire box of Q-tips.

THE FRUIT SAGA

June 4–11, 2003 Kara and Brenna completely detest the Fruit Fucker, and would prefer that he didn't exist, so the next time we needed a storyline we decided to investigate that. The reason we needed a storyline was because Brenna and I had decided to see what was going on over in Europe, specifically Germany and Italy.

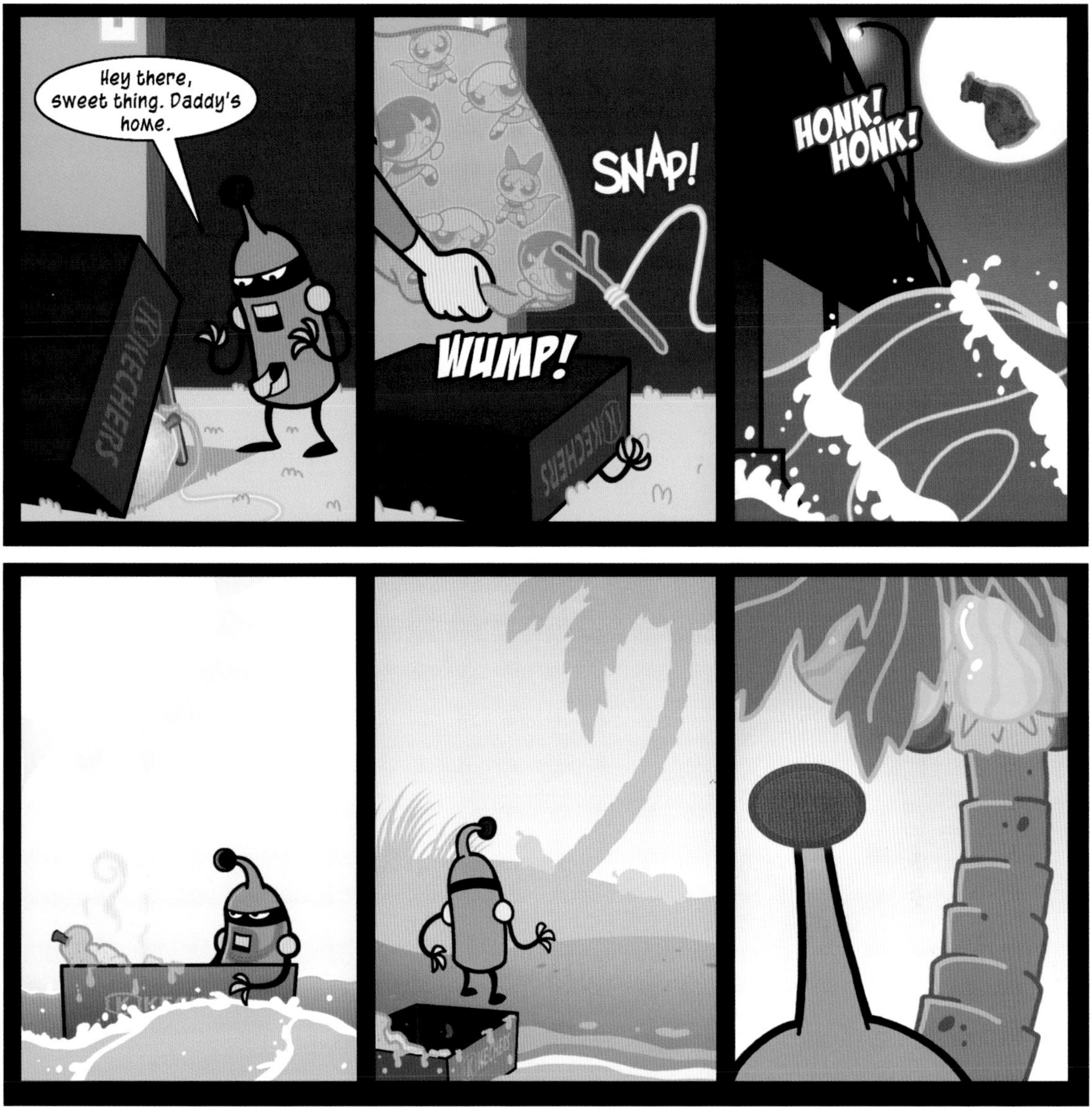
Hey there, sweet thing. Daddy's home.
SNAP!
WUMP!
HONK! HONK!

(CONTINUED)

I don't vacation especially well, partially because I'm a perpetually nervous wreck of a man who finds relaxation impossible. But it is also because, given what my job actually entails, I don't really feel like I deserve a break from it. So while I was over there, I wrote more posts than I ever would have if I'd been at home. You'll find them on the very next page, completely remastered (they have not been remastered).

Italy / Germany Travelogue

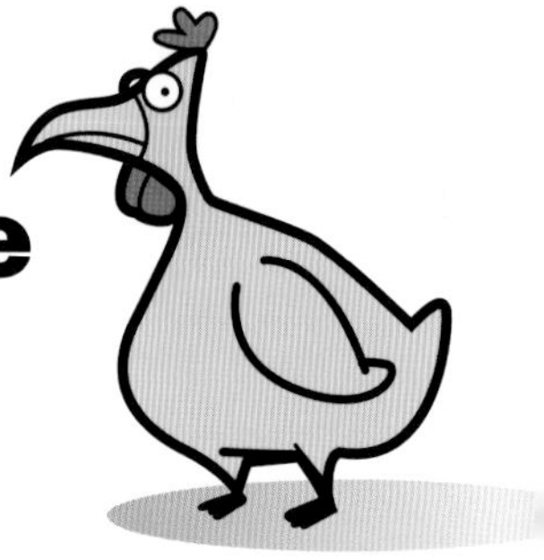

A CENTURY OF FLIGHT

Mon, June 02 2003—07:25 A.M.

Any person who has flown internationally knows that the airplane, at some point in your trajectory, becomes a sort of flying asylum. Time loses meaning. You are buffetted by wailing of all kinds as you try to retain a grip on the steady operation of your mind. Children keen and shriek as though being murdered, and you hold on to your in-flight cookie like it's a life preserver.

To make things worse, I was sitting next to some kind of mutant. I don't know if they just grow them that big where he's from, or what, but he was eight feet tall if he was a foot. We immediately took a dislike to one another. I try not to touch other human beings if I can help it—it's just a personal rule—but his gargantuan legs splayed in all directions and made it difficult to exist in that space. When they brought out breakfast, however, something wonderful happened.

They had given me a raspberry yogurt that was sealed on the top with tinfoil. There was also some sort of Air Quiche, but it's best if we don't discuss it. I opened the treat as carefully as I could, but after the initial resistance the cup practically exploded. Covered from head to toe in stunning pink, the mutant looked like a carnival float in a gay pride parade.

CARROTO MACHINE

Wed, June 04 2003—08:00 A.M.

There is a sort of public market right where I leave the hotel called *Campo del Fiori*, which literally translated means Campo of Something. That's not the point of the story.

I do not, generally speaking, have a high opinion of public markets. Someone clearly must, because people keep marketing things publicly, and I don't dislike them enough to start a movement or something, so it's not a big deal. The sort of market they have around my house can be accurately described as a sort of hippie gauntlet, where you are buffeted on all sides by odors and hacky sacks until you tell your wife you're going home.

I told Brenna that I would rather not attend it, if it's all the same to her. This apparently meant "go there" thanks to the bizarre prism through which she interprets my clear words, so she subjected me to it immediately. It actually turned out sort of interesting, but I would appreciate it if that didn't get back to her.

It appeared to be a haphazard jumble of canopies and vegetables, but there was an ecosystem that governed it. Brenna bought spices, fruit, and something I can't really describe from three separate booths, and each time she had to go to this sort of shifty character in the middle of them, as all their areas were lashed to his. I envisage him as a sort of Spice Lord whose word is law everwhere left of the meat guy.

I started to walk on my own to another part of the *Campo Whatever*, when a man shouted at me with a vigor that belied his advanced age.

"Carroto machine!"

I stopped and stared at him.

He raised his voice, this time approaching religious fervor.

"Carroto Machine!"

I'm sorry, but any man who can speak with such passion about a grater deserves my time. So . . . let's see what this Carroto Machine of his can do.

If you must know, it isn't much to look at. It's hardly a machine at all; it's the kind of twisted metal you might find at the scene of an auto accident. What compels him to rub, straining it against carrots, potatoes, and fish is a matter for philosophy to determine. The state it leaves the grated object in is really quite hideous, I don't know what you would do with the results. I bought it mainly so I could tell you this story. Oh, and get this. Instead of the change he owed me, he gave me the most ineffectual juicer. I bought an orange at the market and endeavored to manipulate it with "the best juicer ever," and it didn't juice for shit. Let this be a lesson to you! Never accept small pieces of plastic instead of actual money.

VATICAN CITY
Wed, June 04 2003—08:00 A.M.

In much the same way that XSN makes me wish I enjoyed sports, visiting the Vatican made me wish I was into gods. *MTV Cribs* needs to talk to the Pope about maybe getting in there with some cameras and shit. I had heard that it was considered a city in and of itself, with its own post office and police force, but I didn't know it was surrounded by a huge wall. It is. It's actually surrounded by two walls, the outer one being comprised entirely of guys selling holy knick-knacks. It is nearly impenetrable.

Once you get your ticket for the Vatican Museum, I think they usually expect you to follow a tour or something but we didn't really know any better. It can take quite a while if you do it right, taking in profoundly beautiful art of every variety. Near the end of the museum itself is the Sistine Chapel, which you might have heard of. Holy shit. It is in that room that they lock the, um . . . Cardinals (I don't really know) up without food until they pick a new Pope. It's cool; there's like a cage for them. In any case, Michelangelo's huge fresco that covers one of the walls is only one element of a room that was so breathtaking that it left me drained as I shambled out of there. That was my definition of the Vatican, the Sistine Chapel, so when I got out of there and went around the corner I wasn't ready.

St. Peter's Basilica practically destroyed me.

There is an amazing square outside of it with extremely refreshing fountains. As you approach the church itself, you'll see a sign that shows people in shorts not getting in there, and people with pants getting in. They're not kidding about it, either. I'm sure their thinking goes something like this: if you want to come into God's house, you can put some fucking pants on.

I was still in a jovial mood when I ascended the front stairs and stood before the doors. I recall the frivolity of the moment because I said it would make a good place for a LAN party. I noticed that the wall opposite the door was actually wired CAT-5, so I was thinking a couple of switches and we'd be ready to go.

If you can look at the *Pieta*—I know the accents aren't right on that word, I don't know how to produce them—if you can look at Michelangelo's *Pieta* and then crack some fucking jokes, then something other than human blood animates you. I kept trying to remind myself that a person made it.

They keep bodies in that place, remains of saints and so forth, honored by gigantic statues placed above their tombs. I can't describe how still it made me. There is a statue of a seated St. Peter whose stone foot has been worn completely smooth—it looks like a hoof—by a procession of human beings long beyond numbering. Even as a person who is not really down with this sort of thing, it had a very pronounced effect on me. It is beautiful, and you can appreciate it either because it's the house of God or because human beings of tremendous talent and passion created something immortal.

There is a room, divided from the rest of the church by a curtain and a guard, that is reserved for prayer only. I went in because I was there and I might as well see it, and once through the curtain I was struck as though by a physical force to kneel. I've never done anything like this, Catholics have a special kind of bench they pray on, and it is not a position natural to me, so I nearly lost my balance. Where do my arms go?

I won't inflict the particulars of my prayer on you. I just needed to tell someone what happened.

ROME, ITALY.
Wed, June 04 2003—10:55 P.M.

Not bad at all.

For one thing, there's Goddamn gelato every hundred feet or so. Gelato is the Italian super ice cream developed—but never unleashed—during World War II. I think they whip it or something. Also, you can walk pretty much anywhere you want to go. I guess there's some kind of a law that says you can't build anything higher than the dome of St. Peter's, which would just be interesting trivia if we hadn't had to use that fact to get us home one day. Of course, using a church dome as your landmark isn't a great idea here, but we lucked out in this case.

It is very hot all the fucking time. I believe that part of the reason Catholicism was able to secure such a grip is that these people are truly frightened of a place that could possibly be hotter than it is already. Fountains aren't just for decoration here; you would die if they weren't all over. There are also these spigots from hell to breakfast that just spill out ice-cold water all day. You can convert any one of them into a fountain by covering where the water comes out at the bottom.

I come here to the Hello Hello internet access place because it is opposite a store called Shoes and Bags. I used to go to the Western Union on the other side, but every time I came out she would have a new pair of shoes. She stressed that buying shoes is simply what one does in Italy, and I suggested to her that perhaps it was what they didn't do ever again. I stood outside that store waiting for her once, and it has a terrible attraction for the women who pass it. I saw a nun walk by with no intention of entering, when suddenly her neck snapped back and she was hauled in by an invisible cord.

Guys keep hitting on my wife, which I can understand, so it doesn't bother me. She looks pretty good, all's fair. But please, don't tell me I'm So Lucky or that I'm A Lucky Man. Brenna could not understand why this would make me angry when them kissing her arm or whatever would not. I let her in on a little man secret. When you tell a guy that he is a Lucky Man, you aren't saying it because she seems like a really nice person. What you are telling him is that you would so fuck that. You would fuck that to pieces.

Gabriel's fondest wish—though not his life's dream, as you'll see next week—is that he never be exposed to the smell of other people's urine. I think that this is a good wish to have, it's just that they keep putting the good stuff right next to the bad stuff on our planet. Big cities just smell like that. They do. When I look at a, you know, *something* by Michelangelo or Raphael or Bernini, I know that I am not seeing everything. I just don't have the eye for it. I mean, shit. I stared at a piece at the Museum of Modern Art for about five minutes—really getting it, man—until I realized it was a fucking fire extinguisher. If only there were some way to combine his capacity to appreciate beauty and my tolerance of—and in some cases, appreciation for—human waste.

HEY HEY, WE'RE THE MONKS
Mon, June 09 2003—03:01 A.M.

We saw something our last day in Rome that shut me right up. We went to something called the *Cappuchine Crypt*, where an order of monks made sculptures out of the bodies of brothers that had been returned to them. Each of five or six small rooms had their floors spread with earth from Jerusalem, and over this the monks had combined different bones into patterns, flowers, and other designs. An effigy of death itself held an hourglass also made out of bones, for example, and a scythe made out of shoulder blades. Between Venice and Rome, I've seen about nine different varieties of monks, priests, and nuns. What do these differences represent, I wonder—is it for intramural sports? At the very least, I'd imagine that each type has different skills and bonus feats.

TRAFFIC AS A DOUBLE ENTENDRE
Mon, June 09 2003—03:35 A.M.

My grandfather once told me that he could make smoke come out of my ears, and I believed him. We were talking about a being who could produce money virtually on demand, and also appeared to have a limitless supply of bubblegum. I was willing to see this for myself. People made smoke rings and so forth; perhaps this procedure was related to that. He took a long drag, and then stared intensely at me. Then he burned my leg under the table with his cigarette.

I was shocked and hurt. What the fuck was this? Not only was my granddad exposed as a charlatan of the worst sort; he had also burned my leg. I learned an important lesson: some games are simply not worth playing.

We had been warned by absolutely every person we know about "Italian drivers" and the danger they represent to humanity. I had no interest in trying to actually drive there. That would have been suicide. It would have been committing my body entirely to a game with indistinct rules, playing with a nation of opponents who are professionals at the sport. Walking there is no problem, though. At least, not if you know about Ethernet.

The way we are used to utilizing our streets in, let's say, Seattle is that we as pedestrians cross when we have the light, and we as drivers go when we have the light. It reminds one of the Token Ring network topology: each node, Vehicular or Pedestrian, gets the token and has access to the media. Then it switches, the other guys go, and it goes on like that. By comparison, if you want to see as compelling a demonstration of Ethernet as you are ever likely to see in your life, head on over to Rome and try to cross the fucking street. Don't *wait* to cross it. They'll never stop. Everyone goes at once. That's right, there are forty motorscooters and tiny Smart Cars and what looks like a motorized wheelbarrow going where you're trying to go at the same time you're trying to go there. They're crossing your path right to left as you are walking straight ahead. You may momentarily feel as though you are floating in a sea of careening metal. That is actually fairly accurate. But you are in no danger.

VENICE, ITALY.
Wed, June 11 2003—07:19 A.M.

If Italy were a videogame, Venice would be the second level. You've still got the twisty streets you had in Rome, and plenty of other old cities I've been in, except now you replace over half of those streets (including the main one that runs through the whole town) with water. You know how in first-person games you'll often come upon a grate that hinders your progress, or some other ridiculous piece of design like "the ground just stops here" that seems trite and lazy when you see it? The person who made that level isn't bored with their job or trying to cut corners. They're accurately simulating Venice. You'll just be going along and then, no sign, no nothing, just mute water.

I'm pretty screwed up at this point; thinking of Venice—a human city—as a "level" is just the start of it. Everywhere I look I see the underlying game mechanism. All I have with me is WarioWare, which is cool, but if I don't get something substantial at

some point over here I'm going to freak the fuck out. I see the old ladies with the woven donation baskets pleading with me in a foreign tongue, and all I can think about is whether the pictures of Jesus and Mary they have in there confer some kind of donation bonus. Of course, there's a metagame being played by the entire city: how much money can we make off tourists before our gravy train sinks like Atlantis beneath the waves?

The psychotic break made was practically audible when I walked off streets that looked like the Italy level in CounterStrike only to find myself with twenty people playing the Italy level inside an Internet cafe. Thank God that place had a liquor license.

IT'S FUN WHEN YOUR BALLS SWELL
Fri, June 13 2003—06:13 A.M.

I keep hoping I'll see that fuckhole Rick Steves while I'm over here. Yes, that Rick Steves, PBS Rick Steves, Mr. Knows All About Europe, I'm Going To Punch Him In The Face Rick Steves.

We've got one of his travel books with us, a real treasure trove of fucking wisdom. If you turn to the last page of the book, you can see ads for a series he calls *Europe Through the Back Door*, promising a host of exciting "Back Door Tours." It probably wouldn't hurt him to ask his hip young nephew whether or not his new book titles contain references to anal sex.

We did not have a very high opinion of Venice, and we were glad to leave it on a train for Munich a few days ago. The thing is, it wasn't even Venice's fault. I blame Dick Steves.

We were staying in a hotel that was about 100 Euro—which is to say about a million US dollars—a night. Keep in mind that this is a hotel we found in his Book of Lies. When we went in to get our key, we saw that there is even a Rick Steves tour staying in the hotel; since this was when we still liked him, we thought this was a good sign.

We became very itchy in the night. I thought I was just hot, but it eventually became so intense that I turned the light on and threw back the sheet. What I saw were black columns of insects lining up to take a bite of my business. Me, I mean, that's how I would write about it. Ants were biting my balls. That cockjockey Steves would probably say some shit about "discovering Venice's tiniest citizens." I'm going to choke him with a belt.

MUNICH, GERMANY
Mon, June 16 2003—03:01 A.M.

I just finished a beer that was so large that I had to lift it with both hands. Really, the only reason I ordered it was to wash down a pretzel that was itself so large that it could have eaten me under the right circumstances. I have a very high opinion of Munich, but it may have been artificially produced.

We got here on Monday, and we didn't know it, but it was some kind of holiday. We just started walking through a park, and we came upon a few hundred people drinking a lot. A bunch of old guys wearing lederhosen were playing brass instruments on the second floor of some rickety structure. I saw no way to access that level, so it's possible they got up there as young men and were never able to escape.

I started to cry as I sat down with a gigantic piece of meat, a schnitzel, which is like a fried continent. I mean it, I pulled my hat off my head and covered my face with it and started to cry in the middle of a crowd of five hundred people. This was the thought that crept across my mind, like skywriting: this is what it is all about. If getting drunk at eleven in the fucking afternoon and eating a huge piece of meat is wrong, then I don't want to be right.

Okay, so that was a holiday and people were celebrating. It's not like that all the time. I could live there for the rest of my life, though, if I needed to. We ride rented bikes we have named Bavaratti and Black Power. We ride them through parks as big as my whole district back home. We ride them through wildflowers which are tiny but distinct, like pixels.

In Italy, meals come in discrete phases, like space rockets. In Germany, the best way I can think of to describe the food is "pragmatic." It is there to get the job done, and make sure that the beer has something to keep it company. We have no idea what we're ordering, ever. Brenna did the "Learn Italian" CD-ROM, and I was supposed to do the German one, but once I learned the word for "airplane" I lost interest and got heavily into online Raven Shield. Airplanes are rarely on the menu, so I've sorta let down the team here. We point at menus to get our food, at random items whose origins are mysterious to us.

Every time, I seem to get sausages and sauerkraut. I'm fine with this, I think that pickling things is very prudent and I support the procedure wholeheartedly. But Brenna gets something like a bowl of Turkey Jell-O with a carrot in it or some shit. That's not a joke. Neither was the Venice thing, actually. I will think of Venice every time a red sore leaks white pus.

The best thing about being over here, aside from the bidets, I mean, is listening to all these languages. Someone needs to speak English for about thirty seconds before I even recognize it. I took a lot of French in high school, which is the same as taking no French ever—I used to be able to talk about hair and cheese or whatever, but the extent of my French ability these days is to declare that I am a frozen chicken. Before I came here, I think that I believed Italian and German and French were just other ways to speak English, like a dialect that they persisted in using because they were stubborn or proud. When you hear a person in Italy or whatever talking in some weird way, they aren't trying to be funny; it's a whole language. They talk like that all the time. They even think like that, if you can imagine it.

Italian is cool because it can warp space-time. Let's say that someone is just saying "hi" to you. The "buon" comes out okay; we're good so far. Even the "g" is good. But when we get to the "iornoooooooo," minutes can turn into hours. I was talking to a guy at this place and he was like "buon" and I was like, "Yeah, great. Look, I need to be somewhere this week." German, it's basically like English. English, you know, spoken by a monster, underwater, into a walkie-talkie.

I'll be turning the e-mail back on come Wednesday's post. Europe is great and everything, but I miss my fucking cat and I don't want to be here anymore.

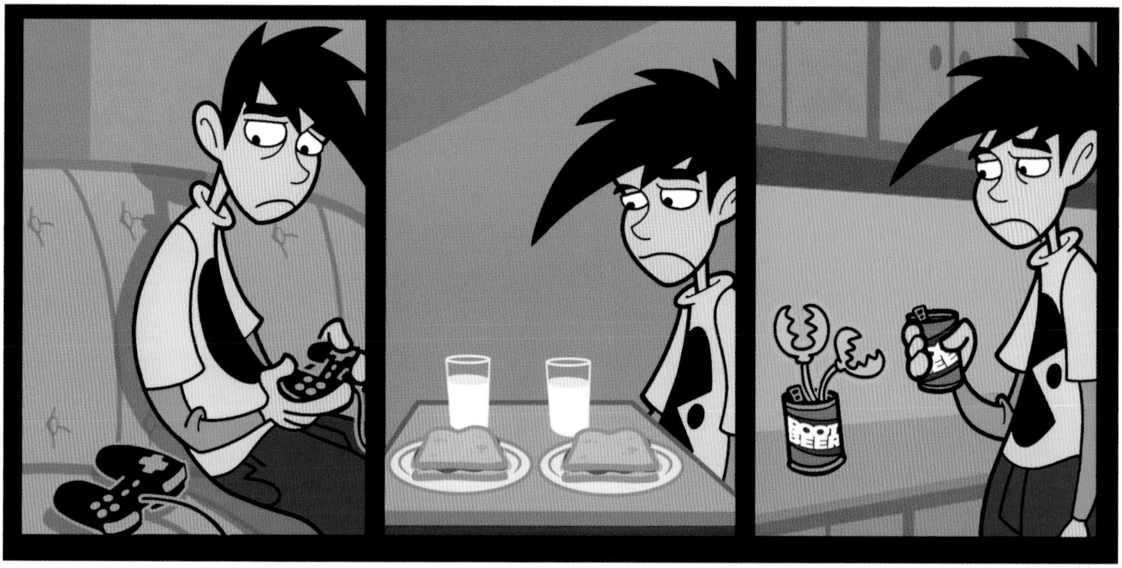

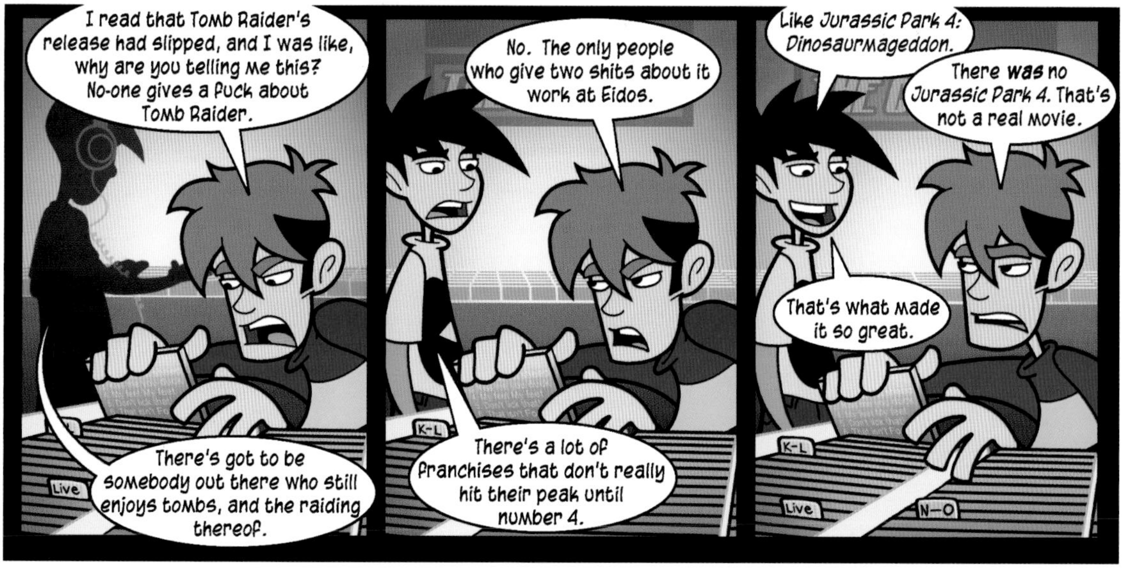
I read that Tomb Raider's release had slipped, and I was like, why are you telling me this? No-one gives a fuck about Tomb Raider.
There's got to be somebody out there who still enjoys tombs, and the raiding thereof.
No. The only people who give two shits about it work at Eidos.
There's a lot of franchises that don't really hit their peak until number 4.
Like Jurassic Park 4: Dinosaurmageddon.
There **was** no Jurassic Park 4. That's not a real movie.
That's what made it so great.
K-L
Live
N-O

I THINK WE'RE ALONE NOW

June 16, 2003 I'm sure his life is richer than *this* when I'm not around . . . Right? Model *trains* or something?

OF TOMBS

June 18, 2003 We could never have imagined during this period that legendary console developer Crystal Dynamics would be given the franchise, let *alone* that they would revive it with such consummate vigor. There were moments I enjoyed less than others—things I covered in the post—but overall it was such a strong relaunch that they've made me a day one customer for Tomb Raider games again—something I would have thought impossible.

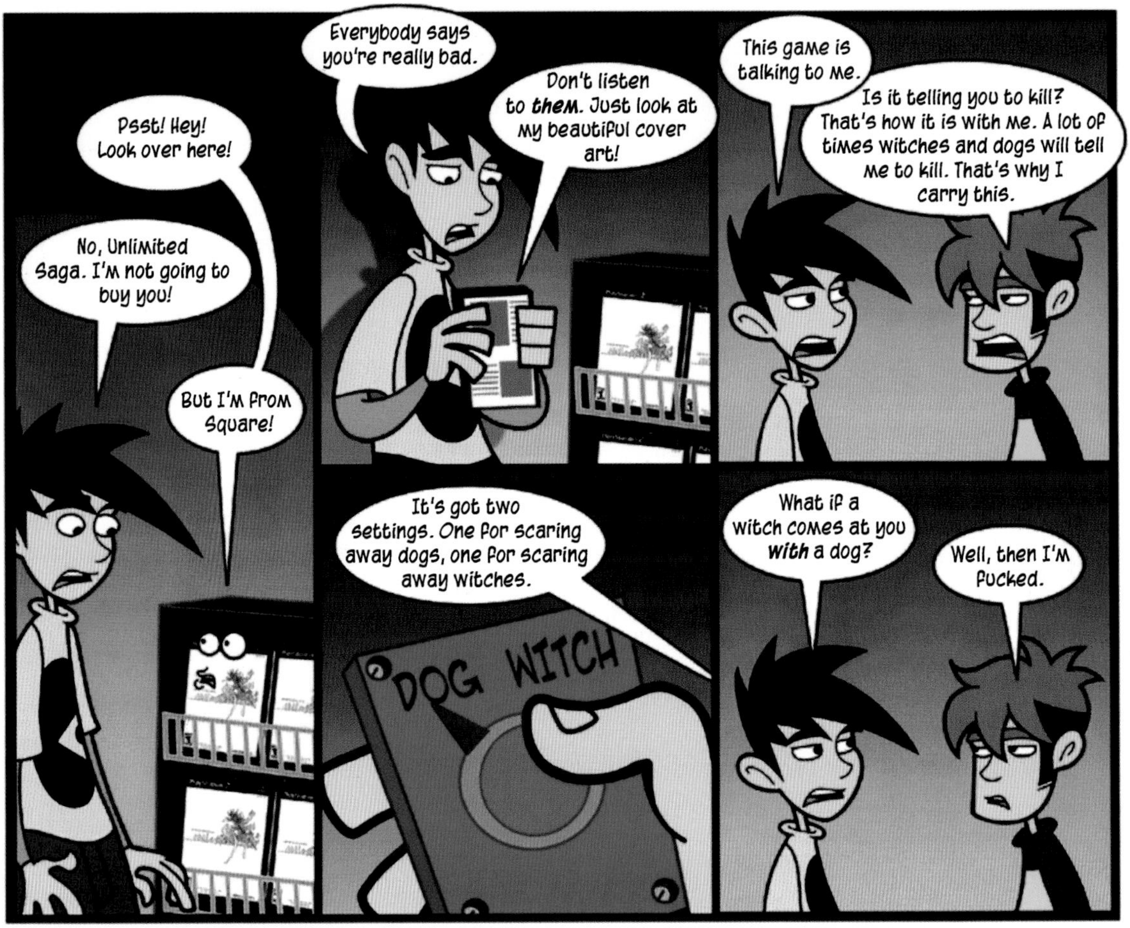
Psst! Hey! Look over here!
No, Unlimited Saga. I'm not going to buy you!
But I'm from Square!
Everybody says you're really bad.
Don't listen to *them*. Just look at my beautiful cover art!
This game is talking to me.
Is it telling you to kill? That's how it is with me. A lot of times witches and dogs will tell me to kill. That's why I carry this.
It's got two settings. One for scaring away dogs, one for scaring away witches.
DOG WITCH
What if a witch comes at you *with* a dog?
Well, then I'm fucked.

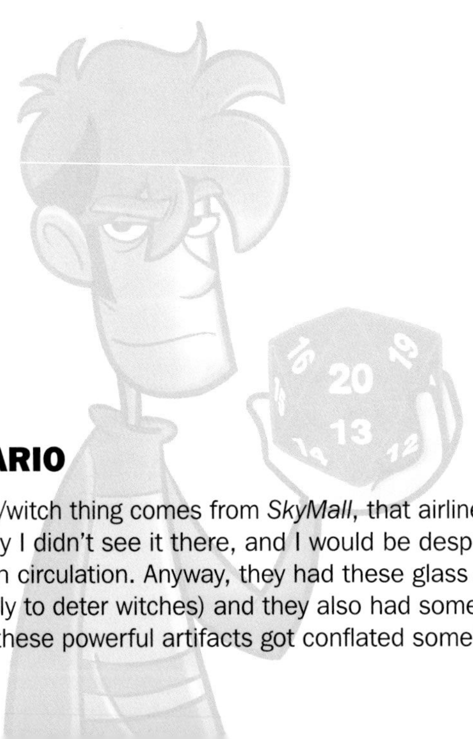
20
13
19
16
12
14

A GRAVE SCENARIO

June 20, 2003 The dog/witch thing comes from *SkyMall*, that airline catalogue thing. The last couple times I was forced to fly I didn't see it there, and I would be despondent to learn that this crucial pamphlet is no longer in circulation. Anyway, they had these glass orbs you're supposed to put in your garden (presumably to deter witches) and they also had some portable dog excruciator; during the writing of the strip these powerful artifacts got conflated somehow.

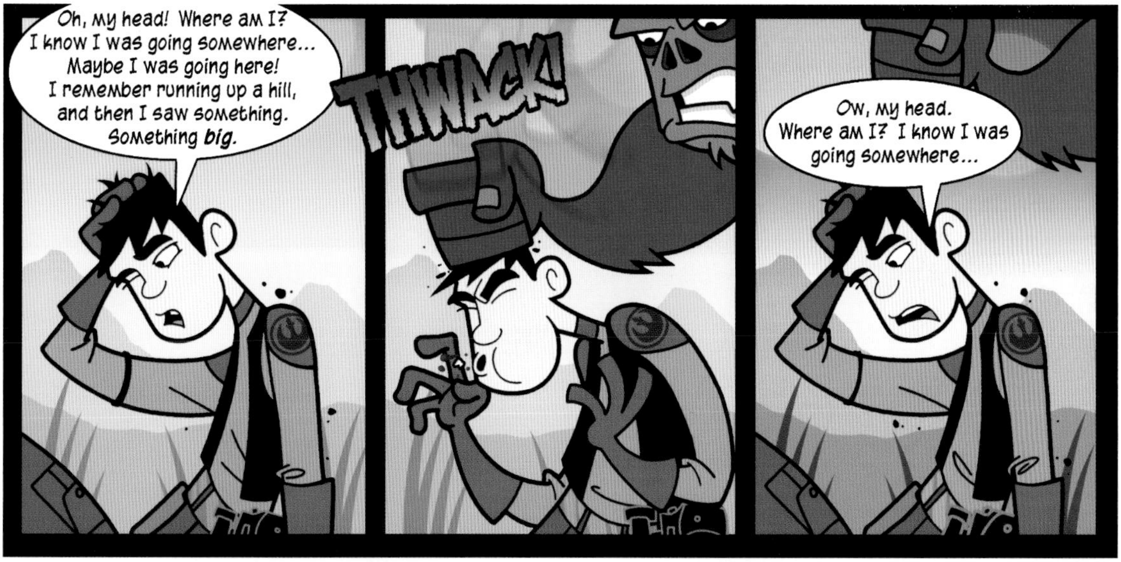
Oh, my head! Where am I? I know I was going somewhere... Maybe I was going here! I remember running up a hill, and then I saw something. Something *big*.
THWACK!
Ow, my head. Where am I? I know I was going somewhere...

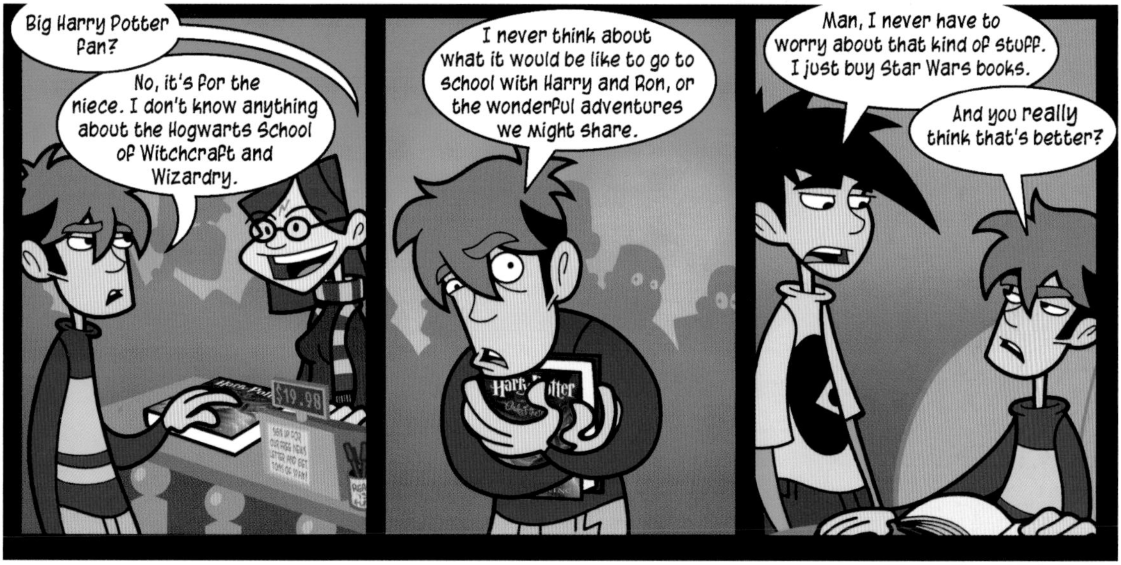
Big Harry Potter fan?
No, it's for the niece. I don't know anything about the Hogwarts School of Witchcraft and Wizardry.
$19.98
I never think about what it would be like to go to school with Harry and Ron, or the wonderful adventures we might share.
Man, I never have to worry about that kind of stuff. I just buy Star Wars books.
And you really think that's better?

WELCOME TO HERE

June 23, 2003 From that day's post: Gabe was often waylaid halfway to some Godforsaken Tatooine shithole he had a mission at, waylaid by some kind of massive troll that would hit him until he fell down; once he groggily regained consciousness, it would bop him like a field mouse in what I'm sure is a highly enjoyable game for trolls.

THE BOY WHO LIVED

June 25, 2003 I think that's *Harry Potter and the Order of the Phoenix* I'm clutching there. The fifth book. It's eight hundred and seventy pages. I read it in a day.

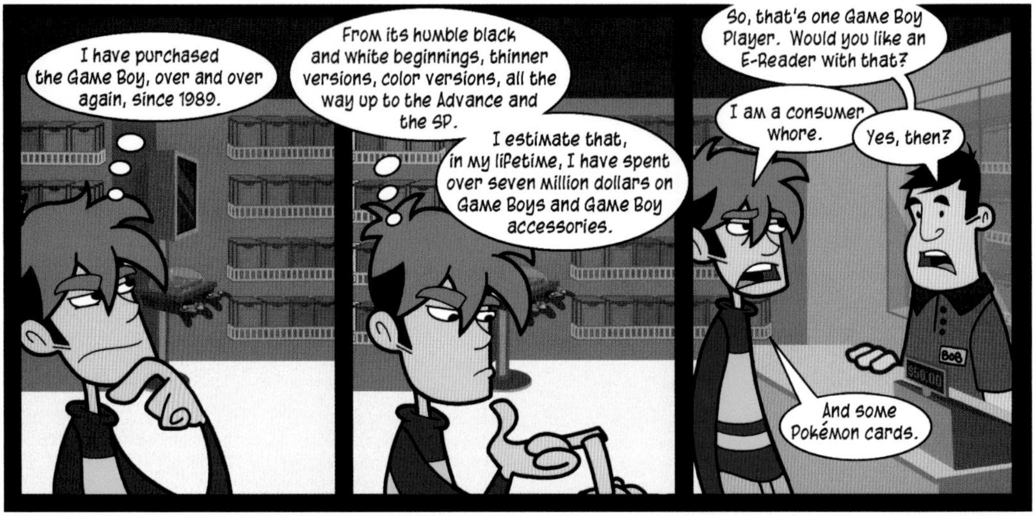

I have purchased the Game Boy, over and over again, since 1989.
From its humble black and white beginnings, thinner versions, color versions, all the way up to the Advance and the SP.
I estimate that, in my lifetime, I have spent over seven million dollars on Game Boys and Game Boy accessories.
So, that's one Game Boy Player. Would you like an E-Reader with that?
I am a consumer whore.
Yes, then?
And some Pokémon cards.
BOB
$50.00

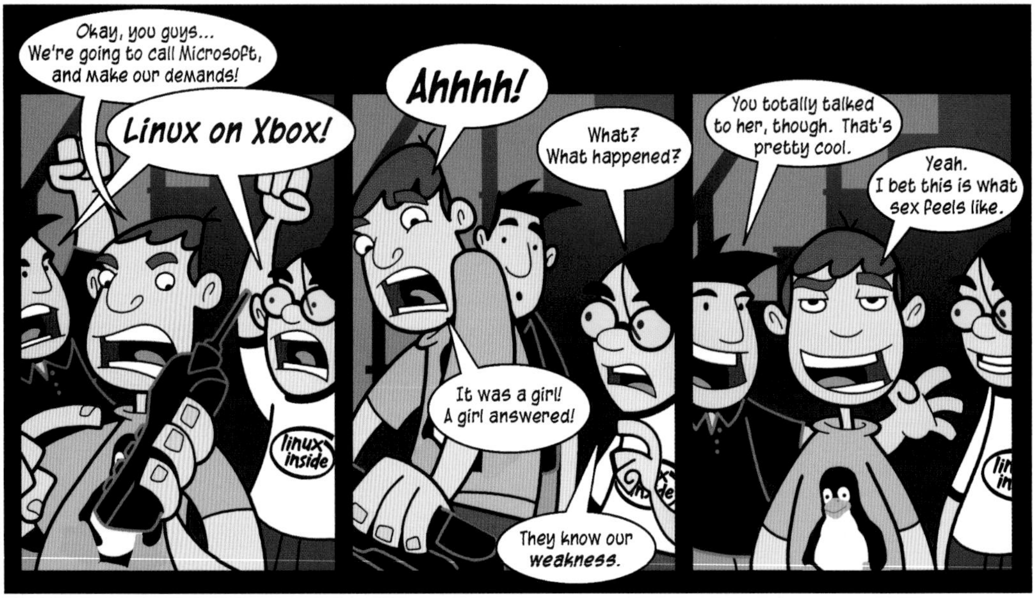

Okay, you guys... We're going to call Microsoft, and make our demands!
Linux on Xbox!
linux inside
Ahhhh!
What? What happened?
It was a girl! A girl answered!
They know our weakness.
You totally talked to her, though. That's pretty cool.
Yeah. I bet this is what sex feels like.

THE ADMISSION

June 27, 2003 Remember the E-Reader? It was this strange wedge you could affix to your Game Boy Advance that read collectible cards. Along one side of the card was what looked like static, and when swiped into your system that static could be any number of things: new characters for your games, apparel or other accessories, even complete games *themselves* which sometimes took several cards to input.

ALSO KNOWN AS BLACKMAIL

June 30, 2003 The story is this: a modding group claimed to have discovered a way to install Linux on the Xbox without a mod chip, and they would release this information to THE WORLD if Microsoft didn't allow legitimate Linux installs. Console makers and modders have been locked in a firmware arms race ever since.

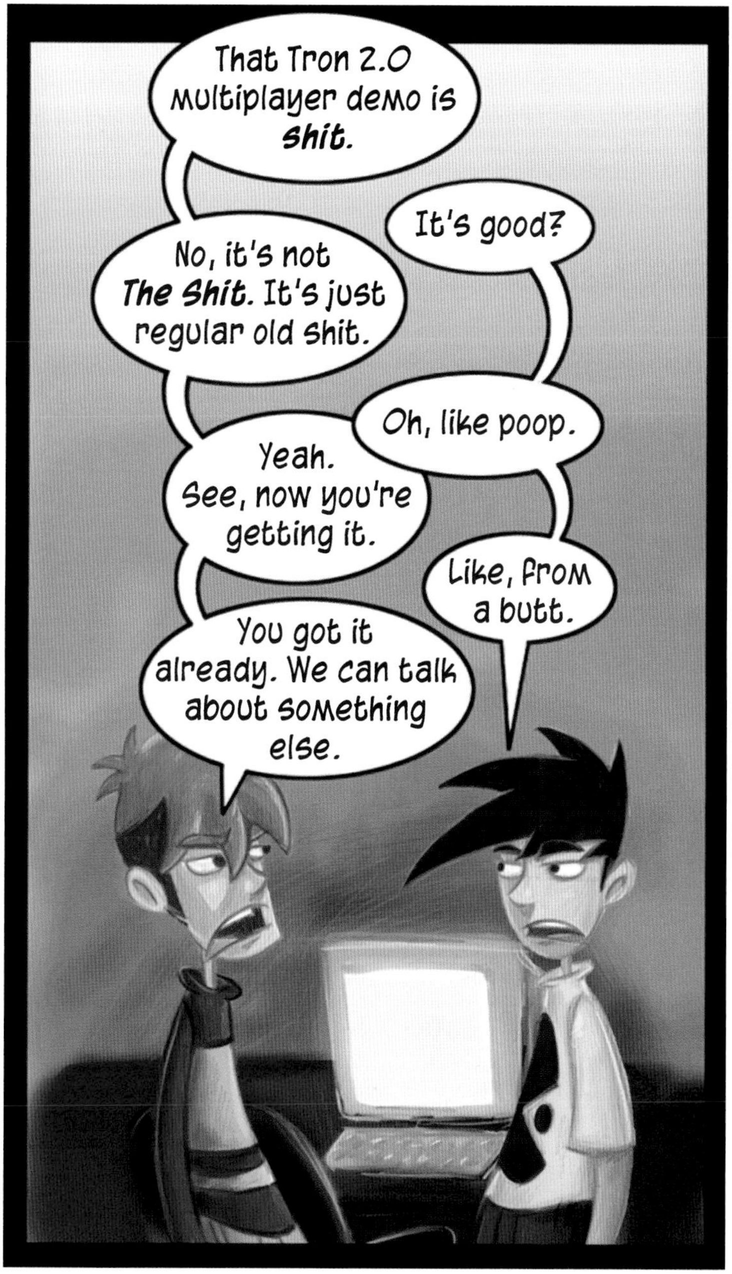
That Tron 2.0 multiplayer demo is *shit.*
It's good?
No, it's not *The Shit.* It's just regular old shit.
Oh, like poop.
Yeah. See, now you're getting it.
Like, from a butt.
You got it already. We can talk about something else.

GARBAGE IS TOO KIND A WORD

July 2, 2003 Gabe did this one on his (then) new Acer TabletPC, which explains the look. It turns out the Tron 2.0 multiplayer demo reviewed here was never meant to see public distribution, and having played it I can absolutely understand why that would be. Much of my opinion at this time was colored by my affection for freeware gem Armegetron, an interpretation of the iconic light cycle combat that really got a lot right. On the other hand, the single-player campaign of Tron 2.0 was unbelievably satisfying—but then, I wrote a brief musical about Tron you might remember from a later comic. I'm not what you would call *neutral* on the subject.

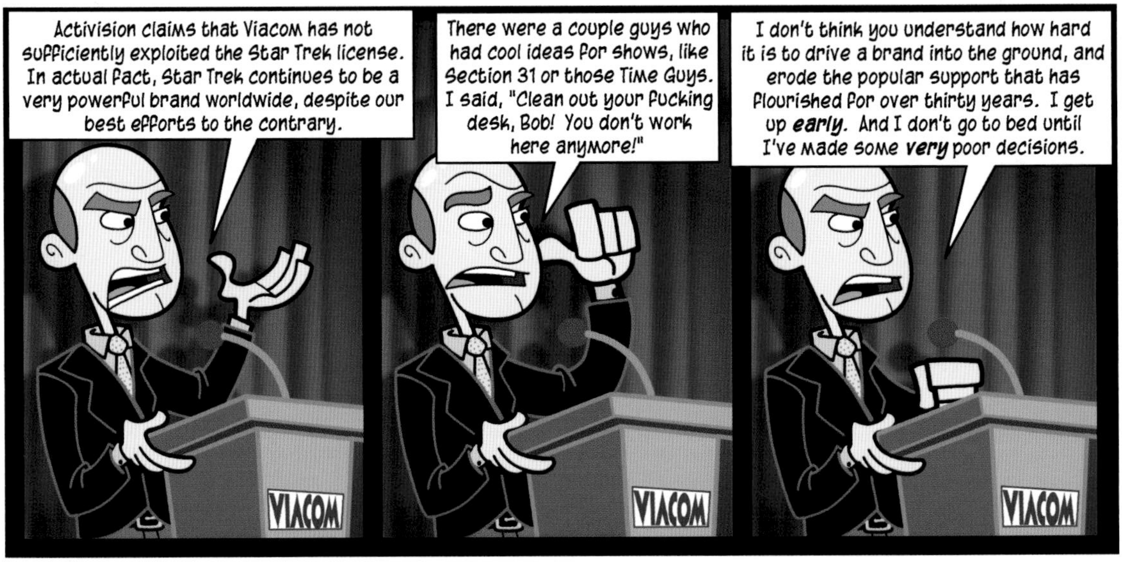
Activision claims that Viacom has not sufficiently exploited the Star Trek license. In actual fact, Star Trek continues to be a very powerful brand worldwide, despite our best efforts to the contrary.
There were a couple guys who had cool ideas for shows, like Section 31 or those Time Guys. I said, "Clean out your fucking desk, Bob! You don't work here anymore!"
I don't think you understand how hard it is to drive a brand into the ground, and erode the popular support that has flourished for over thirty years. I get up early. And I don't go to bed until I've made some very poor decisions.
VIACOM
VIACOM
VIACOM

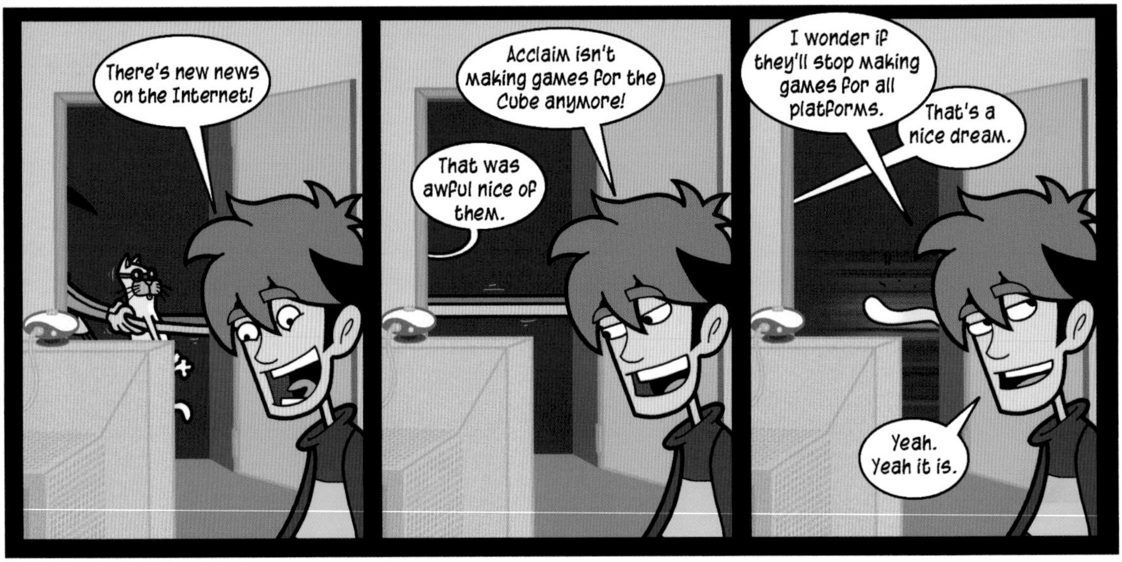
There's new news on the Internet!
Acclaim isn't making games for the Cube anymore!
That was awful nice of them.
I wonder if they'll stop making games for all platforms.
That's a nice dream.
Yeah. Yeah it is.

A UNIQUE PREDICAMENT

July 4, 2003 This strip is still very fresh in my mind, and I think about it a lot. The legal battle between Activision and Viacom came about because Star Trek had basically been run into the ground, and the license Activision had purchased to use the setting had been deprecated as a result. Would that the dedicated fans who *support* these franchises could band together toward the same end, for we have suffered *long*.

CATAPULT

July 9, 2003 And, of course, they *did*. Then they came back somehow? Publishing Korean MMOs or some shit? Who knows anymore. I think someone just bought the name. I don't believe it's the same evil men who rode rough over decency offering to advertise on gravestones. I might have passed on the name "Acclaim," given the opportunity, but that's just me. I think it might be haunted.

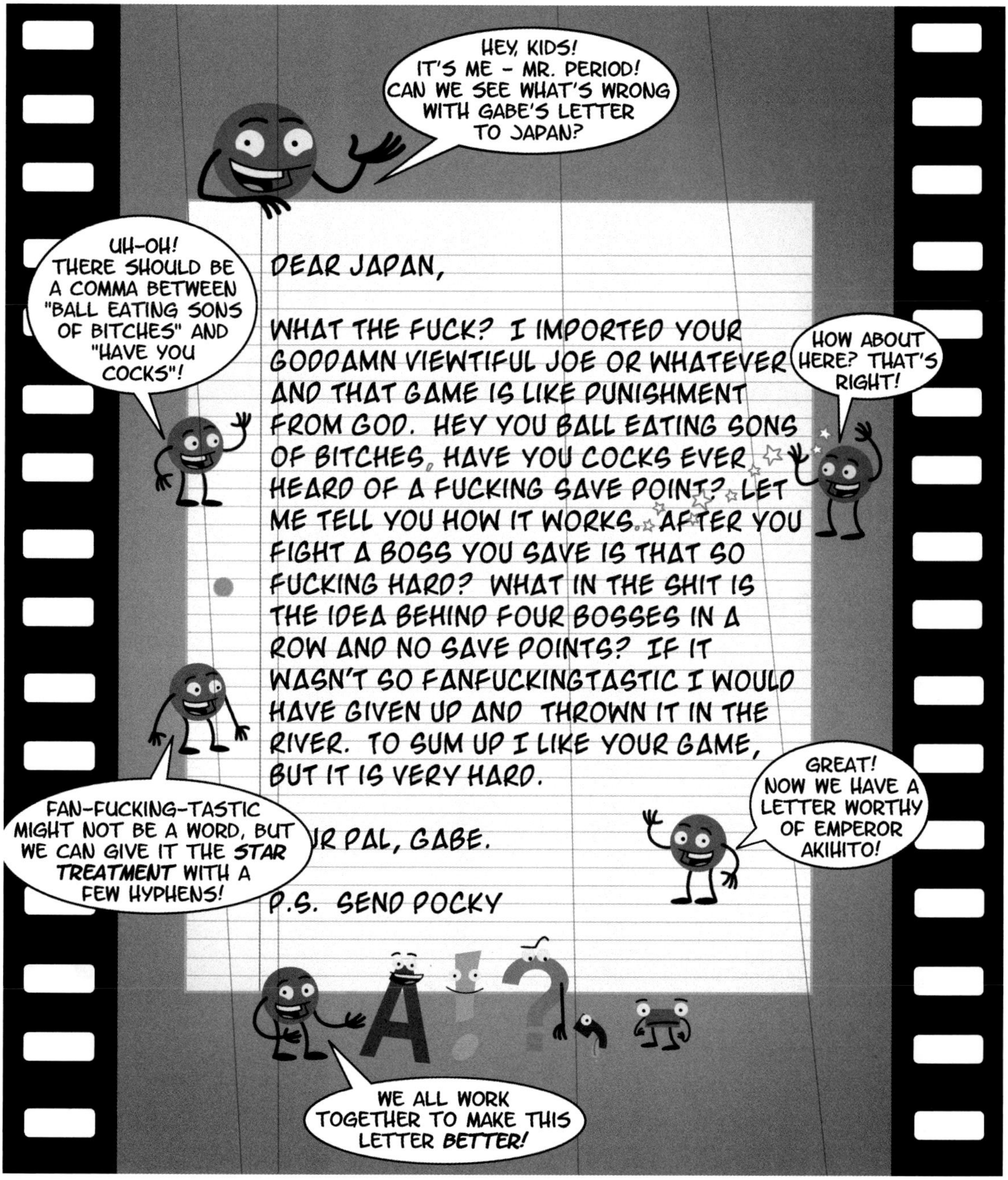
HEY, KIDS! IT'S ME - MR. PERIOD! CAN WE SEE WHAT'S WRONG WITH GABE'S LETTER TO JAPAN?
UH-OH! THERE SHOULD BE A COMMA BETWEEN "BALL EATING SONS OF BITCHES" AND "HAVE YOU COCKS"!
DEAR JAPAN,
WHAT THE FUCK? I IMPORTED YOUR GODDAMN VIEWTIFUL JOE OR WHATEVER AND THAT GAME IS LIKE PUNISHMENT FROM GOD. HEY YOU BALL EATING SONS OF BITCHES, HAVE YOU COCKS EVER HEARD OF A FUCKING SAVE POINT? LET ME TELL YOU HOW IT WORKS. AFTER YOU FIGHT A BOSS YOU SAVE IS THAT SO FUCKING HARD? WHAT IN THE SHIT IS THE IDEA BEHIND FOUR BOSSES IN A ROW AND NO SAVE POINTS? IF IT WASN'T SO FANFUCKINGTASTIC I WOULD HAVE GIVEN UP AND THROWN IT IN THE RIVER. TO SUM UP I LIKE YOUR GAME, BUT IT IS VERY HARD.
R PAL, GABE.
P.S. SEND POCKY
HOW ABOUT HERE? THAT'S RIGHT!
FAN-FUCKING-TASTIC MIGHT NOT BE A WORD, BUT WE CAN GIVE IT THE STAR TREATMENT WITH A FEW HYPHENS!
GREAT! NOW WE HAVE A LETTER WORTHY OF EMPEROR AKIHITO!
WE ALL WORK TOGETHER TO MAKE THIS LETTER BETTER!

THE BAD BOYS OF PUNCTUATION

July 7, 2003 After his debut during the Celda debacle, we liked him so much that we wanted to see him return. The joke (at least, the joke internally) is that my own grammar is pretty terrible. My spelling is decent, as evidenced by the two Spelling Bee medals I am currently wearing, but I am punctuation's natural enemy. Even so, the idea of an animate punctuation "crew"—particularly the panting, canine comma—was always very appealing to me.

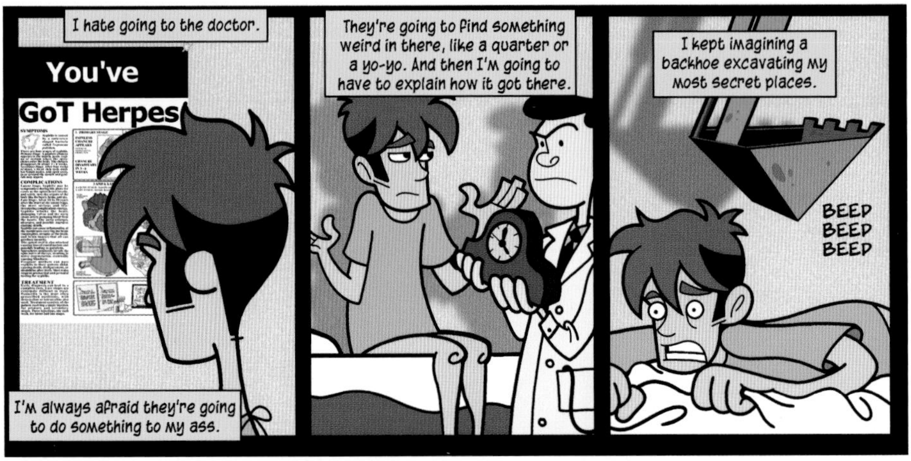
I hate going to the doctor.
You've
GoT Herpes
I'm always afraid they're going to do something to my ass.
They're going to find something weird in there, like a quarter or a yo-yo. And then I'm going to have to explain how it got there.
I kept imagining a backhoe excavating my most secret places.
BEEP
BEEP
BEEP

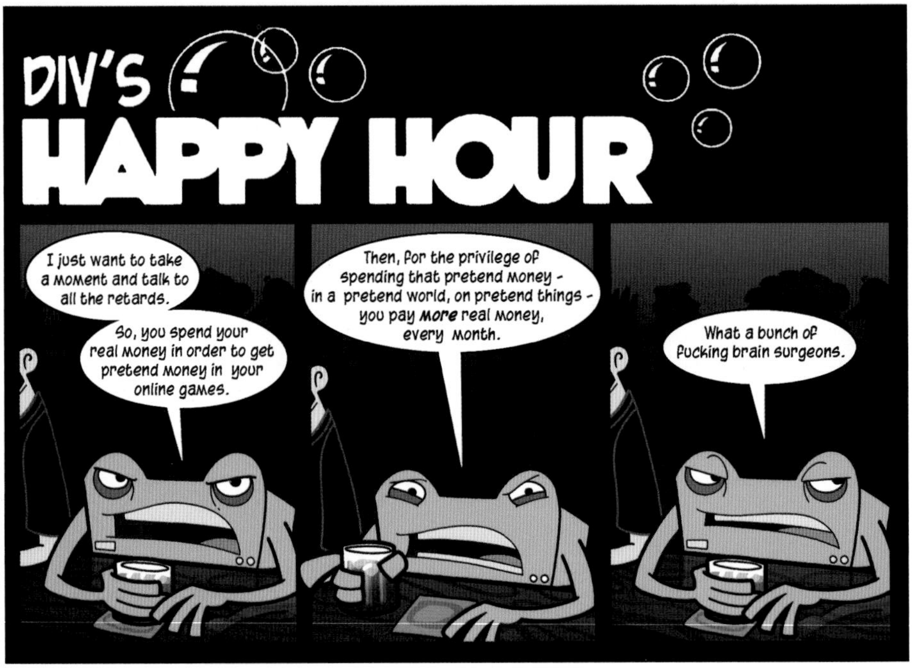
DIV'S
HAPPY HOUR
I just want to take a moment and talk to all the retards.
So, you spend your real money in order to get pretend money in your online games.
Then, for the privilege of spending that pretend money - in a pretend world, on pretend things - you pay *more* real money, every month.
What a bunch of fucking brain surgeons.

A MEDITATION ON FEAR

July 11, 2003 This strip is far, far outside our usual sphere, but my brain needed something to do while I was sitting on that sterile sheet of paper waiting for the doctor to come in and molest me. I had the entire thing put together word for word by the time he burst in the door, which gave me an opportunity to feel some joy before all became darkness.

THAT ADORABLE DEVICE

July 16, 2003 The companies that act as middlemen for this tremendous digital wealth are becoming millionaires in the process, *millionaires*, and given the rage gamers purportedly feel at these services I wonder just how deeply this rage is felt. I wonder how many of our friends' "lucky drops" are not so much a function of luck, but of secret meetings with the shadow bankers that lurk in every crevice of every online game.

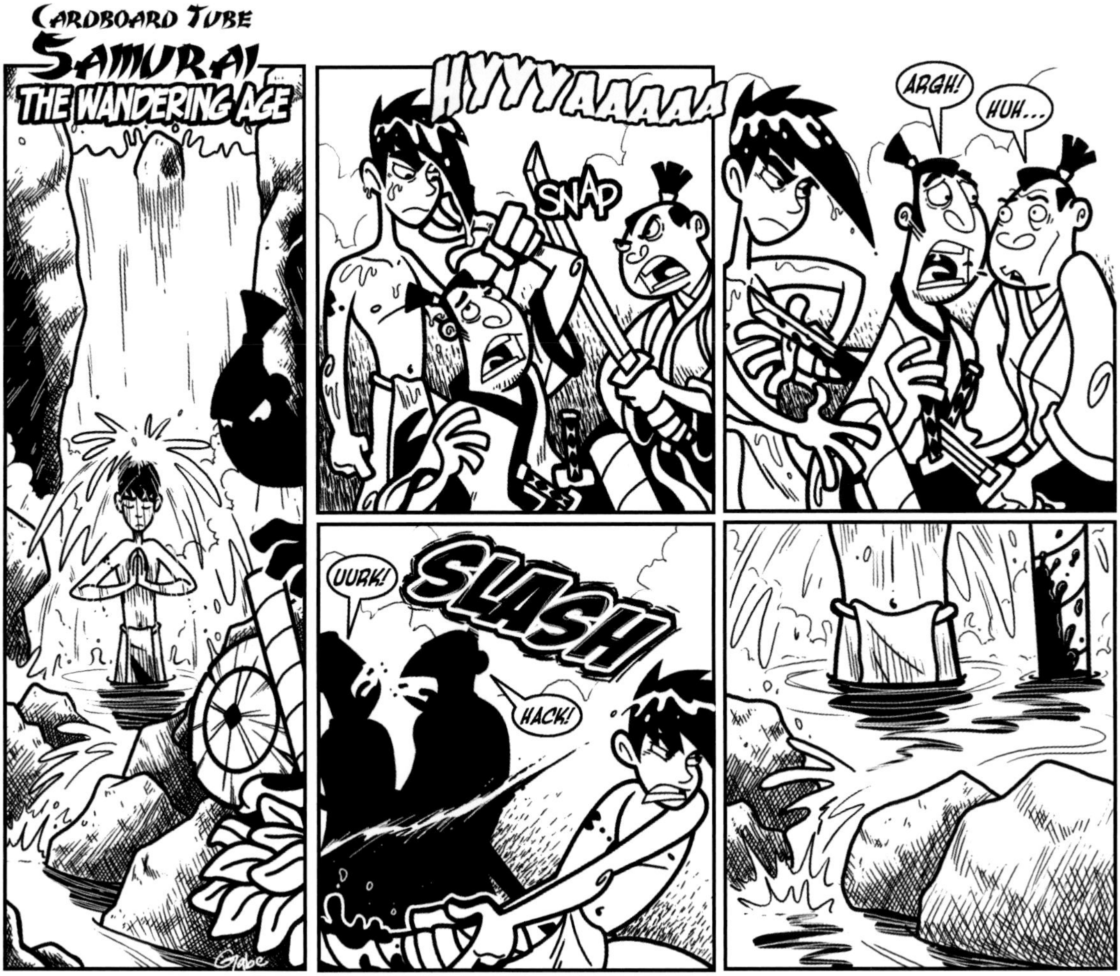
CARDBOARD TUBE SAMURAI
THE WANDERING AGE
HYYYAAAAAA
SNAP
ARGH!
HUH...
UURK!
SLASH
HACK!

THE WANDERING AGE

July 14, 2003 Gabe recently went through every CTS strip we've ever done, adding his analysis, and this is a strip we learned quite a bit from. It was the first time we had experimented with The Wandering Age, that open-ended period of ill-defined adventure introduced in Cardboard and Steel. Typically, our work only covers a couple moments of actual time—we weren't quite ready to tackle a situation like the one we attempted here. We've since learned to give a story—even a very simple story—all the time it needs, and to choose the moments we show the reader much more carefully.

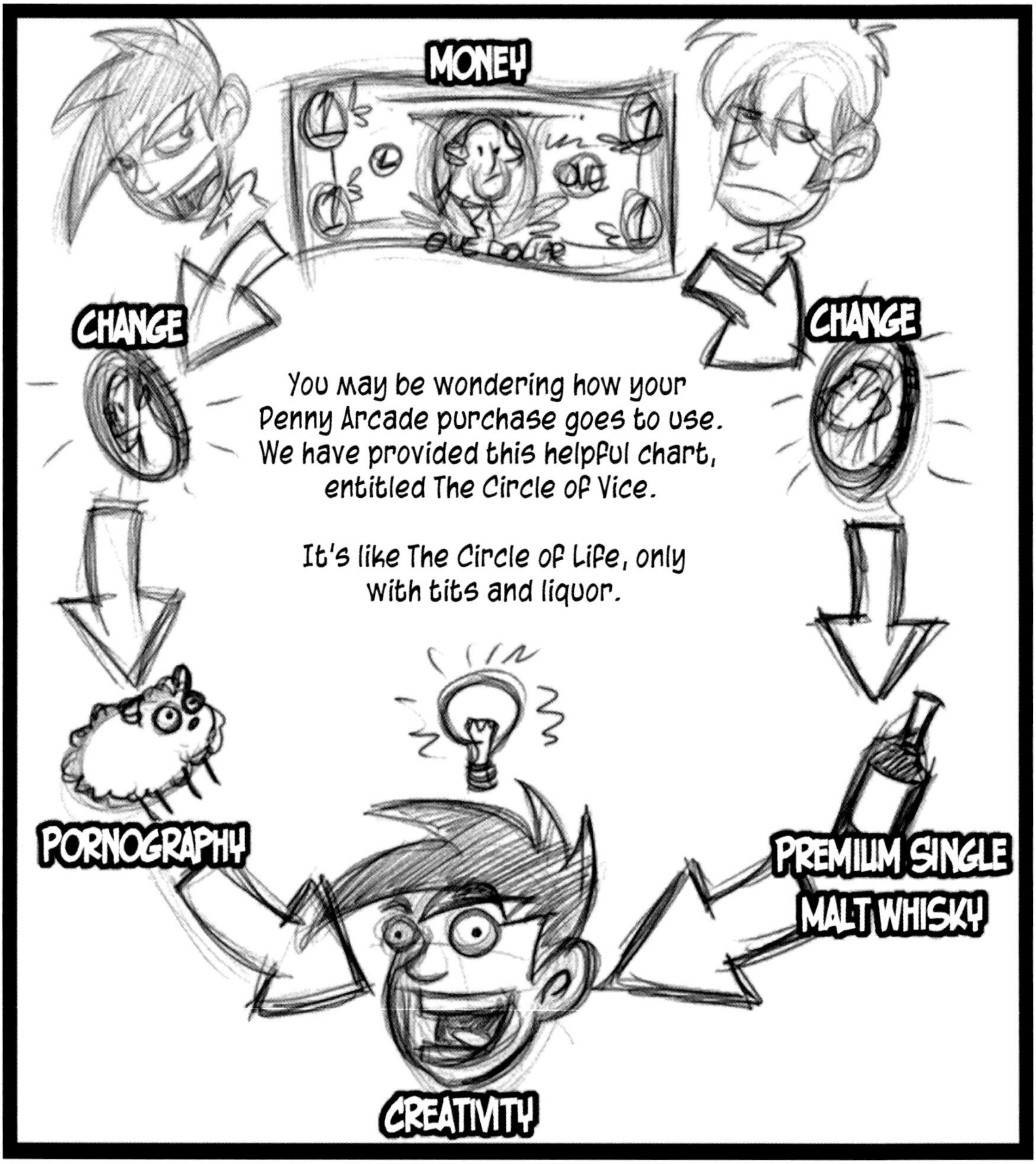
MONEY
CHANGE
CHANGE
You may be wondering how your Penny Arcade purchase goes to use. We have provided this helpful chart, entitled The Circle of Vice.
It's like The Circle of Life, only with tits and liquor.
PORNOGRAPHY
PREMIUM SINGLE MALT WHISKY
CREATIVITY

THE CIRCLE OF VICE

July 18, 2003 For even greater granularity: my beverage of choice is the Balvenie 21 Year Port Wood. The Red Vs. Blue guys bought us a bottle as a gift one year, and since Gabe doesn't drink it was a time of celebration. I can't speak to Gabriel's own predilections, although I *can* say that in a cursory glance beneath his bed I did find a single VHS tape entitled (ahem) "Sheep-Bop-A-Rebop."

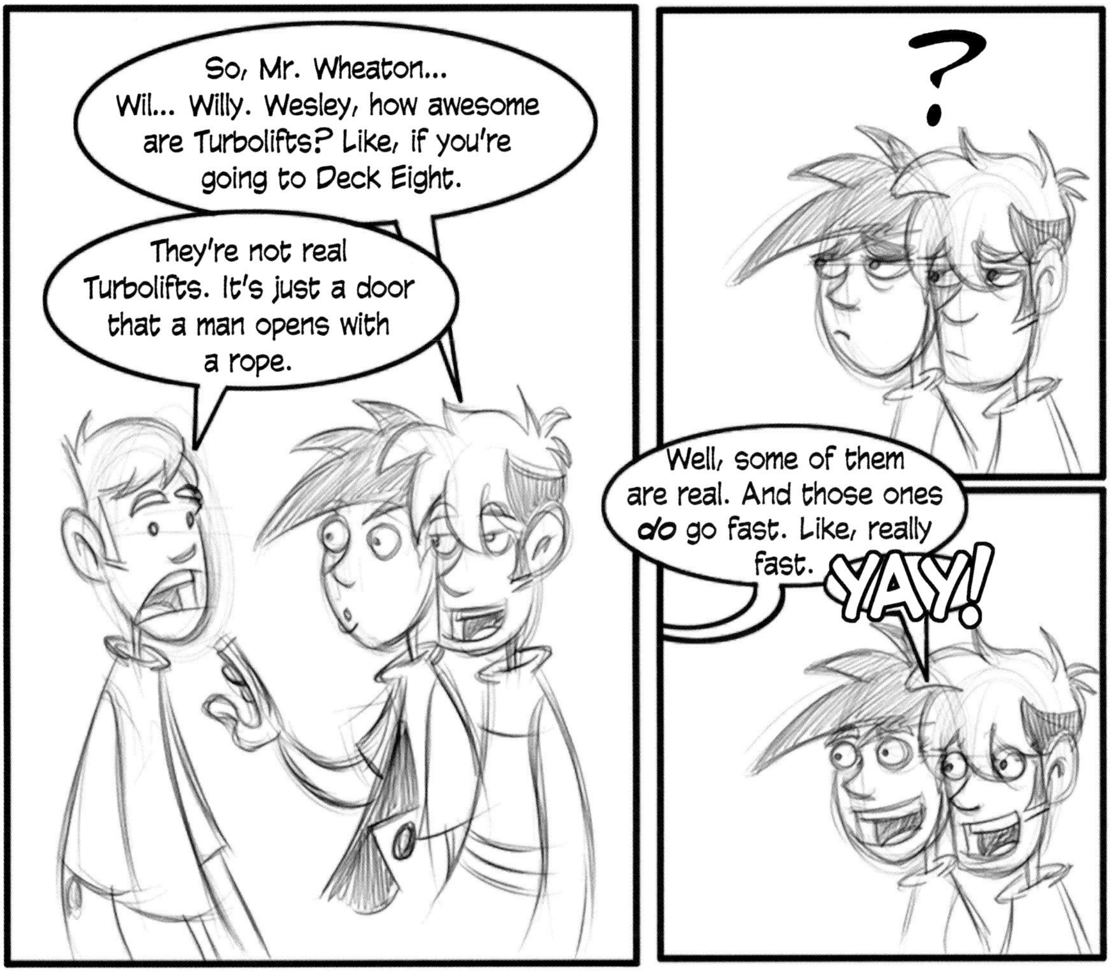
So, Mr. Wheaton... Wil... Willy. Wesley, how awesome are Turbolifts? Like, if you're going to Deck Eight.
They're not real Turbolifts. It's just a door that a man opens with a rope.
?
Well, some of them are real. And those ones *do* go fast. Like, really fast.
YAY!

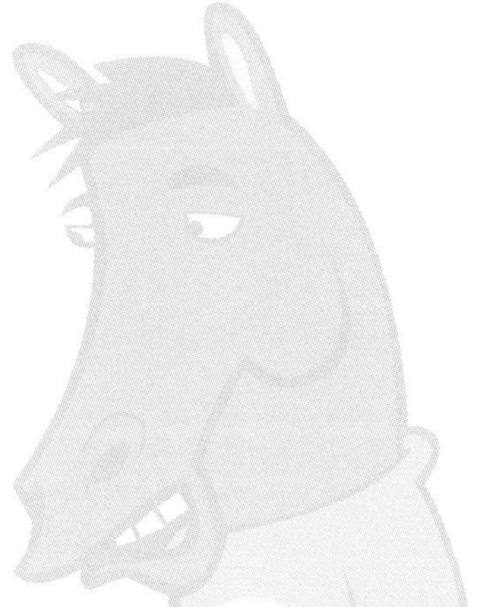

WILLIAM R. WHEATON, ESQ.

July 21, 2003 From that day's post: William Wheaton stopped by our booth and said very nice things to us. Brenna was mad that I did not introduce her to him, as his is the only picture still on her mirror back home. "Wil Wheaton came by to see *you*?" she said. "You're nobody."

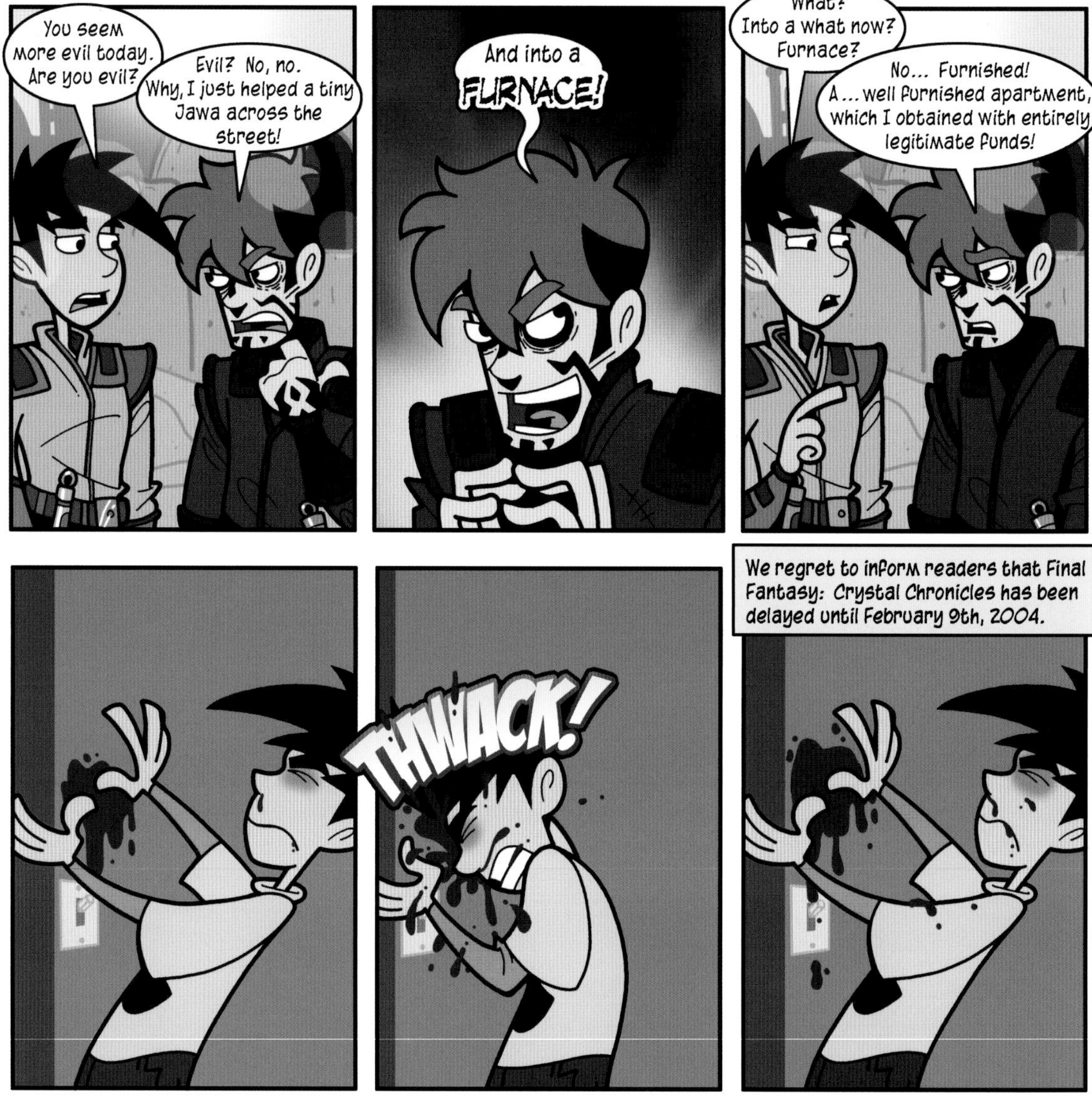
You seem more evil today. Are you evil?
Evil? No, no. Why, I just helped a tiny Jawa across the street!
And into a FURNACE!
What? Into a what now? Furnace?
No... Furnished! A...well furnished apartment, which I obtained with entirely legitimate funds!
THWACK!
We regret to inform readers that Final Fantasy: Crystal Chronicles has been delayed until February 9th, 2004.

THE DARK THIDE OF THE FORTH

July 23, 2003 When we were each playing through Bioware's Knights of the Old Republic, it's probably no surprise that we chose entirely different ways of going about things. Because I was already into Bioware's other role-playing excursions, I had faith that their *bad boy* options would be pretty enjoyable and I was not wrong. In fact, it's fair to say that they went considerably beyond my comfort level.

REPEAT

July 25, 2003 Hearing that Crystal Chronicles had been delayed was momentarily distressing, until I saw the date: February 9th, 2004—more than three years ago, at the time of this writing. It already came out! Man, trawling this archive is an emotional roller coaster.

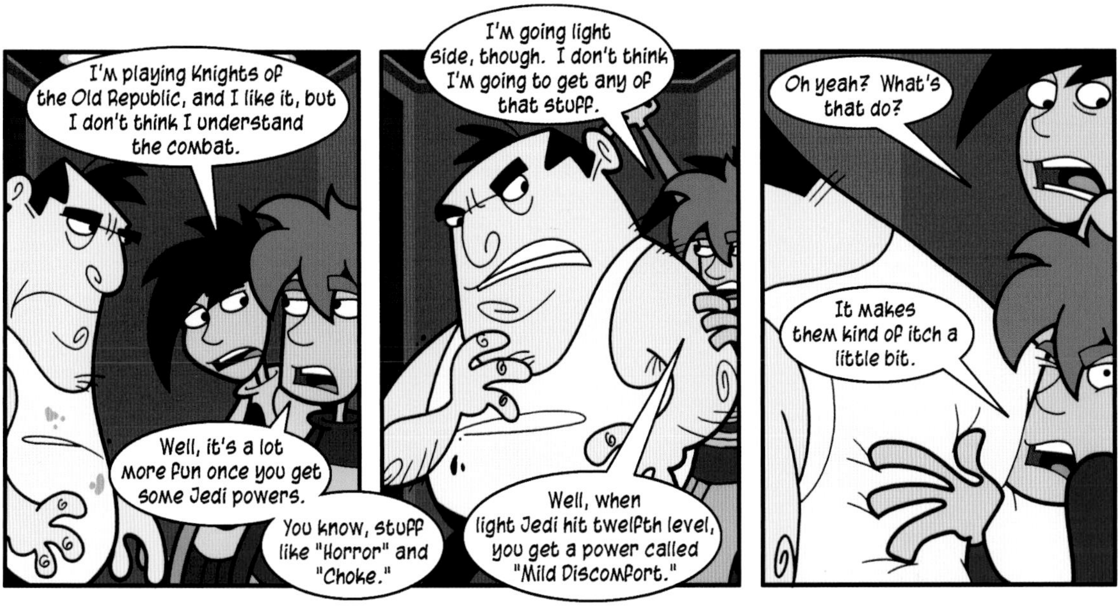
I'm playing Knights of the Old Republic, and I like it, but I don't think I understand the combat.
Well, it's a lot more fun once you get some Jedi powers.
You know, stuff like "Horror" and "Choke."
I'm going light side, though. I don't think I'm going to get any of that stuff.
Well, when light Jedi hit twelfth level, you get a power called "Mild Discomfort."
Oh yeah? What's that do?
It makes them kind of itch a little bit.

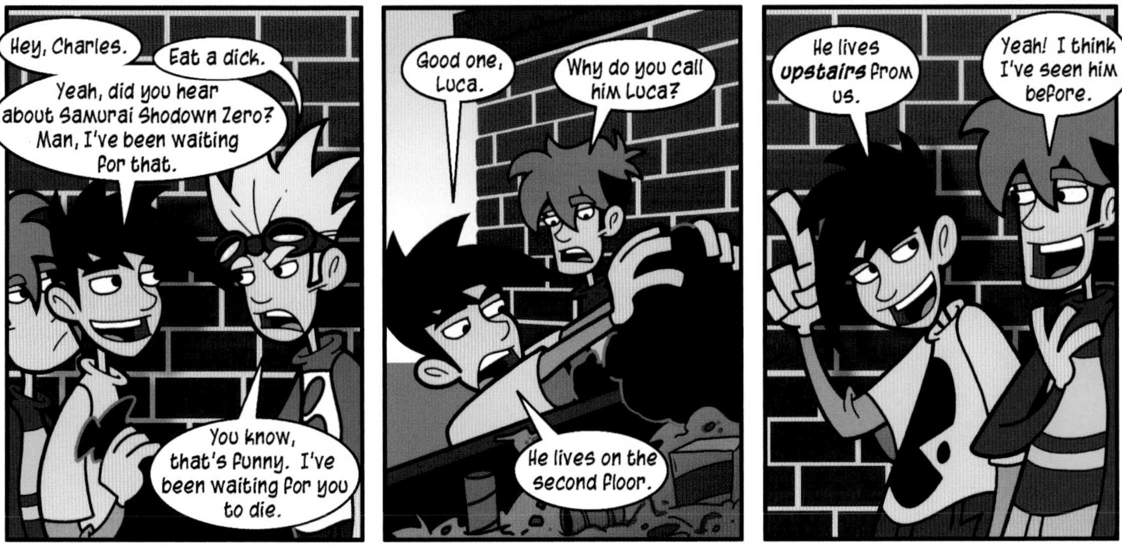
Hey, Charles.
Eat a dick.
Yeah, did you hear about Samurai Shodown Zero? Man, I've been waiting for that.
You know, that's funny. I've been waiting for you to die.
Good one, Luca.
Why do you call him Luca?
He lives on the second floor.
He lives upstairs from us.
Yeah! I think I've seen him before.

THE VERY PICTURE OF DISCOMFORT

July 28, 2003 The differences between the sides are pretty severe, but we don't go into what light side afficionados get for their trouble. I think being able to magically heal wounds and destroy droids with a thought constitute *fairly significant advantages.*

VIVA LAS VEGA

July 30, 2003 We, um . . . We quote songs constantly. I'm not sure if that helps you enjoy this comic or not. We're often accused of producing comics which are essentially inside jokes—*this* is what that would actually look like.

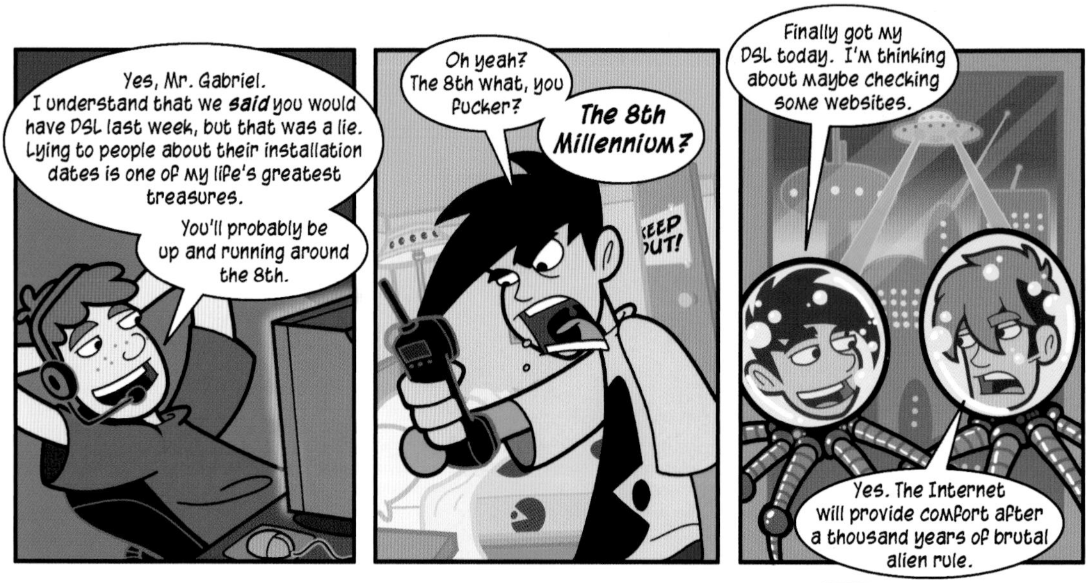
Yes, Mr. Gabriel. I understand that we *said* you would have DSL last week, but that was a lie. Lying to people about their installation dates is one of my life's greatest treasures.
You'll probably be up and running around the 8th.
Oh yeah? The 8th what, you fucker?
The 8th Millennium?
KEEP OUT!
Finally got my DSL today. I'm thinking about maybe checking some websites.
Yes. The Internet will provide comfort after a thousand years of brutal alien rule.

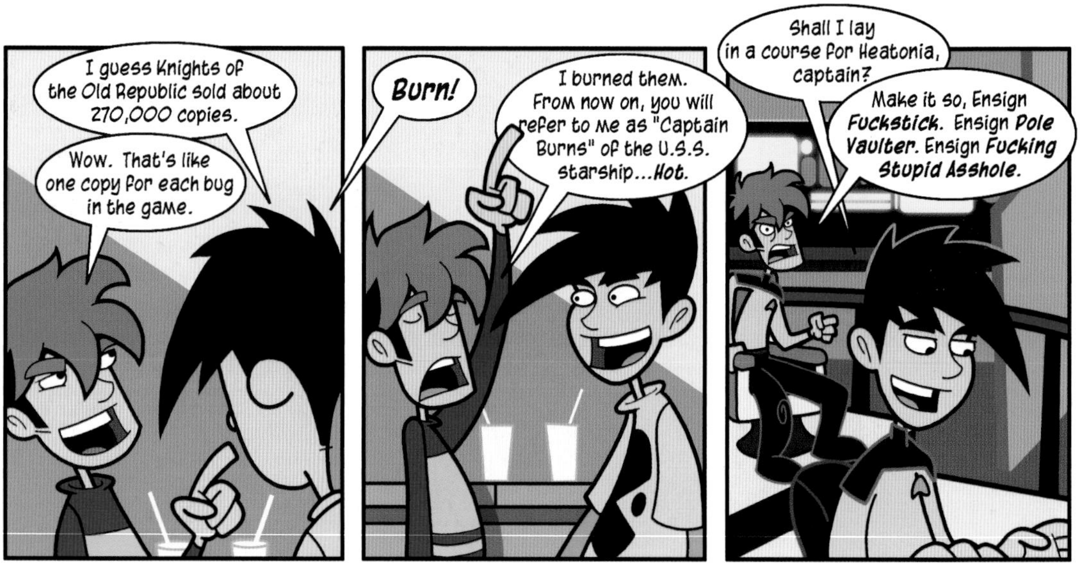
I guess Knights of the Old Republic sold about 270,000 copies.
Wow. That's like one copy for each bug in the game.
Burn!
I burned them. From now on, you will refer to me as "Captain Burns" of the U.S.S. starship... *Hot.*
Shall I lay in a course for Heatonia, captain?
Make it so, Ensign *Fuckstick*. Ensign *Pole Vaulter*. Ensign *Fucking Stupid Asshole*.

THE KRONOS HEGEMONY

August 1, 2003 I'd just helped Gabe and Kara move into the new place, and for the duration of his time there he toiled to keep his DSL healthy. You know, I'm getting the impression that we don't hold out a lot of hope for the future of mankind, because every time we get a chance to depict this doomed period it's either "Rylocks," a millenium of alien domination, or "a race of spacefaring dog-men known as the Canid" to which our race must bend and scrape.

PERHAPS THE BIGGEST DORKS EVER

August 4, 2003 As is probably apparent from the "back-to-back" Knights strips, we liked it a lot—but it was not without technical fault. Among the chilling oversights was the fact that the game would sometimes enter this really odd debug mode that could wreck saves. And, um . . . *Pole Vaulter*? That's quite the mental image.

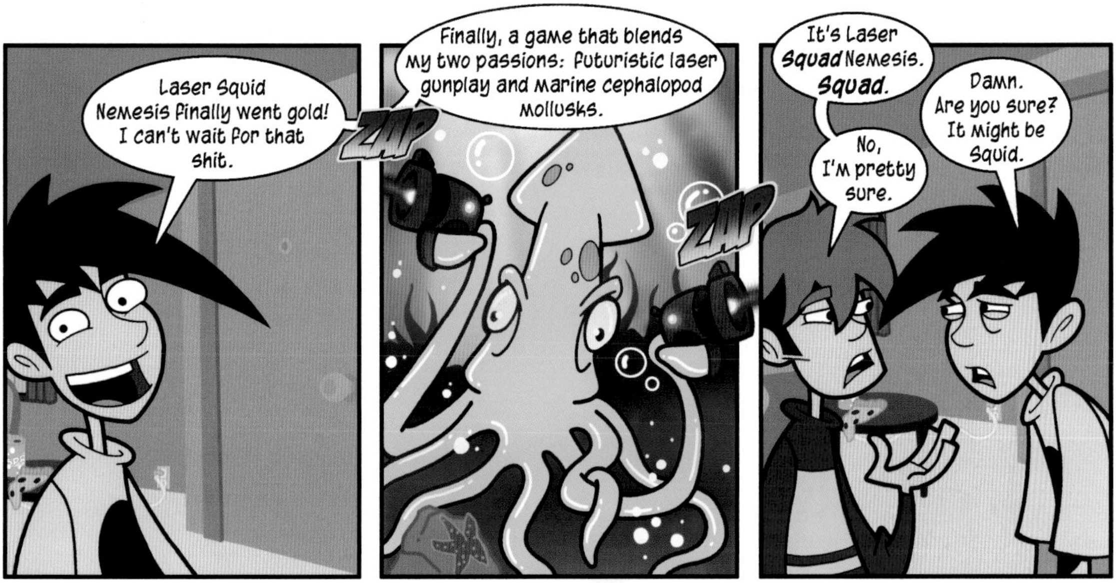
Laser Squid Nemesis finally went gold! I can't wait for that shit.
ZAP
Finally, a game that blends my two passions: futuristic laser gunplay and marine cephalopod mollusks.
ZAP
It's Laser Squad Nemesis. Squad.
Damn. Are you sure? It might be Squid.
No, I'm pretty sure.

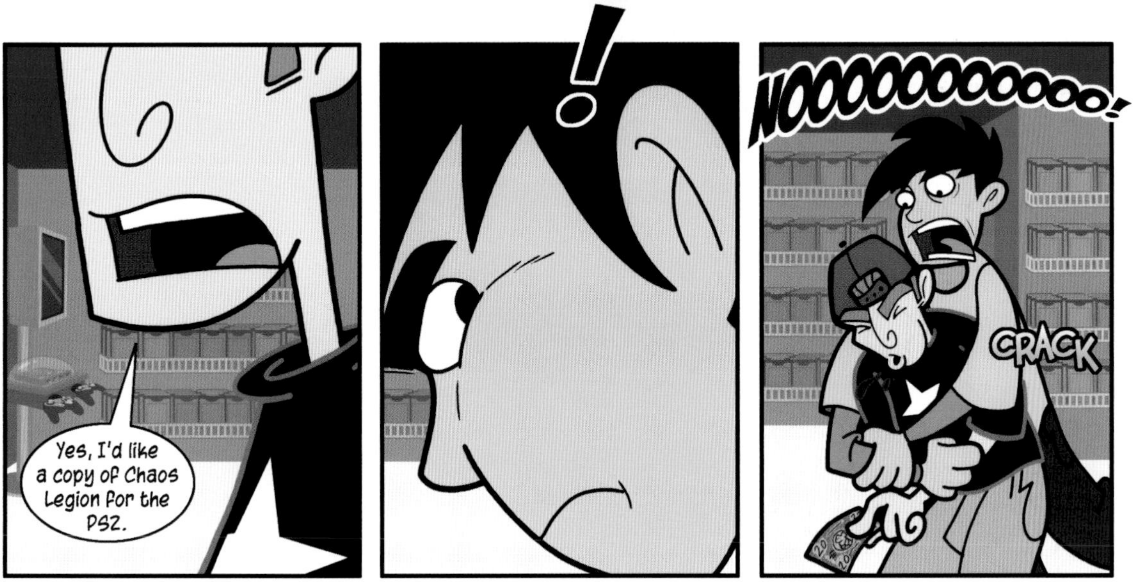
Yes, I'd like a copy of Chaos Legion for the PS2.
!
NOOOOOOOOOOOOO!
CRACK

A COMMON MISCONCEPTION

August 6, 2003 This is one of my favorite *Penny Arcade* strips of all time. I have to say that, *sometimes*, the heady power of the author does go to the head, and the result is a kind of drunkenness. The ability to make another person draw a huge kraken-type thing with akimbo laser guns was, I am afraid, beyond my power to resist.

THE NICK OF TIME

August 8, 2003 That is not a hug! Gabe is sacrificing his body to stop that young man from making bad choices. Chaos Legion not only *features* demons, it was also crafted *by* demons to act as an engine of human misery. We're talking about a game that IGN gave a 6.5. That's *IGN*, whose official scale starts at *seven*.

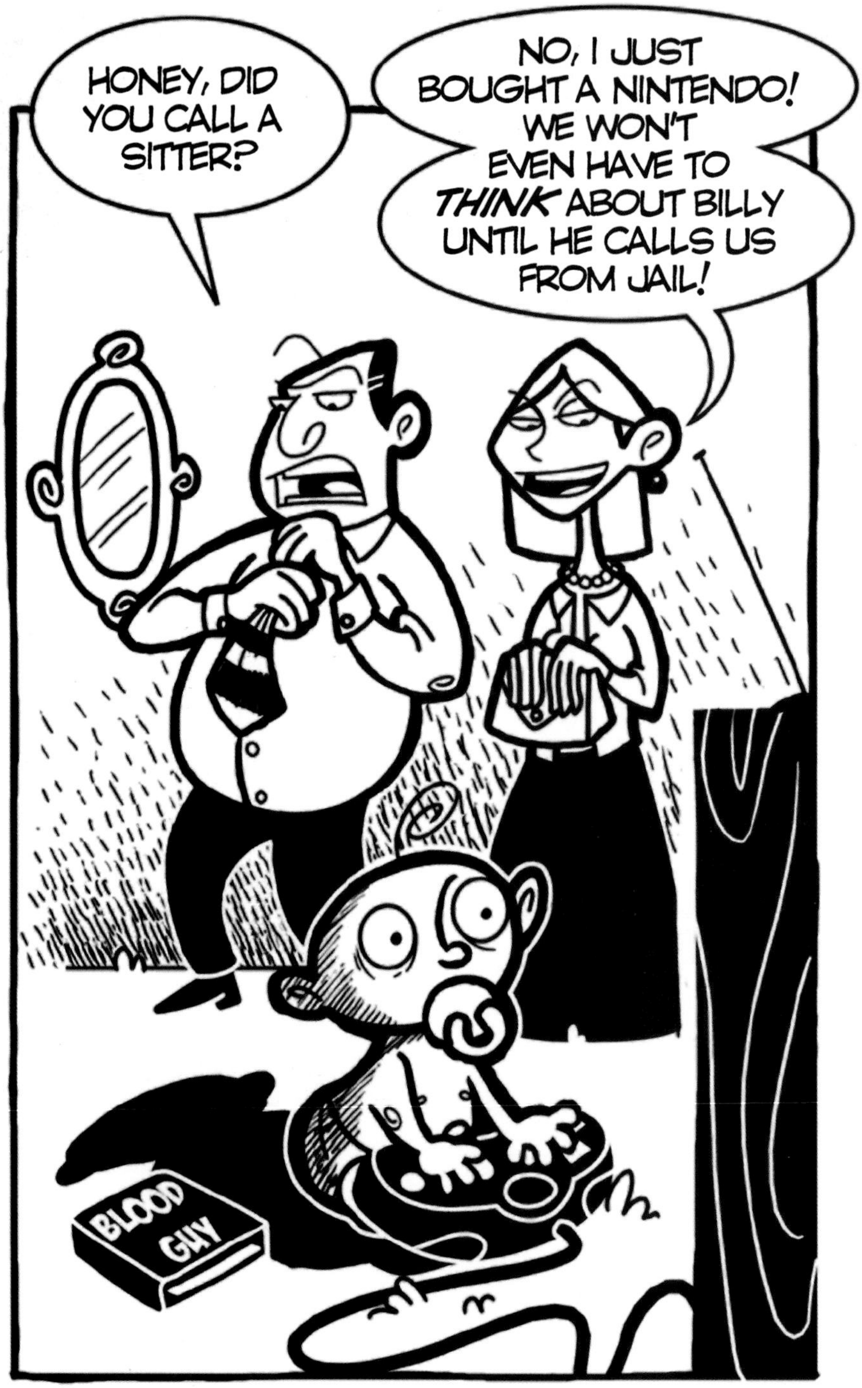
HONEY, DID YOU CALL A SITTER?
NO, I JUST BOUGHT A NINTENDO! WE WON'T EVEN HAVE TO *THINK* ABOUT BILLY UNTIL HE CALLS US FROM JAIL!
BLOOD GUY

SEND THIS TO YOUR LOCAL PAPER

August 11, 2003 A political cartoon by local artist David Horsey depicted the "Video Game Industry" as a vile Dr. Frankenstein, corrupting children and hiding behind the First Amendment to do it. It's a pretty complicated issue, and having to distill ideas is something we understand, but we didn't feel comfortable letting that be the extent of the dialogue.

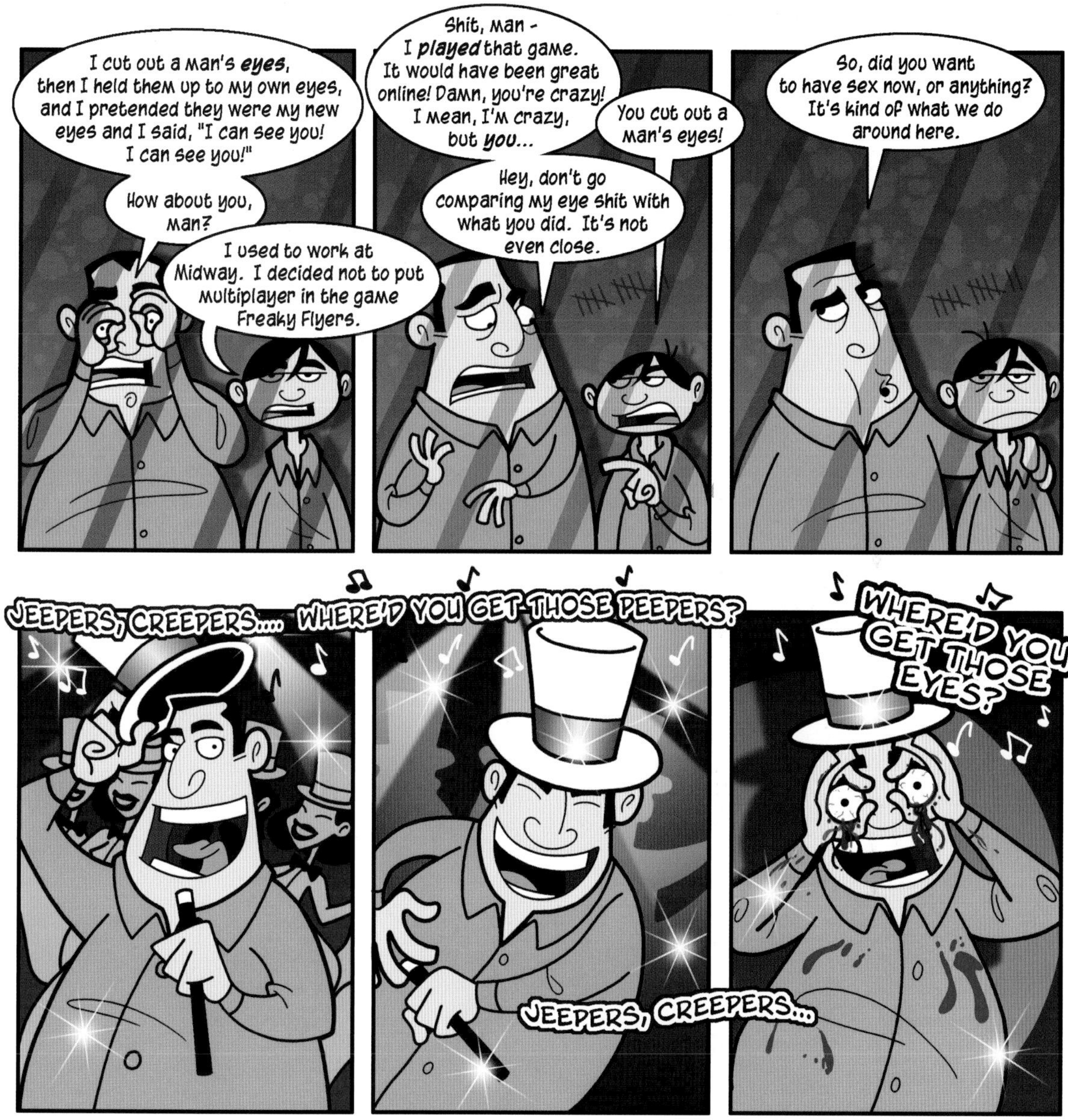
I cut out a man's *eyes*, then I held them up to my own eyes, and I pretended they were my new eyes and I said, "I can see you! I can see you!"
How about you, man?
I used to work at Midway. I decided not to put multiplayer in the game Freaky Flyers.
Shit, man - I *played* that game. It would have been great online! Damn, you're crazy! I mean, I'm crazy, but *you*...
You cut out a man's eyes!
Hey, don't go comparing my eye shit with what you did. It's not even close.
So, did you want to have sex now, or anything? It's kind of what we do around here.
JEEPERS, CREEPERS.... WHERE'D YOU GET THOSE PEEPERS?
JEEPERS, CREEPERS...
WHERE'D YOU GET THOSE EYES?

IT'S FUN TO MEET NEW PEOPLE

August 13, 2003 Freaky Flyers was this weird little airborne racer/platformer thing that would have been great online, but was still great without it—even if no-one seemed to think so. I just went back and looked at the reviews from the period, and I'm finding it hard to reconcile them with what I know to be true in reality. It was also pretty funny, and I don't mean like "videogame funny," I mean actually, really funny for *real*. It contained a number of original songs that I've been trying to track down for years.

FROM ANOTHER HUMAN BEING

August 15, 2003 Man, I just . . . Hm. I guess it's . . . I guess it's a reasonable question.

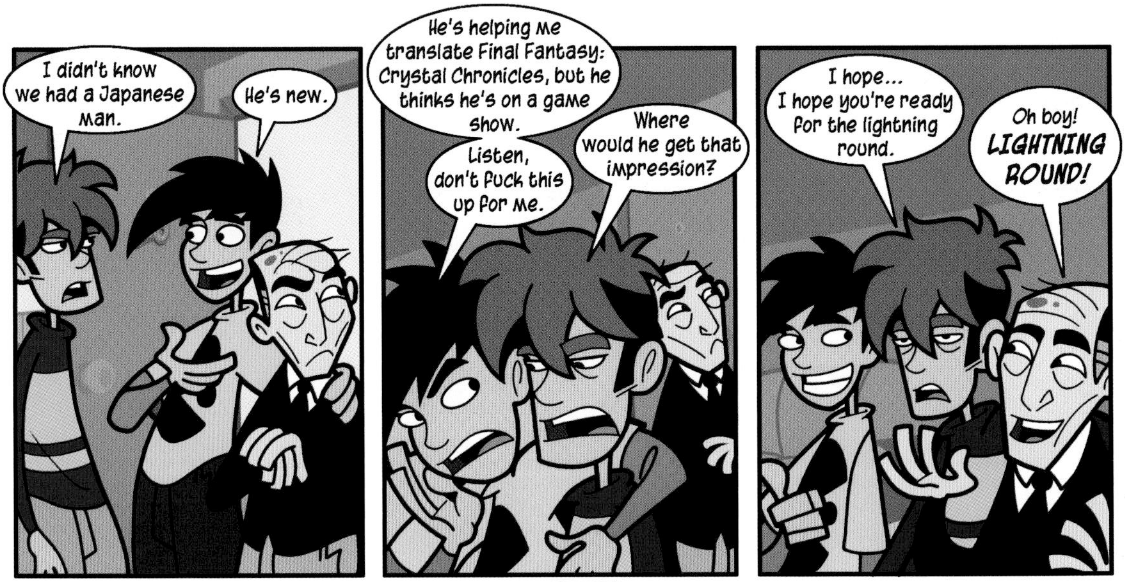
I didn't know we had a Japanese man.
He's new.
He's helping me translate Final Fantasy: Crystal Chronicles, but he thinks he's on a game show.
Where would he get that impression?
Listen, don't fuck this up for me.
I hope... I hope you're ready for the lightning round.
Oh boy! *LIGHTNING ROUND!*

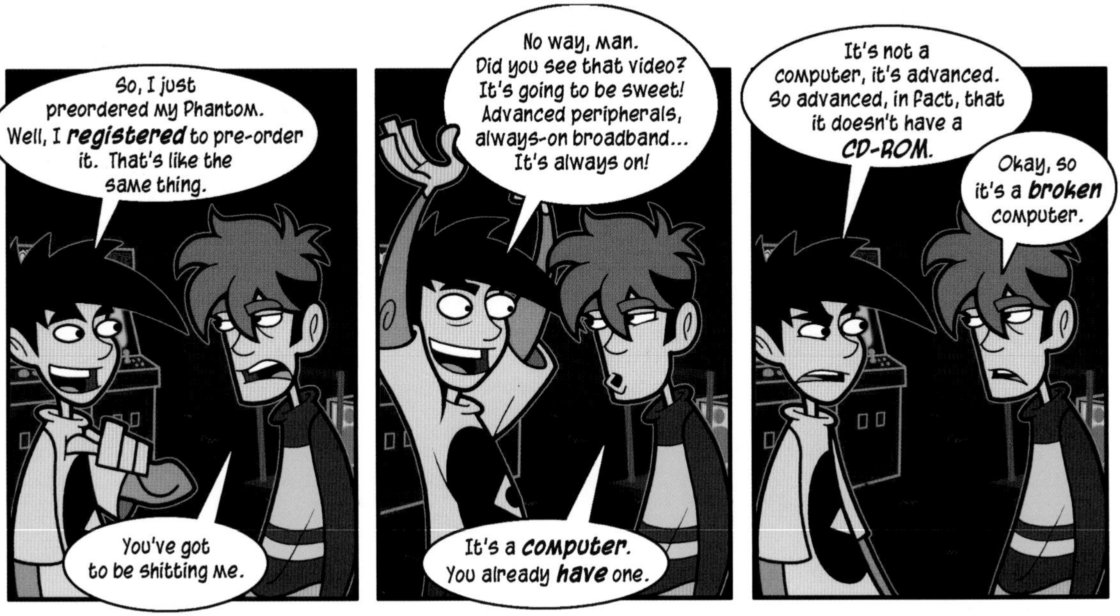
So, I just preordered my Phantom. Well, I ***registered*** to pre-order it. That's like the same thing.
You've got to be shitting me.
No way, man. Did you see that video? It's going to be sweet! Advanced peripherals, always-on broadband... It's always on!
It's a ***computer***. You already ***have*** one.
It's not a computer, it's advanced. So advanced, in fact, that it doesn't have a ***CD-ROM***.
Okay, so it's a ***broken*** computer.

THE OTHER EAST

August 18, 2003 I don't know what we were thinking, but we used to think this kind of thing quite a bit: importing Japanese RPGs is really one of the worst things you can do with your money. Crystal Chronicles had a lot of dialogue in towns, and we didn't realize how much we were missing until the US version came out. Still, the main method of interaction with this game was to swing your sword or sear foes with magic, and as gamers we are well versed in the universal language of *expressed power*.

I HATE THE STUPID PHANTOM

August 20, 2003 I'd forgotten that—there was no way to get media on there without paying for it through the service, and you couldn't futz around inside it because the entire motherboard was covered in glue. Yes, glue! Thick, nutritive glue that tasted *great*.

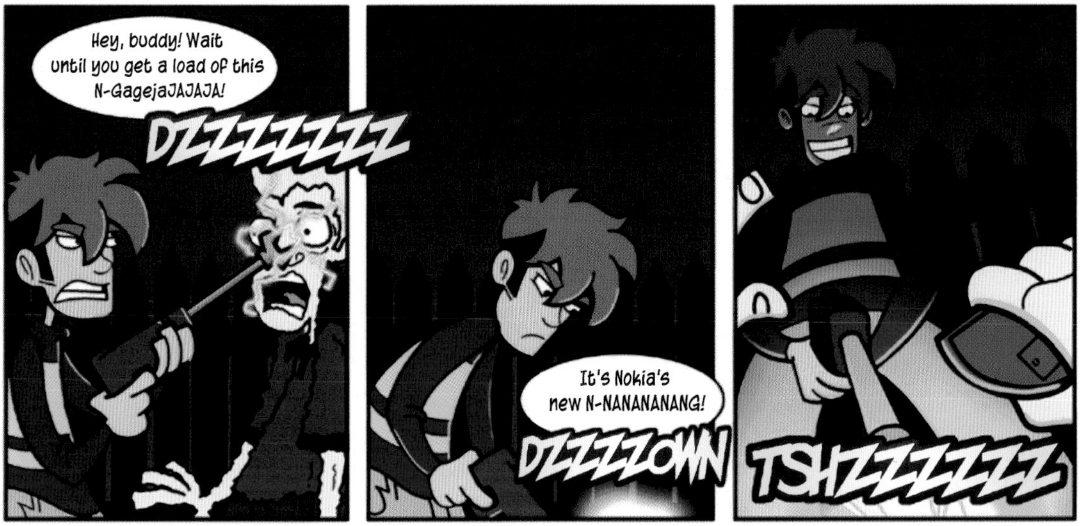
Hey, buddy! Wait until you get a load of this N-GagejaJAJAJA!
DZZZZZZZZ
It's Nokia's new N-NANANANANG!
DZZZZOWN
TSHZZZZZZZ

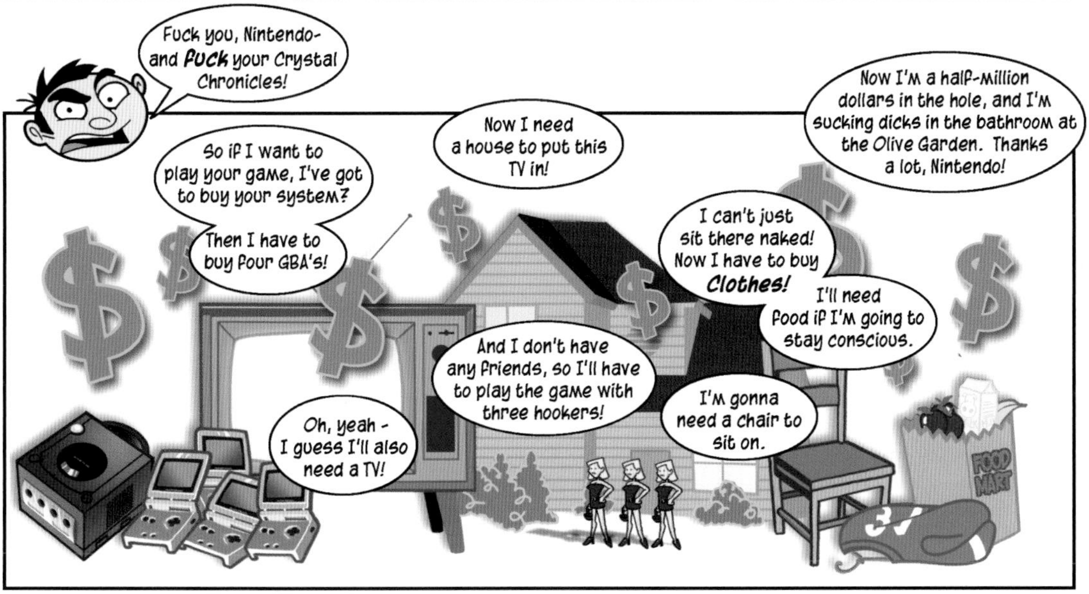
Fuck you, Nintendo- and fuck your Crystal Chronicles!
So if I want to play your game, I've got to buy your system?
Then I have to buy four GBA's!
Oh, yeah - I guess I'll also need a TV!
Now I need a house to put this TV in!
And I don't have any friends, so I'll have to play the game with three hookers!
I'm gonna need a chair to sit on.
I can't just sit there naked! Now I have to buy Clothes!
I'll need food if I'm going to stay conscious.
Now I'm a half-million dollars in the hole, and I'm sucking dicks in the bathroom at the Olive Garden. Thanks a lot, Nintendo!
FOOD MART

NOT JUST FOR COWS

August 22, 2003 Nokia was setting up some kind of street team called The N-Gage Special Forces during this time, and the thought of a person approaching me to describe the many *delights* of the platform was almost impossible to bear. I don't know if it warrants being electrocuted by a cattle prod, but I've always had trouble knowing when (and when *not*) to electrocute someone.

HOW COULD THEY DO SUCH A THING

August 25, 2003 This logic always comes up, but I've never found it especially satisfying. Most recently it came up for *another* Nintendo product, the Wii. People were using a branch of "hater mathematics" to generate a price for the system that was higher than its competitors because you had to buy three more controllers and nunchuks. I guess that's true, but I run with gamers, my crew is like *six deep*, and if they want to play at my house, they can bring their own shit.

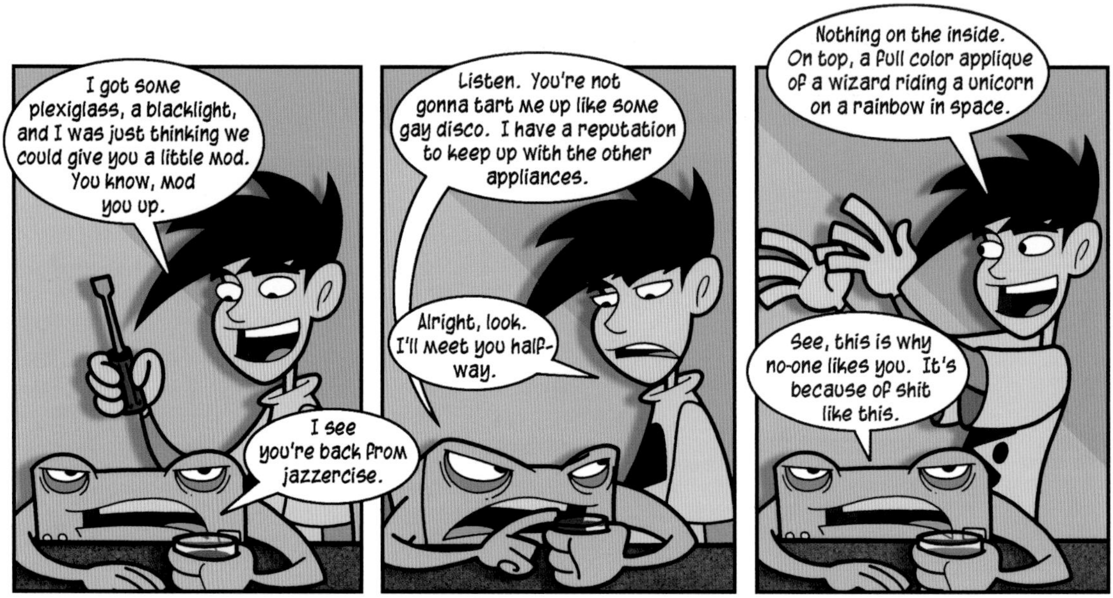
I got some plexiglass, a blacklight, and I was just thinking we could give you a little mod. You know, mod you up.
I see you're back from jazzercise.
Listen. You're not gonna tart me up like some gay disco. I have a reputation to keep up with the other appliances.
Alright, look. I'll meet you half-way.
Nothing on the inside. On top, a full color applique of a wizard riding a unicorn on a rainbow in space.
See, this is why no-one likes you. It's because of shit like this.

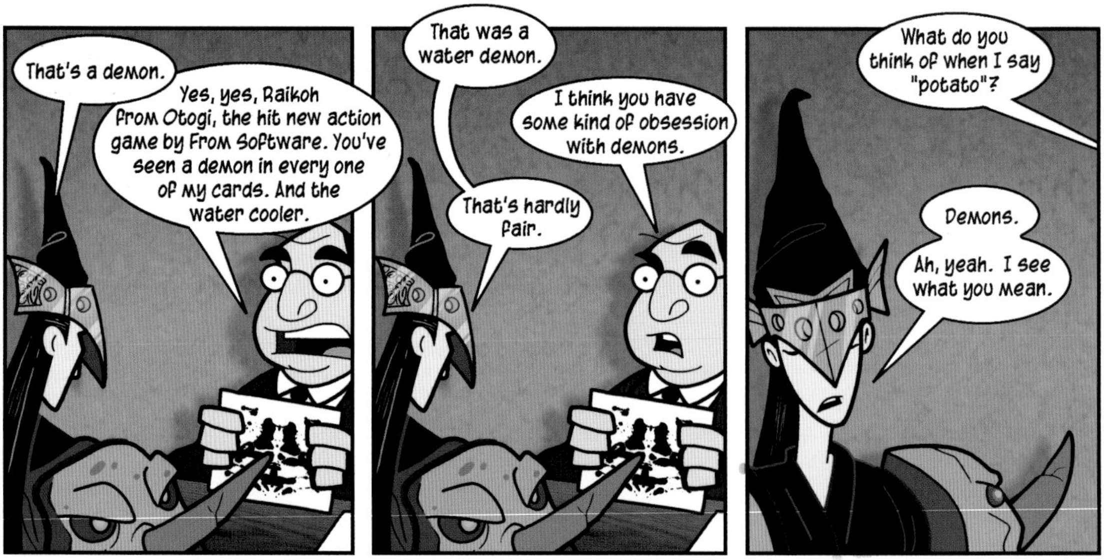
That's a demon.
Yes, yes, Raikoh from Otogi, the hit new action game by From Software. You've seen a demon in every one of my cards. And the water cooler.
That was a water demon.
I think you have some kind of obsession with demons.
That's hardly fair.
What do you think of when I say "potato"?
Demons.
Ah, yeah. I see what you mean.

PUT DOWN THE SCREWDRIVER

August 27, 2003 Gabe freaked out around this time and took on this Toolmaster, Master Craftsman persona. He bought a number of tools and took to improving his Ikea furniture with various . . . I don't know, *lacquers* or something? It was his phase, not mine.

DEMONS, DEMONS EVERYWHERE

August 29, 2003 Otogi was very weird, but it was the good kind of weird that our people actively seek out. The original Xbox was (as you will recall!) not a place that many Japanese developers released on; this is true for the Xbox 360 as well, although to a much lesser extent. In any case, it had the wild art, strange story, and unique combat of the sort one rarely saw on that system. It feels ordinary enough when you're starting out, but then you're destroying an entire temple with a swipe of your sword or fighting some demon while suspended more than a mile off the ground.

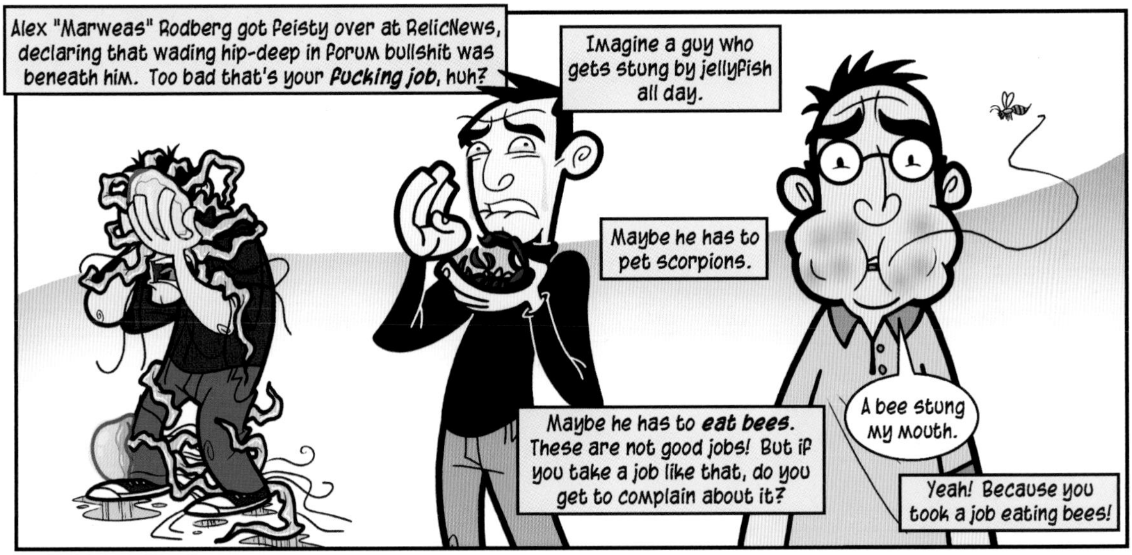
Alex "Marweas" Rodberg got feisty over at RelicNews, declaring that wading hip-deep in forum bullshit was beneath him. Too bad that's your *fucking job*, huh?
Imagine a guy who gets stung by jellyfish all day.
Maybe he has to pet scorpions.
Maybe he has to **eat bees**. These are not good jobs! But if you take a job like that, do you get to complain about it?
A bee stung my mouth.
Yeah! Because you took a job eating bees!

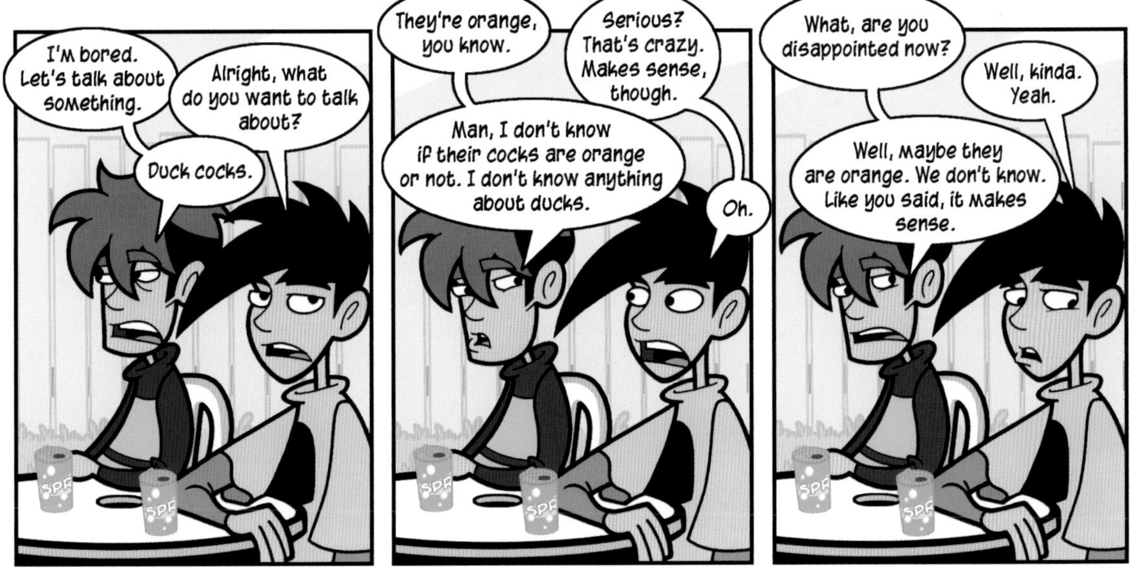
I'm bored. Let's talk about something.
Alright, what do you want to talk about?
Duck cocks.
They're orange, you know.
Serious? That's crazy. Makes sense, though.
Man, I don't know if their cocks are orange or not. I don't know anything about ducks.
Oh.
What, are you disappointed now?
Well, kinda. Yeah.
Well, maybe they are orange. We don't know. Like you said, it makes sense.

SOMEONE IS PROJECTING

September 1, 2003 Alex Rodberg was a Sierra Online community guy who resented having to manage consumer expectations. We crossed swords a couple times over their management of the Tribes franchise. I actually really enjoyed Tribes: Vengeance, quite possibly the last Tribes game ever, but I was in the minority. It was probably the only thing he and I ever agreed on.

ORANGE, OR SOME OTHER COLOR

September 3, 2003 I'm not sure what kind of texture and richness I'm supposed to add to a piece about duck dicks. I can communicate that this was an actual conversation we had, and on that day we had much stranger conversations than this, so that should tell you how surreal things get around here on an average day.

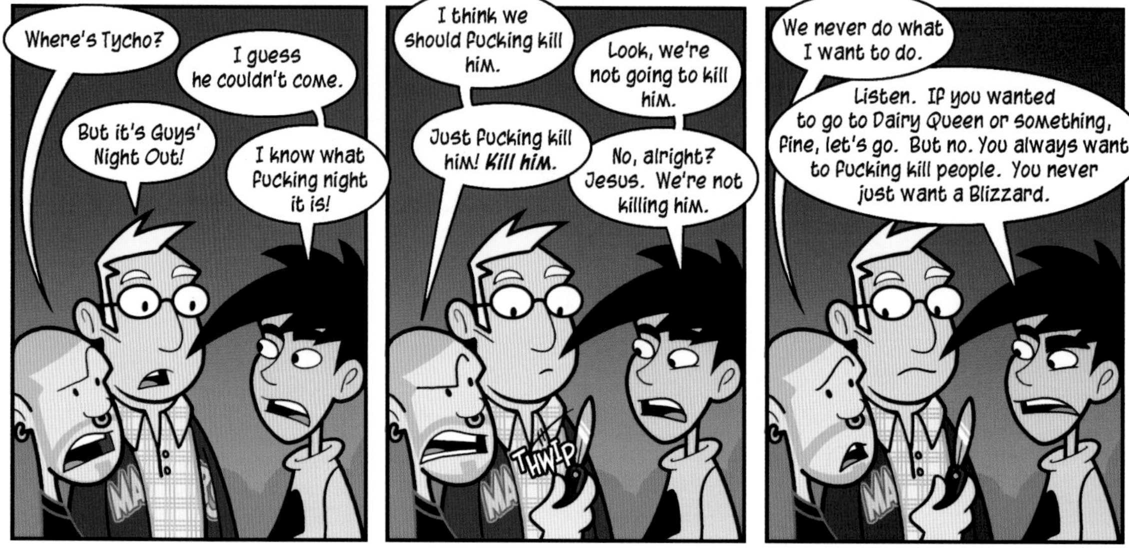
Where's Tycho?
I guess he couldn't come.
But it's Guys' Night Out!
I know what fucking night it is!
I think we should fucking kill him.
Look, we're not going to kill him.
Just fucking kill him! *Kill him.*
No, alright? Jesus. We're not killing him.
THWIP
We never do what I want to do.
Listen. If you wanted to go to Dairy Queen or something, fine, let's go. But no. You always want to fucking kill people. You never just want a Blizzard.

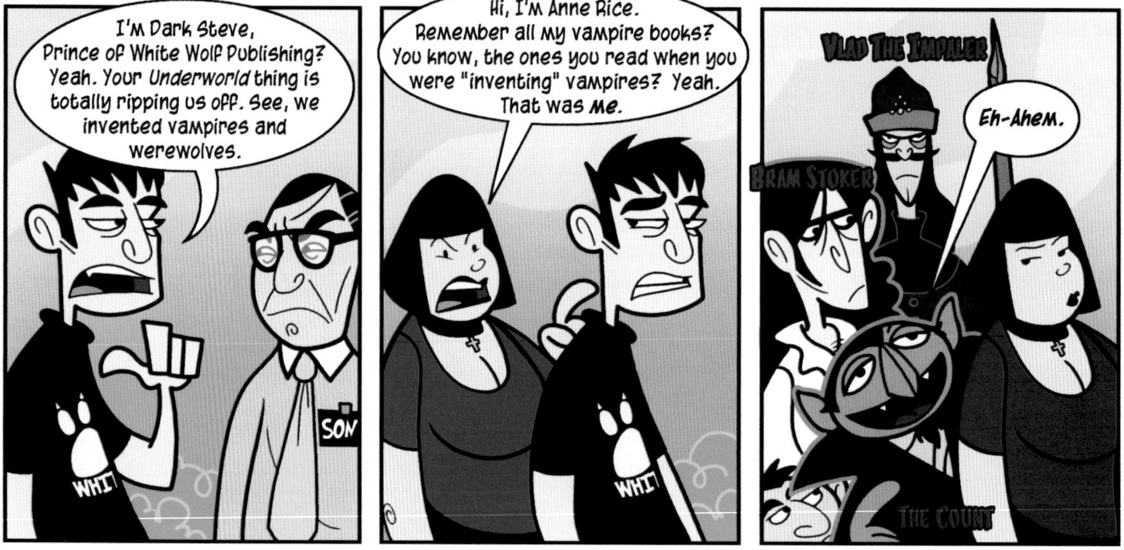
I'm Dark Steve, Prince of White Wolf Publishing? Yeah. Your *Underworld* thing is totally ripping us off. See, we invented vampires and werewolves.
Hi, I'm Anne Rice. Remember all my vampire books? You know, the ones you read when you were "inventing" vampires? Yeah. That was *me*.
VLAD THE IMPALER
BRAM STOKER
Eh-Ahem.
THE COUNT

WHAT THE GIRLS CALL MURDER

September 5, 2003 Pork actually does carry a knife, a real knife, everywhere he goes. He's sad when we have to fly somewhere because he has to leave it at home—he *loves* the thing. He took it to an engraver and had them inscribe "Mr. Stabby" on the side. He gave it to a friend to check out for five minutes, and somehow it managed to sever the man's tendon in that span of time—and it wasn't even *open*. That's how the legend goes, at any rate.

THE DARK PROCESSION

September 8, 2003 White Wolf wasn't really claiming that they had invented vampires and werewolves, just that they had interpreted them in a certain way, and that in their substantial vault of fiction was a story very, very similar to the one portrayed in the movie *Underworld*. It never went their way legally, but *Underworld* is guilty of many crimes, and this might as well be one of them.

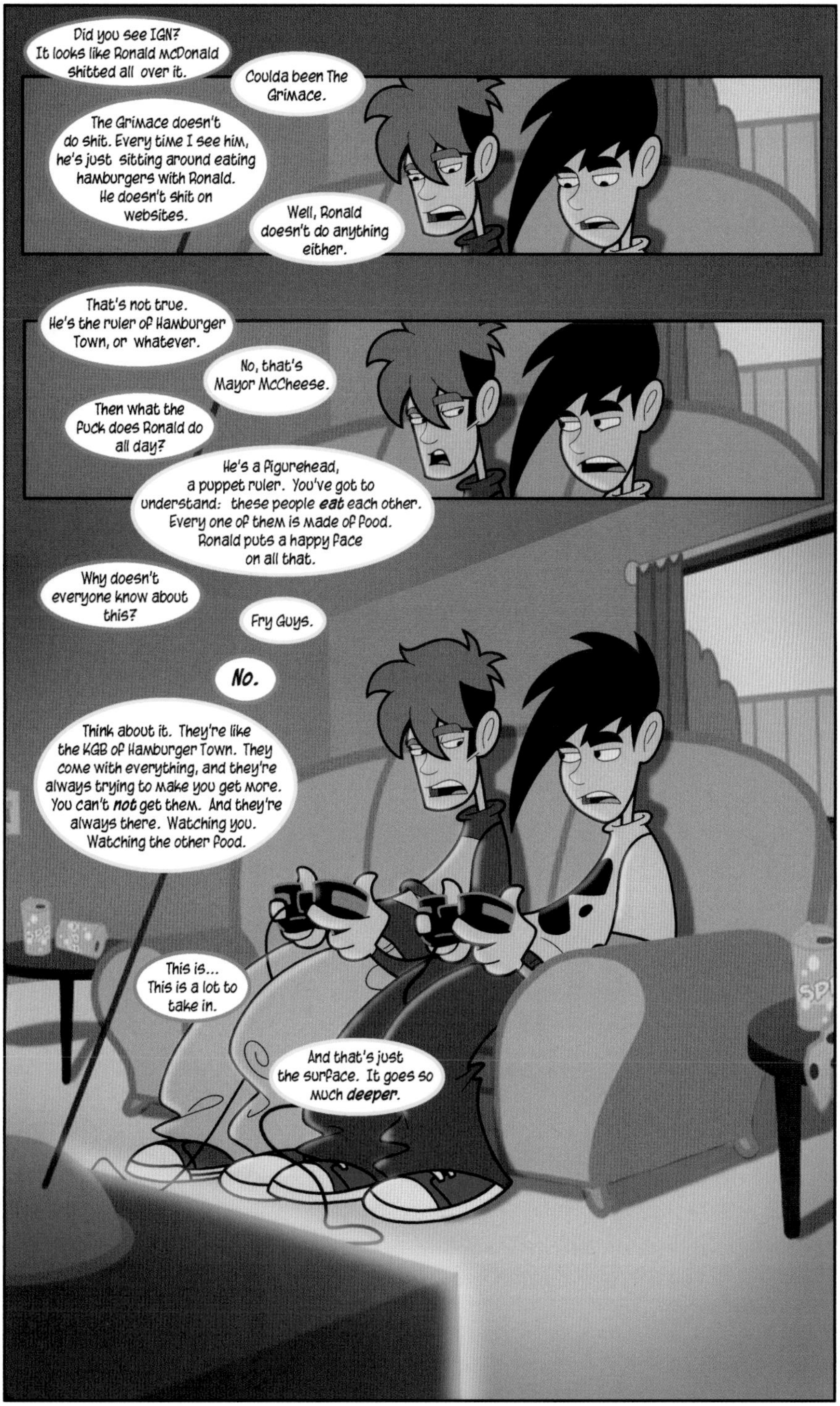
Did you see IGN? It looks like Ronald McDonald shitted all over it.
Coulda been The Grimace.
The Grimace doesn't do shit. Every time I see him, he's just sitting around eating hamburgers with Ronald. He doesn't shit on websites.
Well, Ronald doesn't do anything either.
That's not true. He's the ruler of Hamburger Town, or whatever.
No, that's Mayor McCheese.
Then what the fuck does Ronald do all day?
He's a figurehead, a puppet ruler. You've got to understand: these people eat each other. Every one of them is made of food. Ronald puts a happy face on all that.
Why doesn't everyone know about this?
Fry Guys.
No.
Think about it. They're like the KGB of Hamburger Town. They come with everything, and they're always trying to make you get more. You can't not get them. And they're always there. Watching you. Watching the other food.
This is... This is a lot to take in.
And that's just the surface. It goes so much deeper.

THIS IS TO SAY NOTHING OF THE HAMBURGLAR

September 10, 2003 This harrowing exposé would, ultimately, net us a Pulitzer.

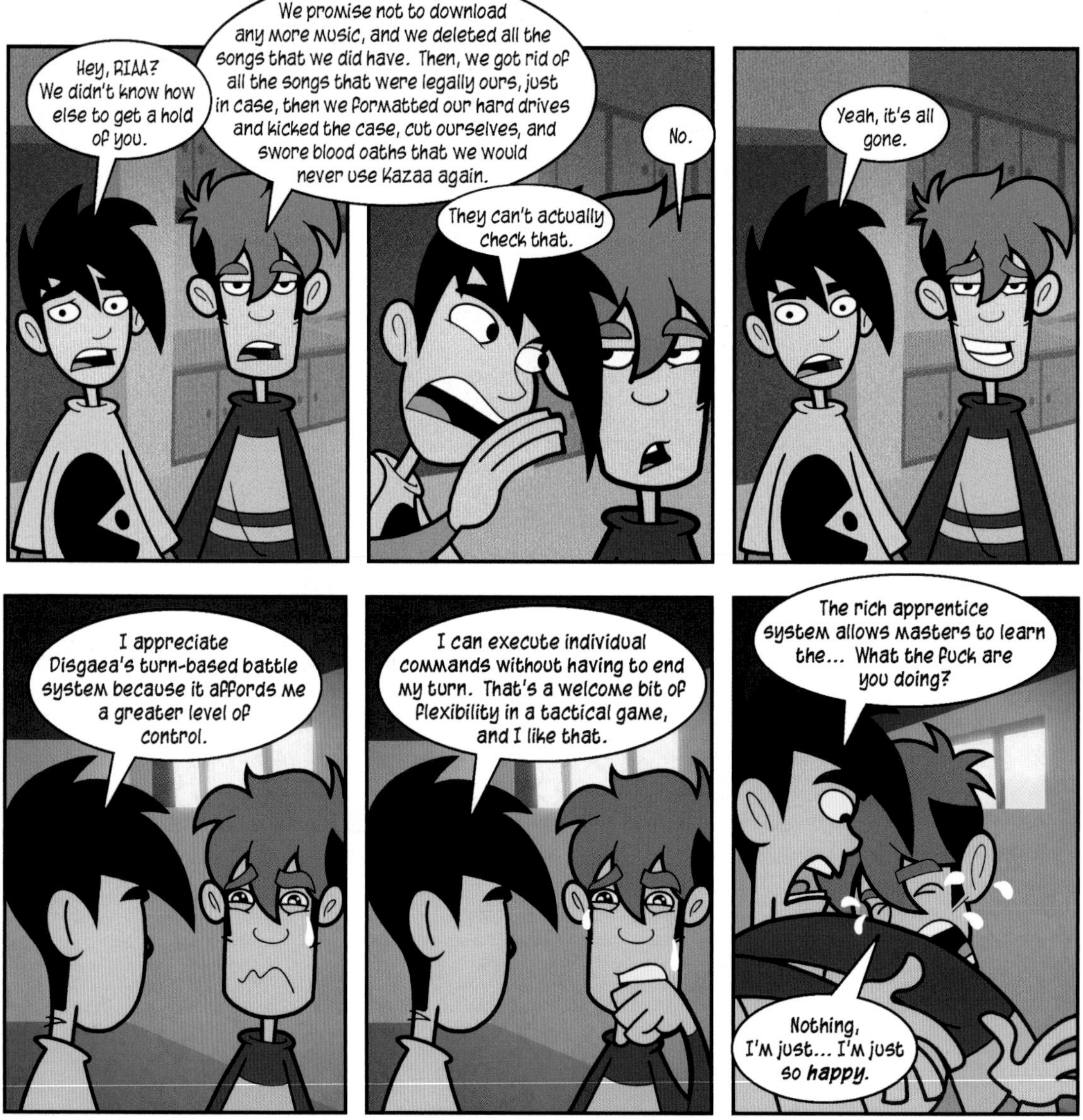
Hey, RIAA? We didn't know how else to get a hold of you.
We promise not to download any more music, and we deleted all the songs that we did have. Then, we got rid of all the songs that were legally ours, just in case, then we formatted our hard drives and kicked the case, cut ourselves, and swore blood oaths that we would never use Kazaa again.
They can't actually check that.
No.
Yeah, it's all gone.
I appreciate Disgaea's turn-based battle system because it affords me a greater level of control.
I can execute individual commands without having to end my turn. That's a welcome bit of flexibility in a tactical game, and I like that.
The rich apprentice system allows masters to learn the... What the fuck are you doing?
Nothing, I'm just... I'm just so *happy*.

A CLOSE ONE

September 12, 2003 Now that there are straightforward and reasonably priced ways to obtain music online, I haven't returned to the web's seedier districts for my digital audio—not even to thumb my nose at multinational corporations! I hardly remember what it was like anymore—that is, during the first Napster's glorious rule. We just downloaded all the songs we wanted, all the time, every day and late into the night? It's hard to believe.

I ALWAYS KNEW THIS DAY WOULD COME

September 15, 2003 Earlier in this very book, you saw the cruel divisions his hatred of strategy games had wrought at E3—and now, he comes forward in contrition. I could have taken this opportunity to shame him, and I believe I may have done so briefly in that day's post, but now there is only joy. Welcome home, Gabriel. Welcome home.

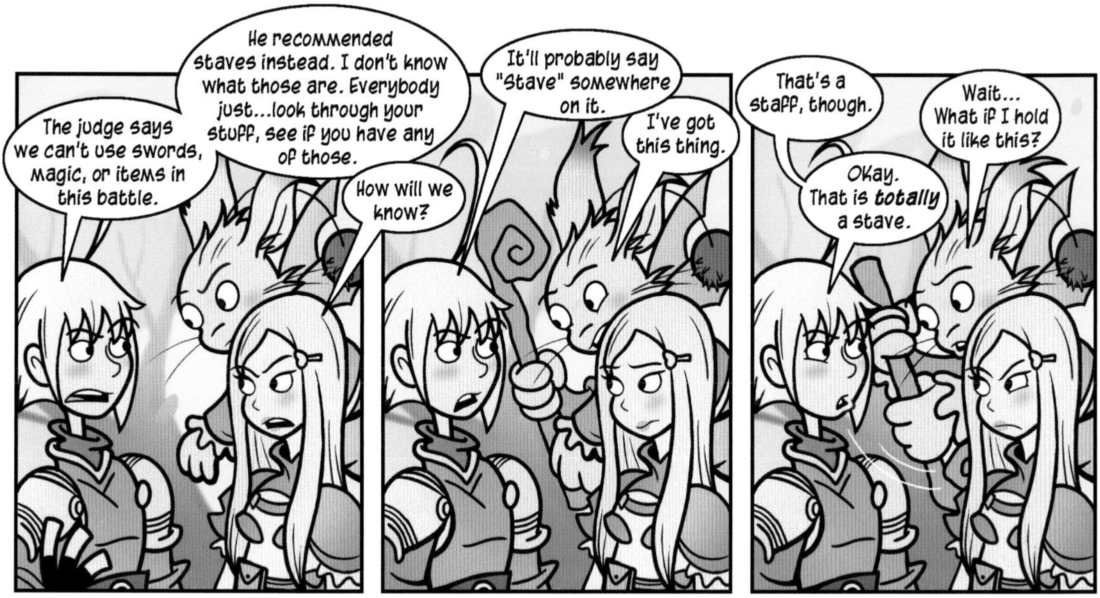
The judge says we can't use swords, magic, or items in this battle.
He recommended staves instead. I don't know what those are. Everybody just...look through your stuff, see if you have any of those.
How will we know?
It'll probably say "Stave" somewhere on it.
I've got this thing.
That's a staff, though.
Wait... What if I hold it like this?
Okay. That is *totally* a stave.

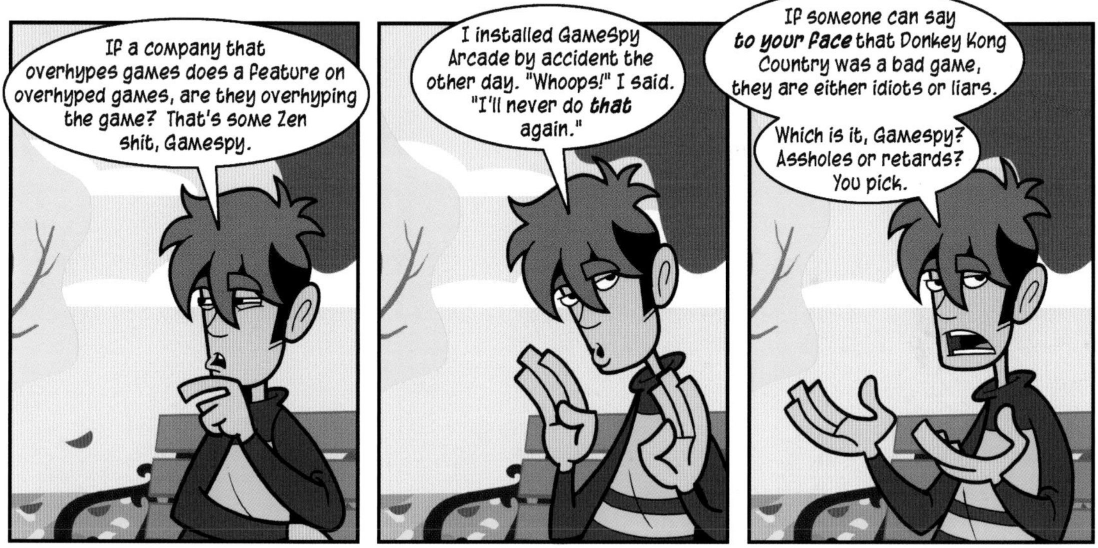
If a company that overhypes games does a feature on overhyped games, are they overhyping the game? That's some Zen shit, Gamespy.
I installed GameSpy Arcade by accident the other day. "Whoops!" I said. "I'll never do *that* again."
If someone can say *to your face* that Donkey Kong Country was a bad game, they are either idiots or liars.
Which is it, Gamespy? Assholes or retards? You pick.

LEST YE BE JUDGED

September 17, 2003 So now we're playing games like Final Fantasy Tactics Advance in parallel, and it's like pure light streaming in every window. He's playing his save on the television with the Game Boy Player, and I'm focused on my own campaign on the portable. Not once does he refer to me as a cock jockey. I guess that's a person who rides cocks? Anyway, he manages not to call me that for several *hours*, and it's a nice change of pace.

CRITICAL STRIKE

September 19, 2003 Their piece also had stupid things to say about Quake II and Final Fantasy VII, games which occupy high seats in Gaming Olympus, but since the entire purpose of the piece was to manufacture traffic from enraged gamers it no doubt delivered the intended results. And here we are, discussing this same article years after the fact, giving the stupid thing a kind of corrupt *unlife*.

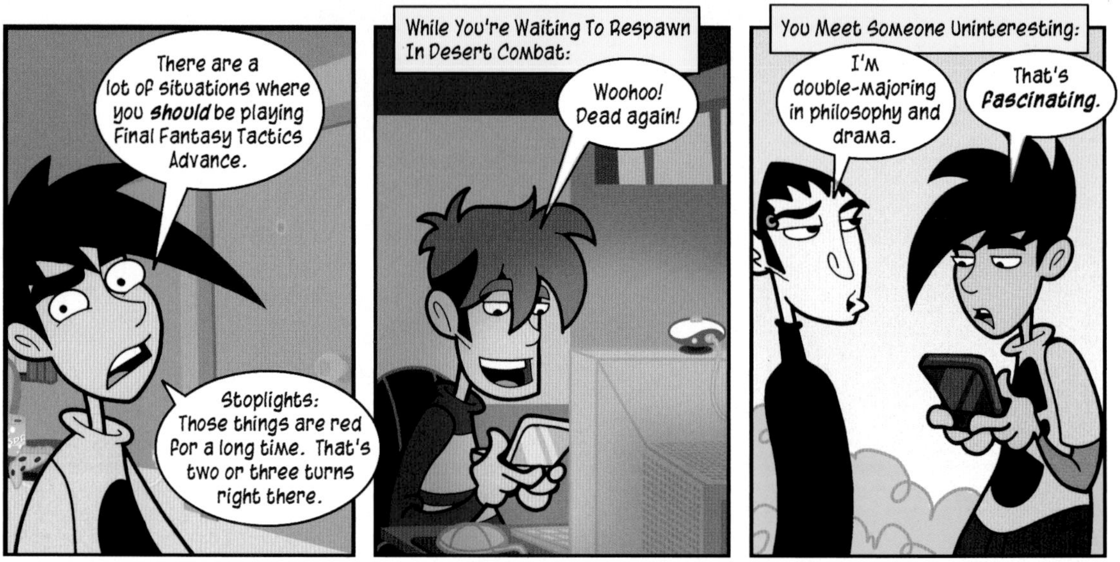
There are a lot of situations where you *should* be playing Final Fantasy Tactics Advance.
Stoplights: Those things are red for a long time. That's two or three turns right there.
While You're Waiting To Respawn In Desert Combat:
Woohoo! Dead again!
You Meet Someone Uninteresting:
I'm double-majoring in philosophy and drama.
That's *fascinating.*

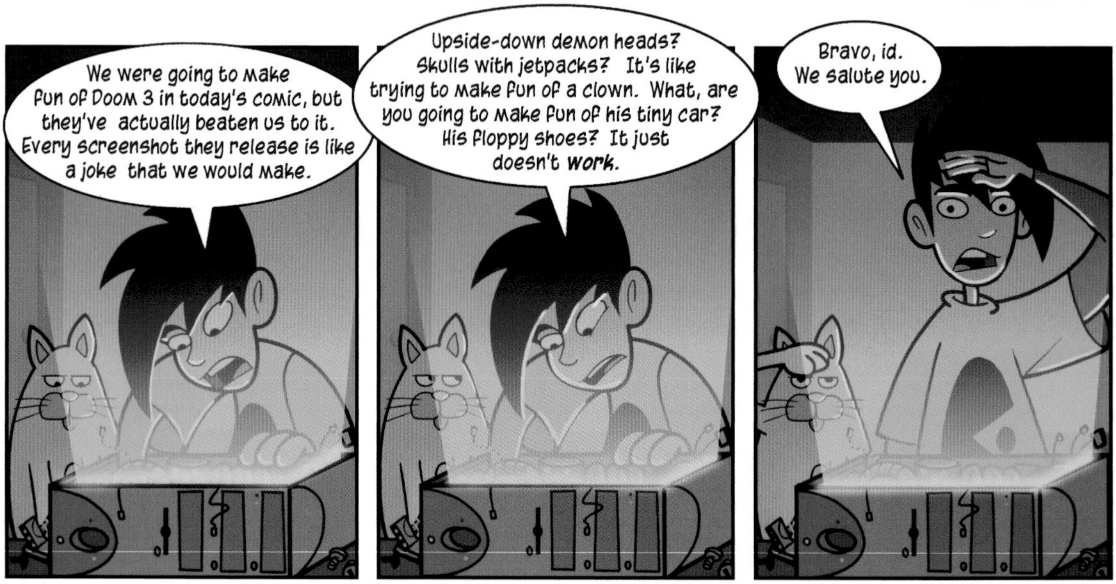
We were going to make fun of Doom 3 in today's comic, but they've actually beaten us to it. Every screenshot they release is like a joke that we would make.
Upside-down demon heads? Skulls with jetpacks? It's like trying to make fun of a clown. What, are you going to make fun of his tiny car? His floppy shoes? It just doesn't *work.*
Bravo, id. We salute you.

THE DAY IS FULL OF MOMENTS

September 22, 2003 My friend Blake *was* double-majoring in philosophy and drama, so this isn't really his favorite strip. And the middle panel there is a reference to Porkfry, whose powerful ADHD makes him ravenous for stimuli even while playing another *videogame*. That, my friends, is true brain hunger.

BELIEVE ME, WE TRIED

September 24, 2003 I had a lot of fun with the final product, having recently upgraded my video hardware to something that could better satisfy that engine's endless appetite. Because of the way light works in the game, clinging to surfaces in real time, no screenshot is going to help you understand why their technology was important. Unfortunately, their screenshots also included their silly monster designs, which work *in place* but do not thrill in still shots.

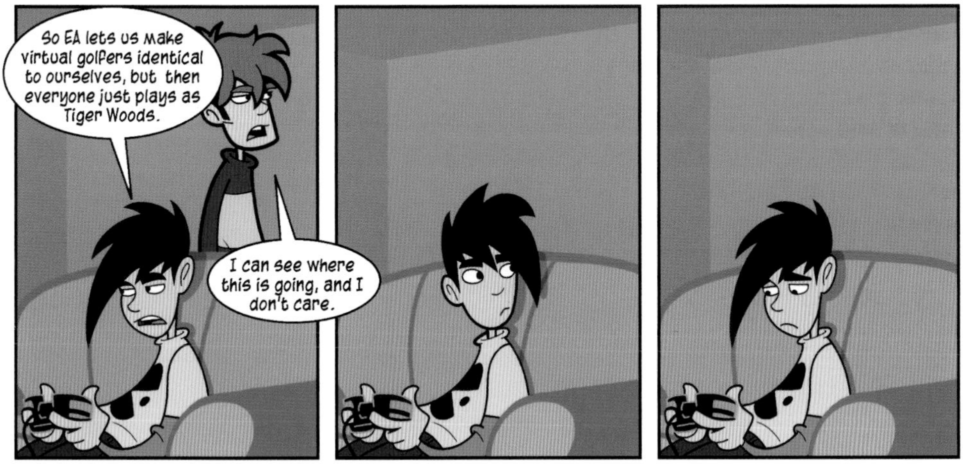
So EA lets us make virtual golfers identical to ourselves, but then everyone just plays as Tiger Woods.
I can see where this is going, and I don't care.

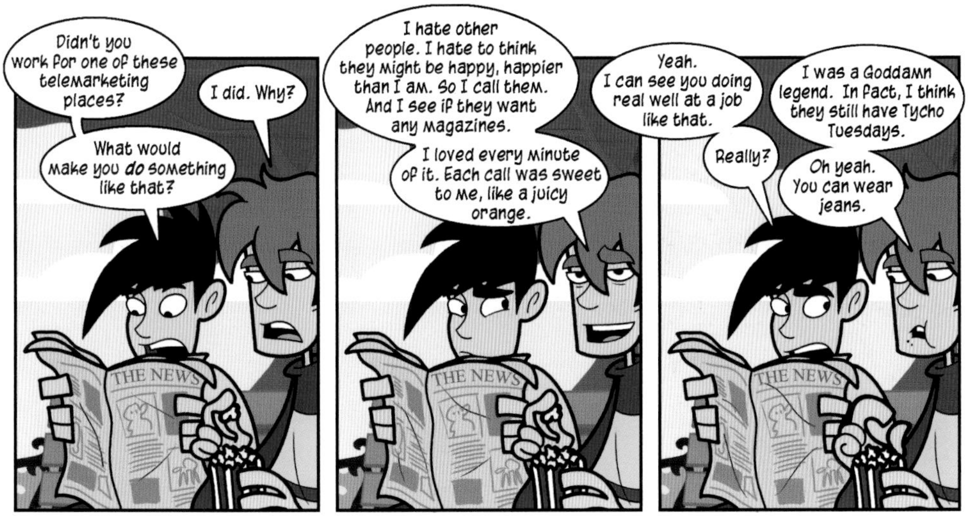
Didn't you work for one of these telemarketing places?
I did. Why?
What would make you *do* something like that?
I hate other people. I hate to think they might be happy, happier than I am. So I call them. And I see if they want any magazines.
I loved every minute of it. Each call was sweet to me, like a juicy orange.
Yeah. I can see you doing real well at a job like that.
I was a Goddamn legend. In fact, I think they still have Tycho Tuesdays.
Really?
Oh yeah. You can wear jeans.

(TIGER) WOO

September 26, 2003 But see, now, I *do* care. We're becoming the same Goddamn person! Constant exposure to his . . . his rays is starting to dim my own true light. I must retain my own flavor at all costs! There has to be a kind of Tycho-oriented calisthenics I can do. Maybe *curls* and *reps* with the substantial *Oxford Unabridged*.

THE MARKETEERS

September 29, 2003 From that day's post:

The reason people work at telemarketing places is because, no matter how bad things are, even if a meteor penetrates North America and night falls on the Earth for the last time, these calling centers will still be hiring. It follows, then, that they're also *firing*, but we'll get to that.

The first thing I had to sell was a service from US West. See, they had sold us thousands of unlisted numbers, and they wanted to sell these people a service that kept companies like mine from *getting* their number. The customers were often incoherent with rage, betrayed—it was as though I had called a bear. It had just occurred to me that death might be the answer when I was sent to the copy room to get some, I don't know, copies of something. One of the managers, Marie, was in there already; I didn't need to see the nametag because I had already loved her, desperately, at Bible Camp. I believe that I was staring at her—at least, that may have been the manifestation on *this* plane of existence—but at a level undetectable by equipment I was communicating data, years' worth, exquisitely compressed.

Bible Camp is just like any other camp, except they have a special guest—Christ Jesus! Certainly the activities are Christ-centered, even soccer, but in practice what this does is add even more drama to a demographic with no shortage of it to begin with. Now, instead of you meeting a girl and it just being regular old run-of-the-mill destiny, a divine hand is at play. The architect of *being* had invented this union. Many churches used the same camp—they owned it, actually—so you saw a lot of people you might not have encountered otherwise, even at the multi-faith Halloween alternatives. It seemed plain to me that Jesus wanted me to spend a lot of time with girls. I was happy for the help, because I had already exhausted the supply at my own church. It may be hard to imagine this, but I was considered somewhat weird.

I don't recall what church Marie was from. The thing I liked best about her was that she wasn't stupid. Like many geeks, I'm used to excluding fifty percent of my vocabulary from conversations, but she knew what I was talking about. We reminisced about how many daughters you could lose to cholera travelling the Oregon Trail. We saw the Oregon Trail heaped high with discarded daughters, the road itself a valley between dead girls.

It was standing room only on the bus back from the lake, and holding the railing overhead, the jostling of the bus put my arm around her. I swear, I didn't do it. It was as though God was winking at me. The next night at dinner, they had a Chastity Dance where they chose your dates based on what they *claimed* was a complex computer algorithm when *in reality* they just watched who you ate lunch with. When our names were announced, we just smiled at other. It was right and proper that they should be spoken together. It was everything *up* to this point that had been wrong.

The last night, the rest of the youth groups from all the churches came up for a final Revival whatever thing. Her *actual* boyfriend came up, too. Vaughn. Just as the man who is gutshot is made instantaneously aware of previously unknown internal geographies, it became suddenly clear that there was a vast expanse in me, a region, a continent, perhaps even a universe that could contain a truly stunning volume of pure pain. She squeezed my hand in the prayer circle, and we looked at each other while Vaughn's head was bowed. My hand started to hurt with it, actually. But I understood that she was deploying a form of compression. She was trying to communicate something. I got the message.

Every call a telemarketer makes is recorded, because when you're calling people on behalf of another company they want to be sure you aren't telling people that US West Would Like To Pee On Them, or interesting trivia like "fortune cookies are actually ninety-percent *rat*." You stick to the script on the screen, and you don't deviate from it. The scripts usually don't reference the composition of fortune cookies.

I wasn't really cut out for this job. I would sing a lot in-between calls, and that's not okay. Also, I completely fucking hated it. So when Marie called me into her office and started playing the tape of my call, my humming somewhat off-pitch, I sort of understood why she might be doing something like that.

How could such a contrived cheap shot make it into my life? She had absolutely no idea who I was. She made it clear that though I could still work there, she really didn't want me to. That was fine by me. But it worried me. If I turned in some videos late, would she just appear in the Blockbuster and revoke my membership? What if I handled a cantaloupe somewhat roughly in the produce aisle? I was afraid she might now be my omnipresent nemesis.

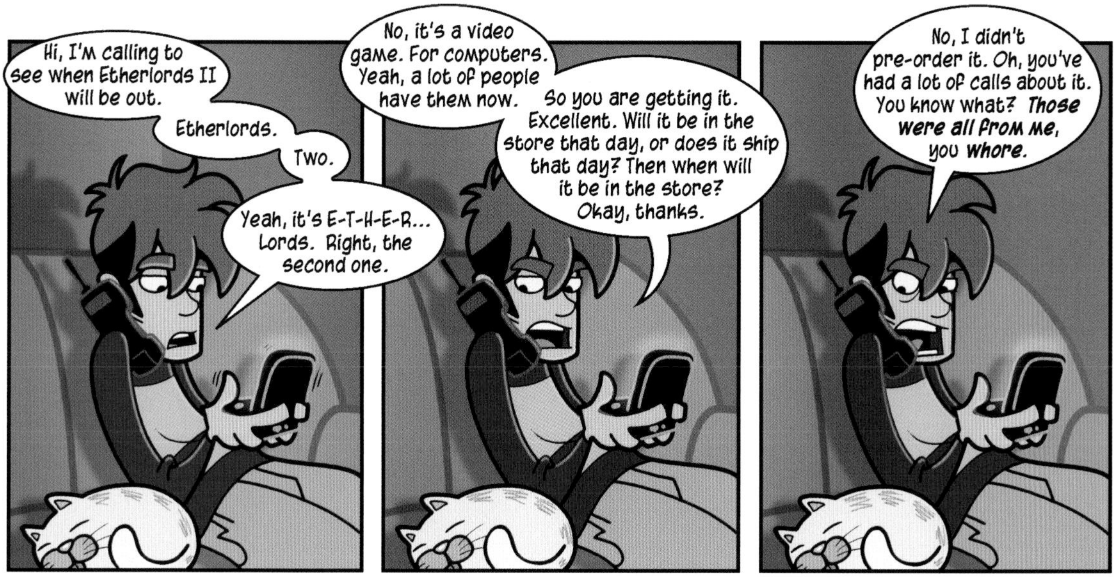
Hi, I'm calling to see when Etherlords II will be out.
Etherlords.
Two.
Yeah, it's E-T-H-E-R... Lords. Right, the second one.
No, it's a video game. For computers. Yeah, a lot of people have them now.
So you are getting it. Excellent. Will it be in the store that day, or does it ship that day? Then when will it be in the store? Okay, thanks.
No, I didn't pre-order it. Oh, you've had a lot of calls about it. You know what? **Those were all from me,** you **whore.**

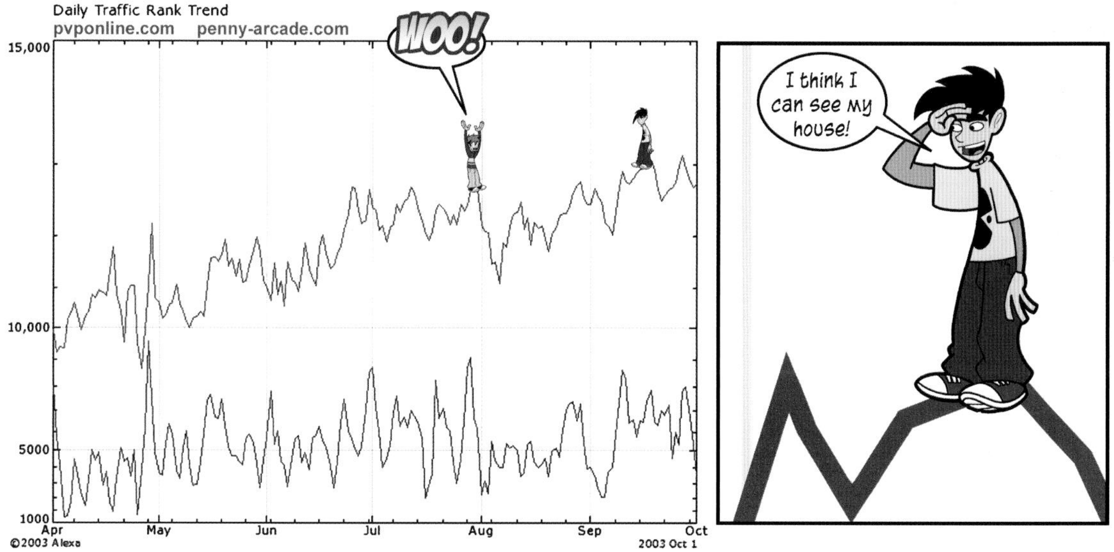
Daily Traffic Rank Trend
pvponline.com penny-arcade.com
15,000
10,000
5000
1000
Apr
May
Jun
Jul
Aug
Sep
Oct
©2003 Alexa
2003 Oct 1
WOO!
I think I can see my house!

MY HALF

October 1, 2003 I don't think the Etherlords series was an especially big deal, but I certainly enjoyed it. I'm into card games, collectible or otherwise, though the costs (and the difficulty of finding people to play against) tend to limit my access. This was a solution that basically fixed everything: a purely *electronic* collectible card game that *doubled* as a crafty opponent. It was by Nival Interactive, which specializes in great strategy games with *terrible* translations.

ZING!

October 3, 2003 Scott Kurtz of the infamous *PvP* kept trying to start some shit with us in his comic (as happened from time to time in those days), and so we responded with this low blow. Scott's best work is done when he is on the warpath, at least in our opinion, but then we are *bad men* who love driving people into that state.

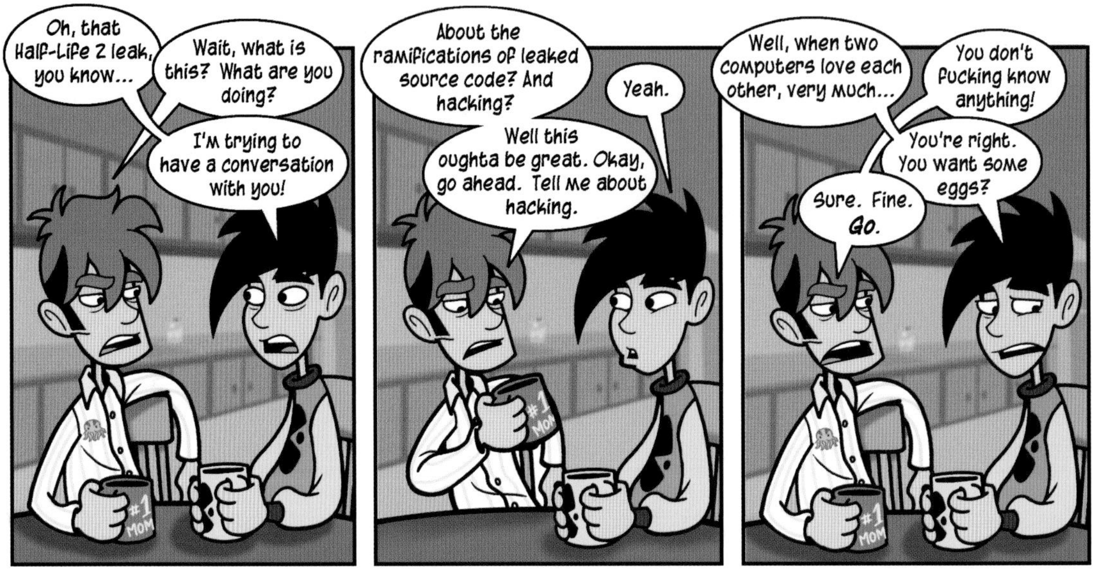
Oh, that Half-Life 2 leak, you know...
Wait, what is this? What are you doing?
I'm trying to have a conversation with you!
About the ramifications of leaked source code? And hacking?
Yeah.
Well this oughta be great. Okay, go ahead. Tell me about hacking.
Well, when two computers love each other, very much...
You don't fucking know anything!
You're right. You want some eggs?
Sure. Fine. Go.
#1 MOM

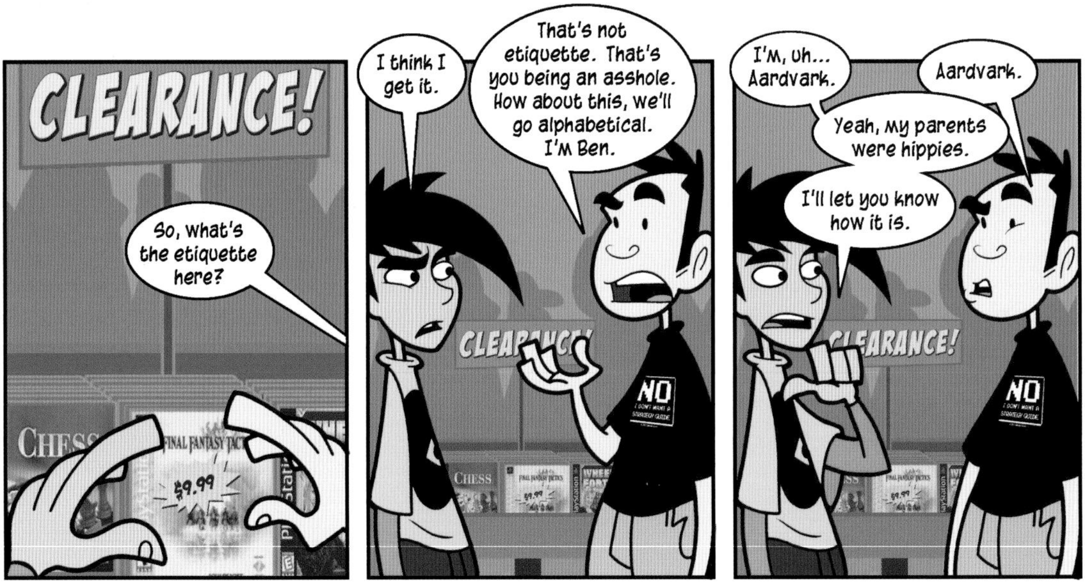
CLEARANCE!
So, what's the etiquette here?
FINAL FANTASY TACT
$9.99
I think I get it.
That's not etiquette. That's you being an asshole. How about this, we'll go alphabetical. I'm Ben.
NO
I'm, uh... Aardvark.
Aardvark.
Yeah, my parents were hippies.
I'll let you know how it is.

A RARE GLIMPSE

October 4, 2003 This was huge news at the time. The shadowy forces known collectively as "the hax0r" managed to get their hands on the source code for Half-Life 2, and revealed that it was nowhere *near* completion. This strip went up on a Saturday, which is for us exceedingly rare, but Gabe felt bad that we had used up one of our weekly comics just to take a shot at Scott, and he felt like our readers deserved more from us.

YOU CAN CALL ME ORYCTEROPUS

October 6, 2003 I have no idea how he was able to come up with a copy of FFT used; that shit is a king's ransom now. They're re-releasing it on the PSP, which is an opportunity for people to share my (perhaps unreasonably) high opinion of the game. Now perhaps my trove of Final Fantasy Tactics jokes will find a waiting audience.

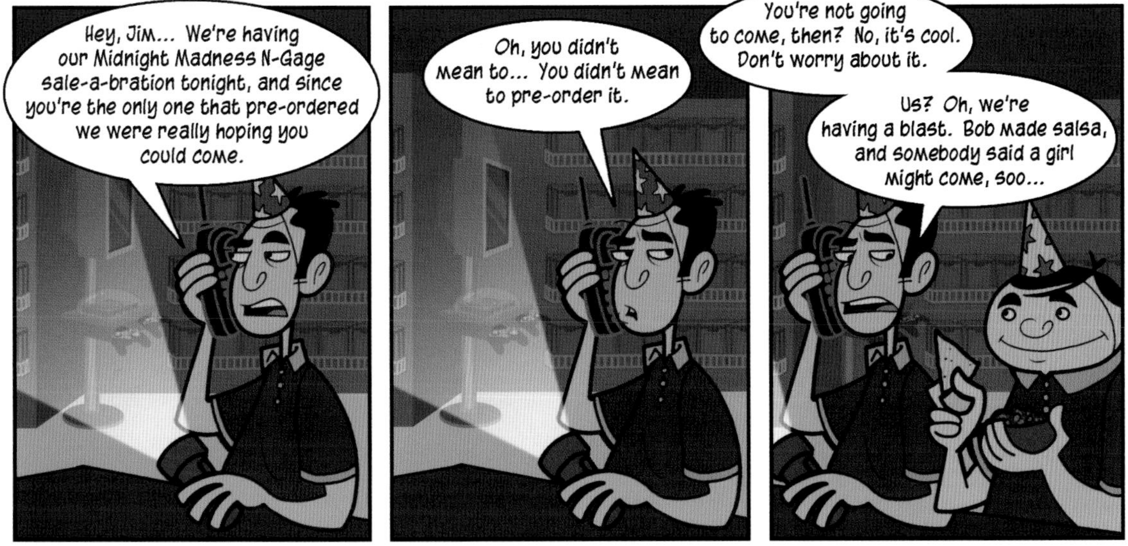
Hey, Jim... We're having our Midnight Madness N-Gage sale-a-bration tonight, and since you're the only one that pre-ordered we were really hoping you could come.
Oh, you didn't mean to... You didn't mean to pre-order it.
You're not going to come, then? No, it's cool. Don't worry about it.
Us? Oh, we're having a blast. Bob made salsa, and somebody said a girl might come, soo...

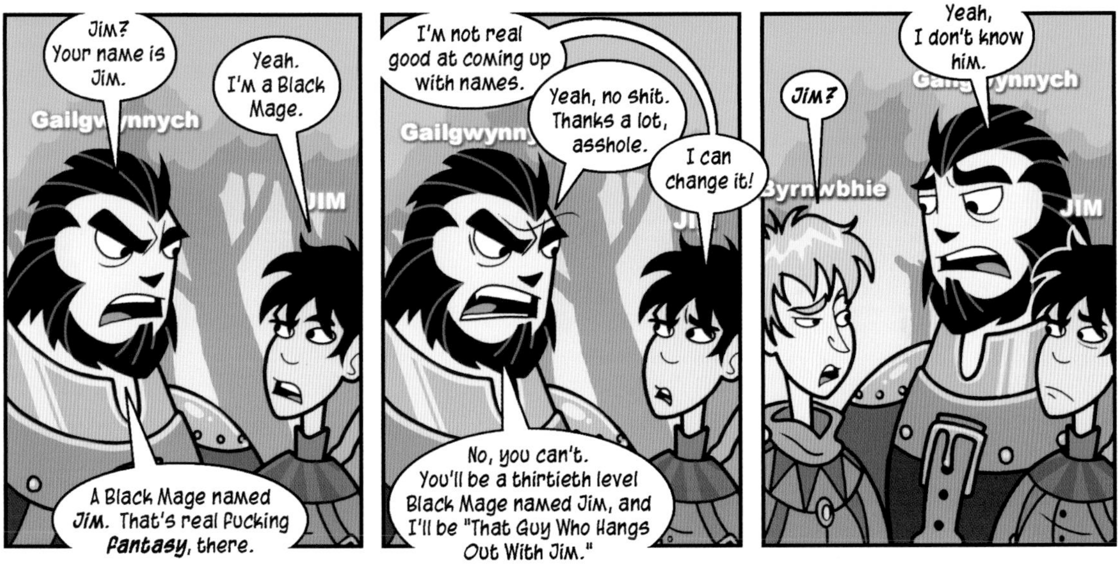
Jim? Your name is Jim.
Yeah. I'm a Black Mage.
JIM
A Black Mage named Jim. That's real fucking fantasy, there.
I'm not real good at coming up with names.
Yeah, no shit. Thanks a lot, asshole.
I can change it!
No, you can't. You'll be a thirtieth level Black Mage named Jim, and I'll be "That Guy Who Hangs Out With Jim."
Jim?
Yeah, I don't know him.
JIM

THE SOUND OF CRICKETS

October 8, 2003 I considered going to one of these things, just because I felt kind of bad and I didn't want those guys to be lonely. Actually, it looks like Bob there is having a pretty good time. You know? Maybe they did all right.

THAT'S ME ON THE LEFT

October 10, 2003 I didn't actually go with "Gailgwynnych" myself, but you can be assured that the name I settled on was *quite* elaborate, and that many consonants were nestled up close to one another. He left the genre alone for a while after Final Fantasy XI, returning to World of Warcraft with . . . (sigh) . . . *Dudefella*.

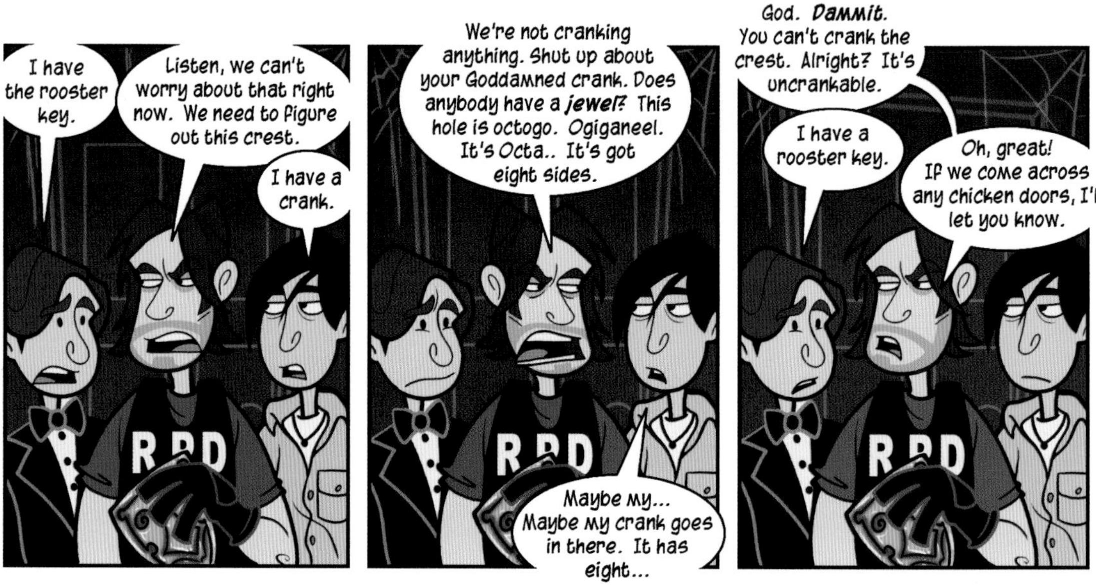
I have the rooster key.
Listen, we can't worry about that right now. We need to figure out this crest.
I have a crank.
We're not cranking anything. Shut up about your Goddamned crank. Does anybody have a *jewel*? This hole is octogo. Ogiganeel. It's Octa.. It's got eight sides.
Maybe my... Maybe my crank goes in there. It has eight...
God. *Dammit.* You can't crank the crest. Alright? It's uncrankable.
I have a rooster key.
Oh, great! If we come across any chicken doors, I'll let you know.

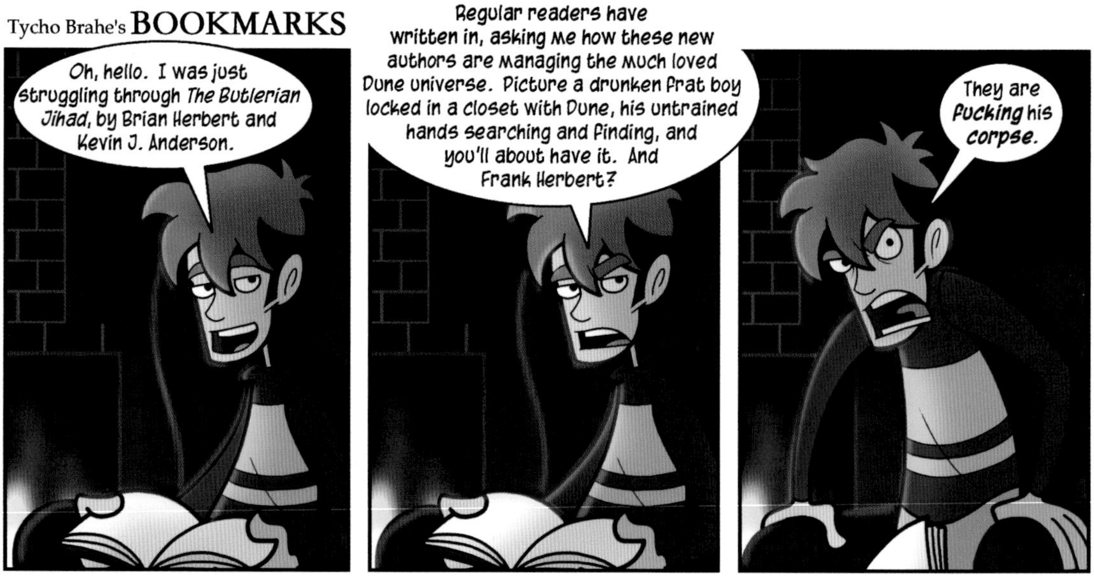
Tycho Brahe's BOOKMARKS
Oh, hello. I was just struggling through *The Butlerian Jihad*, by Brian Herbert and Kevin J. Anderson.
Regular readers have written in, asking me how these new authors are managing the much loved Dune universe. Picture a drunken frat boy locked in a closet with Dune, his untrained hands searching and finding, and you'll about have it. And Frank Herbert?
They are *fucking* his *corpse*.

OF CRESTS AND CRANKS

October 13, 2003 I will forgive you for not remembering, but there was—briefly—a multiplayer branch of the Resident Evil franchise. It saw a sequel in Japan for whatever reason, but there were some serious issues with it. No voice chat, for one. Second, in a game where you're being chased around by the undead, load times of a minute or more tend to *dissipate the tension*.

HONESTY TIME

October 15, 2003 I've come around to some—*some*—of the Expanded Universe fiction being written for Star Wars, but Dune is (for me) sacrosanct and if you start putting the Dune name on books then those books had better be excellent. These were not. I was reading one on a plane, and after we landed I left it behind in the seat pouch—like I would leave *garbage*.

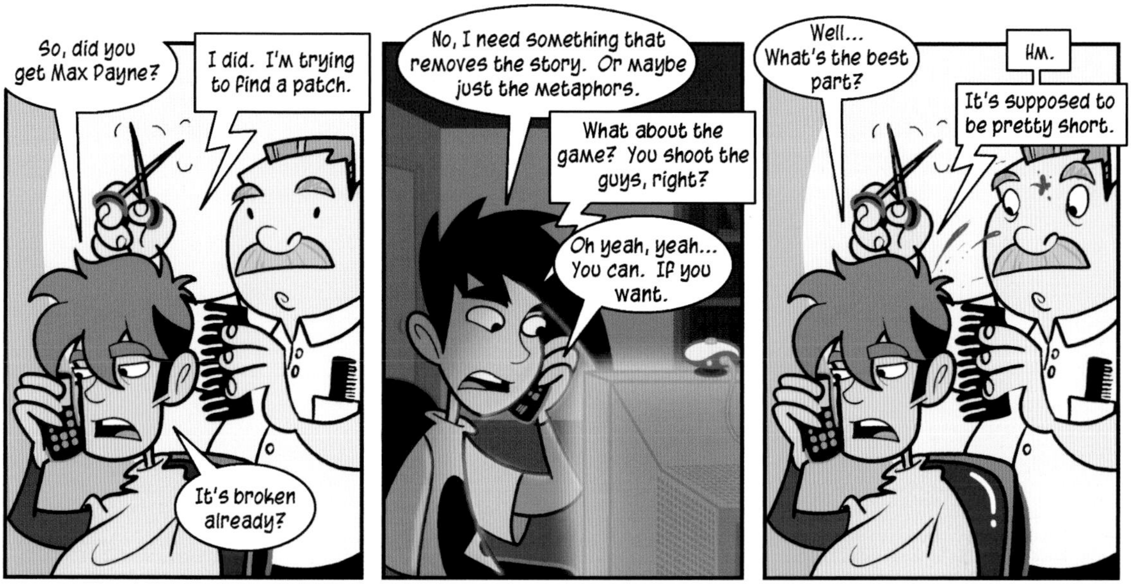
So, did you get Max Payne?
I did. I'm trying to find a patch.
It's broken already?
No, I need something that removes the story. Or maybe just the metaphors.
What about the game? You shoot the guys, right?
Oh yeah, yeah... You can. If you want.
Well... What's the best part?
HM.
It's supposed to be pretty short.

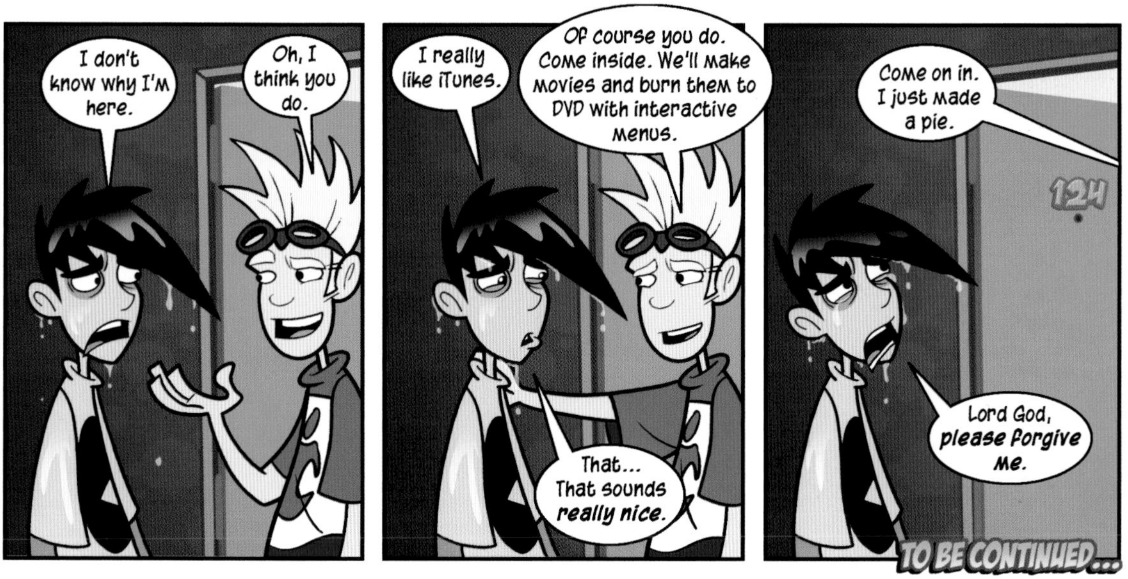
I don't know why I'm here.
Oh, I think you do.
I really like iTunes.
Of course you do. Come inside. We'll make movies and burn them to DVD with interactive menus.
That... That sounds *really nice.*
Come on in. I just made a pie.
124
Lord God, *please forgive me.*
TO BE CONTINUED...

BARBERISM

October 17, 2003 I found a method by which I could enjoy the story in Max Payne 2, a process my cohort never discovered. It's quite simple, really. I systematically lowered all of my expectations until even the sound of a *phone* ringing was like the *second coming of Christ*.

THE PIED PIPER

October 20, 2003 I don't know if it's rude, I think it might be, but sometimes we like to say that a strip is "TO BE CONTINUED . . ." when we don't really have any intention of continuing it. Besides, in this *particular* case, I'm not sure we need what happened there in apartment 124 made absolutely explicit.

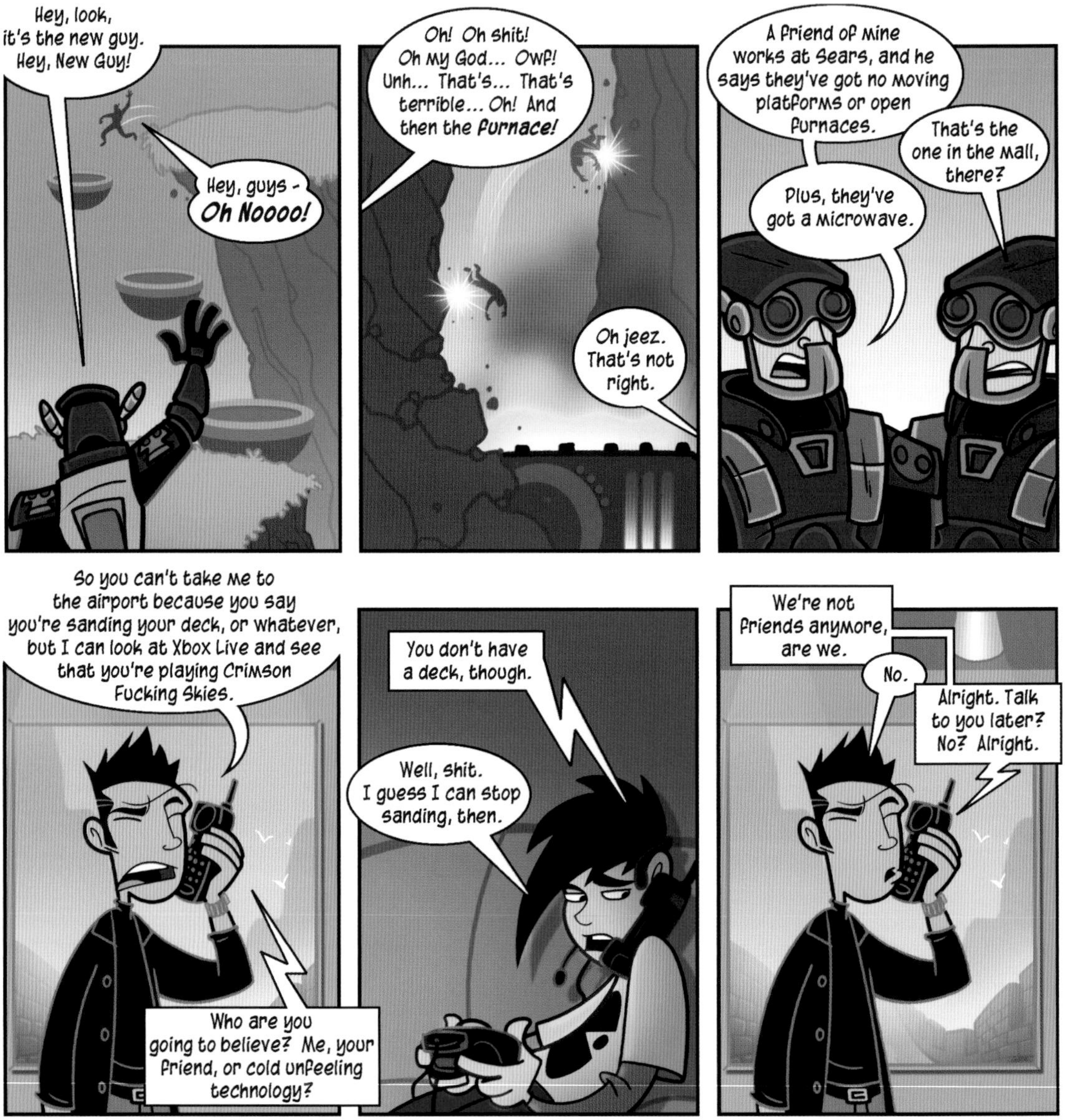
Hey, look, it's the new guy. Hey, New Guy!
Hey, guys - Oh Noooo!
Oh! Oh shit! Oh my God... Owf! Unh... That's... That's terrible... Oh! And then the furnace!
Oh jeez. That's not right.
A friend of mine works at Sears, and he says they've got no moving platforms or open furnaces.
That's the one in the mall, there?
Plus, they've got a microwave.
So you can't take me to the airport because you say you're sanding your deck, or whatever, but I can look at Xbox Live and see that you're playing Crimson Fucking Skies.
Who are you going to believe? Me, your friend, or cold unfeeling technology?
You don't have a deck, though.
Well, shit. I guess I can stop sanding, then.
We're not friends anymore, are we.
No.
Alright. Talk to you later? No? Alright.

SAFETY IN THE WORKPLACE

October 22, 2003 The second Jak and Daxter game was very good, and the series continued to be good, and then there was a racing game, and then Daxter got his own game on the PSP, and *whatever.* But let's be clear: actually going to work in that world is a Goddamn death sentence. If the whirling blades don't get you, or the liquid darkness, odds are good that you will find yourself consumed by a perpetual fire.

CRIMSON LIES

October 24, 2003 I think this might have been the first time we showed Robert in the strip. Unfortunately, Xbox Live proved a very effective way for Robert to spy on us when we were first working together. We didn't have a very good work ethic, because that's an *ethic*, and we don't have ethics of *any kind*.

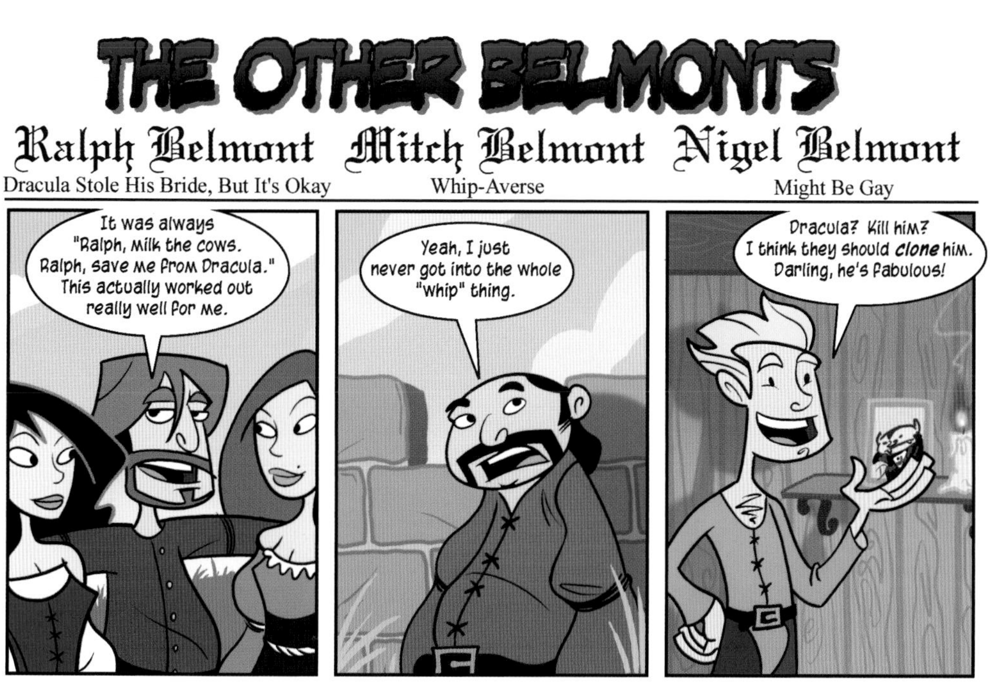
THE OTHER BELMONTS
Ralph Belmont
Dracula Stole His Bride, But It's Okay
Mitch Belmont
Whip-Averse
Nigel Belmont
Might Be Gay
It was always "Ralph, milk the cows. Ralph, save me from Dracula." This actually worked out really well for me.
Yeah, I just never got into the whole "whip" thing.
Dracula? Kill him? I think they should clone him. Darling, he's fabulous!

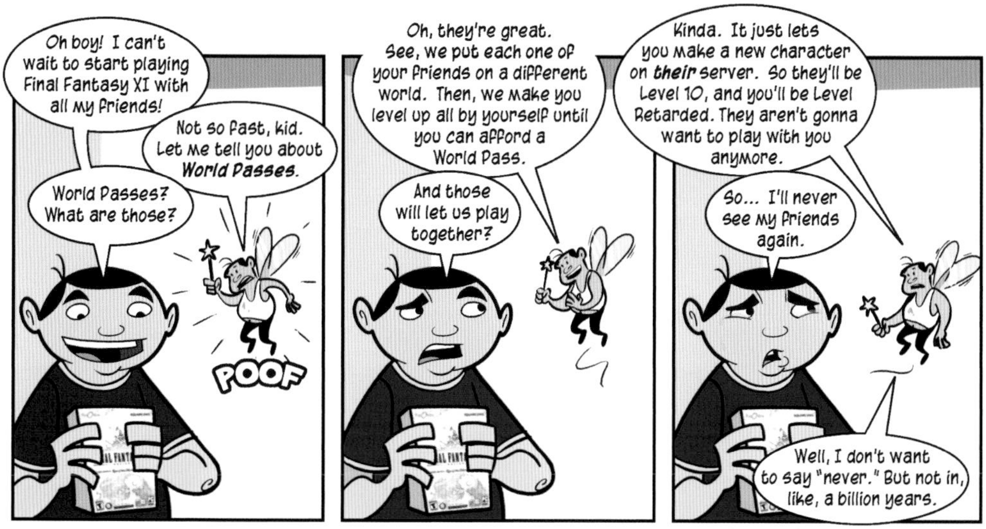
Oh boy! I can't wait to start playing Final Fantasy XI with all my friends!
Not so fast, kid. Let me tell you about World Passes.
World Passes? What are those?
POOF
Oh, they're great. See, we put each one of your friends on a different world. Then, we make you level up all by yourself until you can afford a World Pass.
And those will let us play together?
Kinda. It just lets you make a new character on their server. So they'll be Level 10, and you'll be Level Retarded. They aren't gonna want to play with you anymore.
So... I'll never see my friends again.
Well, I don't want to say "never." But not in, like, a billion years.

THE OTHER BELMONTS

October 27, 2003 This comic came out around the same time as Castlevania: Lament of Innocence. I never got a chance to play it much, as my Playstation 2 decided to stop reading discs around this time. I've had three different PS2s all told, and I've never once regretted the purchase. The machine is—quite simply—a necessity.

THE INCONVENIENCE FAIRY

October 29, 2003 The World Pass system isn't all that bad if you've got people in the game playing already but, as we didn't, this strip was the result. As a new player, you've just installed what feels like a million discs, and then updated the game online, and then signed into *two* separate services to find yourself penniless and alone.

VEGAS SKETCHBOOK 2003

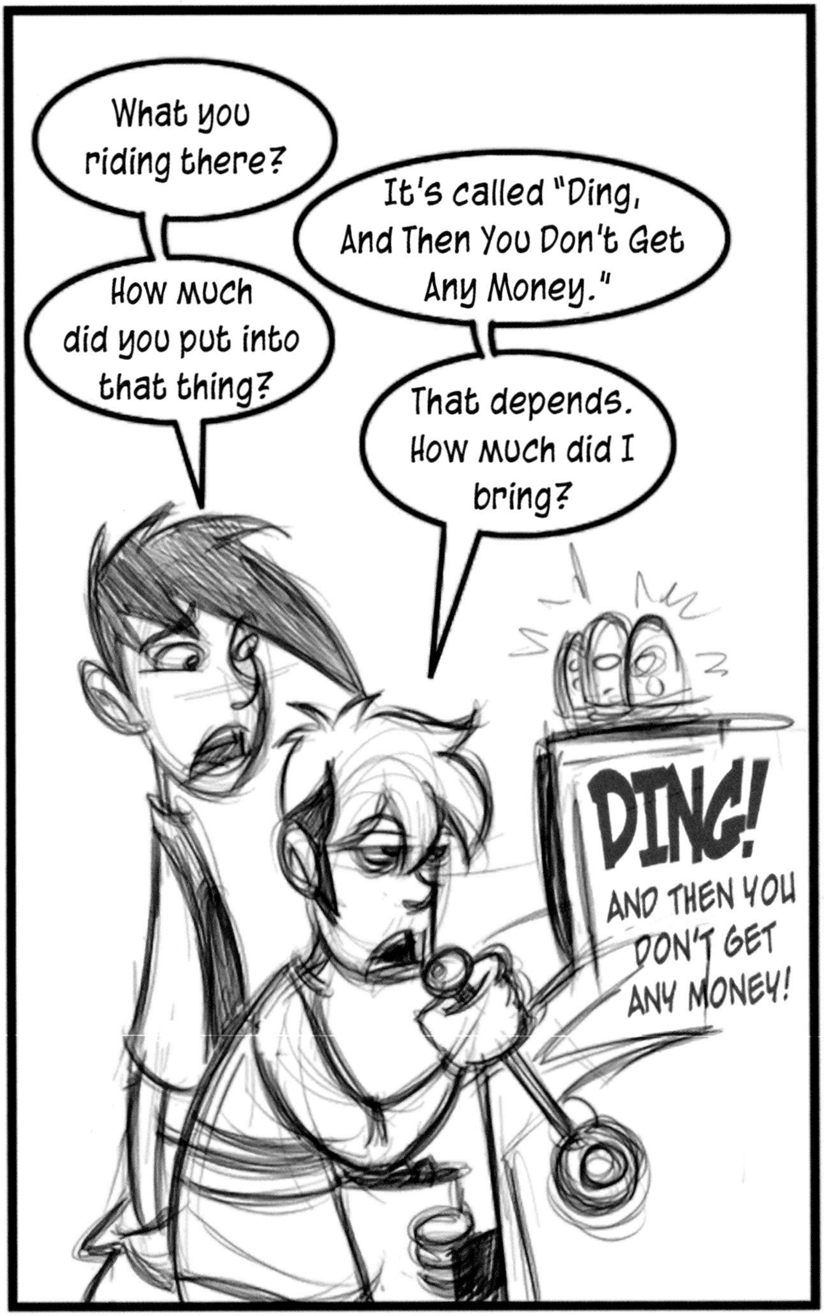
What you riding there?
It's called "Ding, And Then You Don't Get Any Money."
How much did you put into that thing?
That depends. How much did I bring?
DING!
AND THEN YOU DON'T GET ANY MONEY!

SIN CITY SKETCHBOOK, VOLUME ONE

October 31, 2003 The truth is that the only time I ever play slots *ever* is when I am walking to and from a craps table. I never understood how a person could get addicted to losing money until the first time I stood at one of these devil tables, the red dice heavy in my hand. It's essentially co-operative gambling, and that social facet has a terrible, terrible pull.

VEGAS SKETCHBOOK 2003

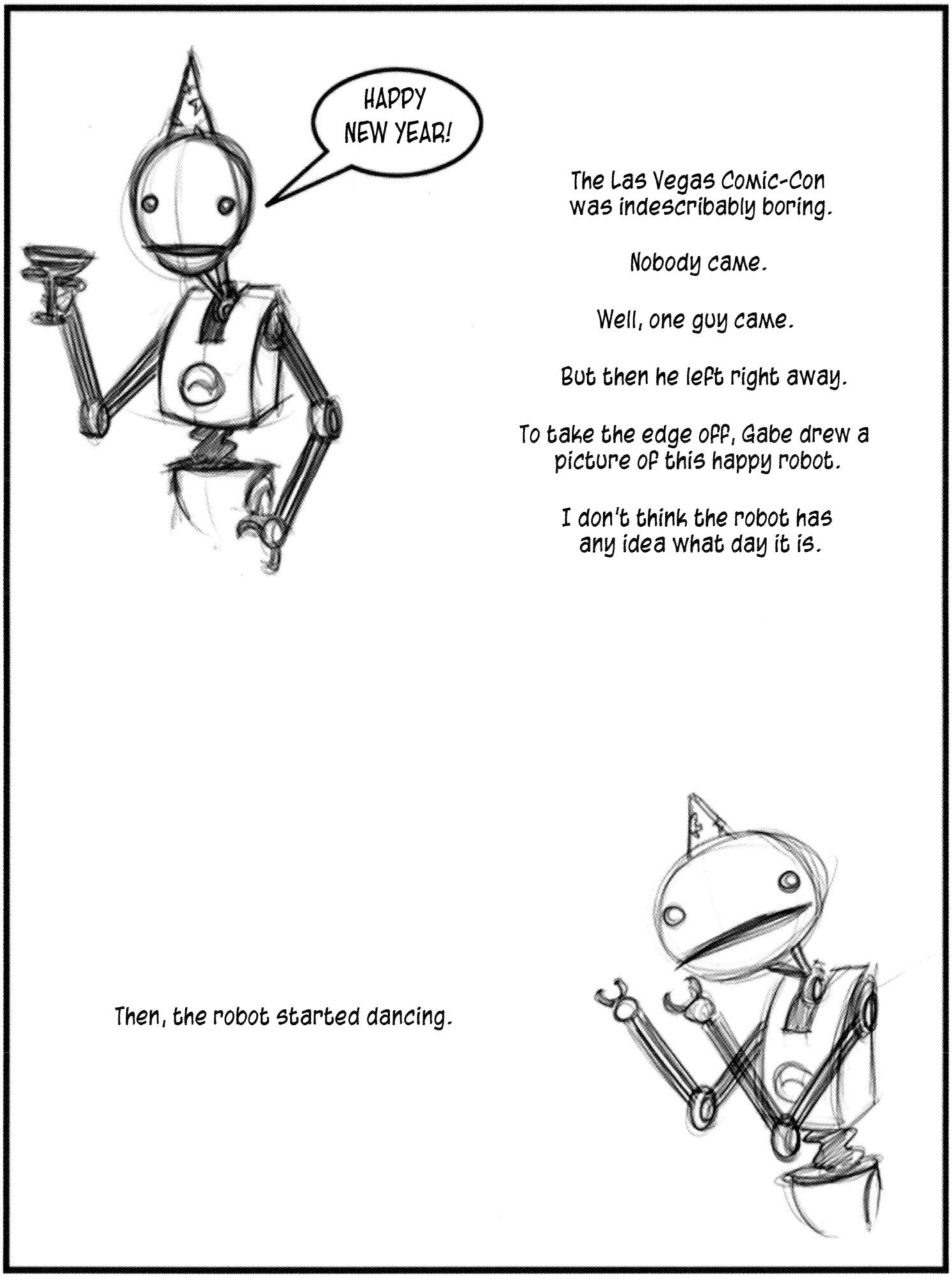

HAPPY NEW YEAR!
The Las Vegas Comic-Con was indescribably boring.
Nobody came.
Well, one guy came.
But then he left right away.
To take the edge off, Gabe drew a picture of this happy robot.
I don't think the robot has any idea what day it is.
Then, the robot started dancing.

SIN CITY SKETCHBOOK, VOLUME TWO

November 3, 2003 The Las Vegas Comic-Con was an absolute nightmare as a business trip; we gave away more shirts than we sold. In every other respect, it was marvelous. The dancing robot was born there. I count the best night of my life as having taken place in Las Vegas, specifically at Quark's Bar in The Star Trek Experience. I don't know if you've heard, but if you ask for it those guys will bring you a *fishbowl* full of rum.

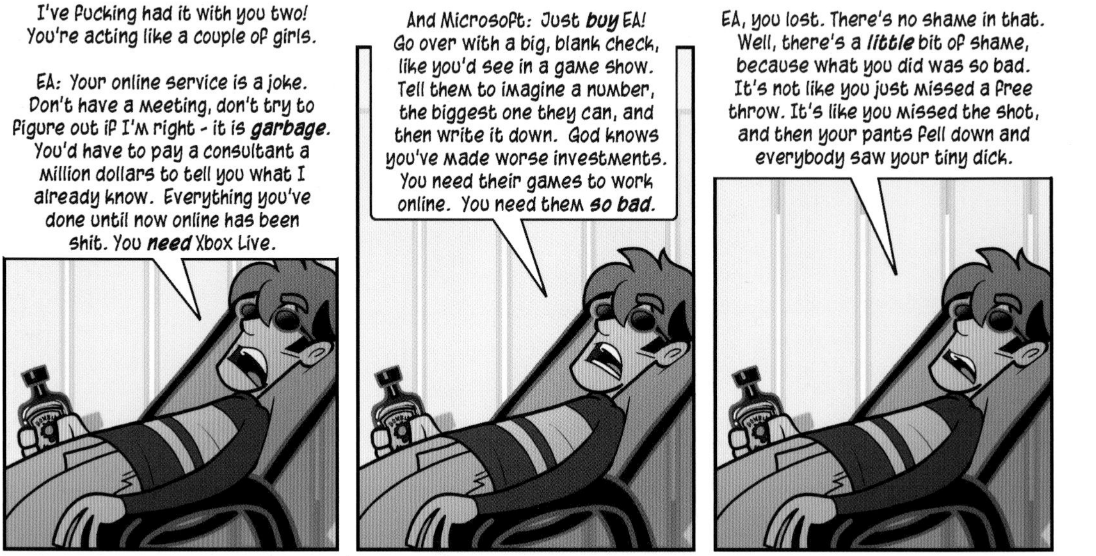
I've fucking had it with you two! You're acting like a couple of girls.
EA: Your online service is a joke. Don't have a meeting, don't try to figure out if I'm right - it is **garbage**. You'd have to pay a consultant a million dollars to tell you what I already know. Everything you've done until now online has been shit. You **need** Xbox Live.
And Microsoft: Just **buy** EA! Go over with a big, blank check, like you'd see in a game show. Tell them to imagine a number, the biggest one they can, and then write it down. God knows you've made worse investments. You need their games to work online. You need them **so bad**.
EA, you lost. There's no shame in that. Well, there's a **little** bit of shame, because what you did was so bad. It's not like you just missed a free throw. It's like you missed the shot, and then your pants fell down and everybody saw your tiny dick.

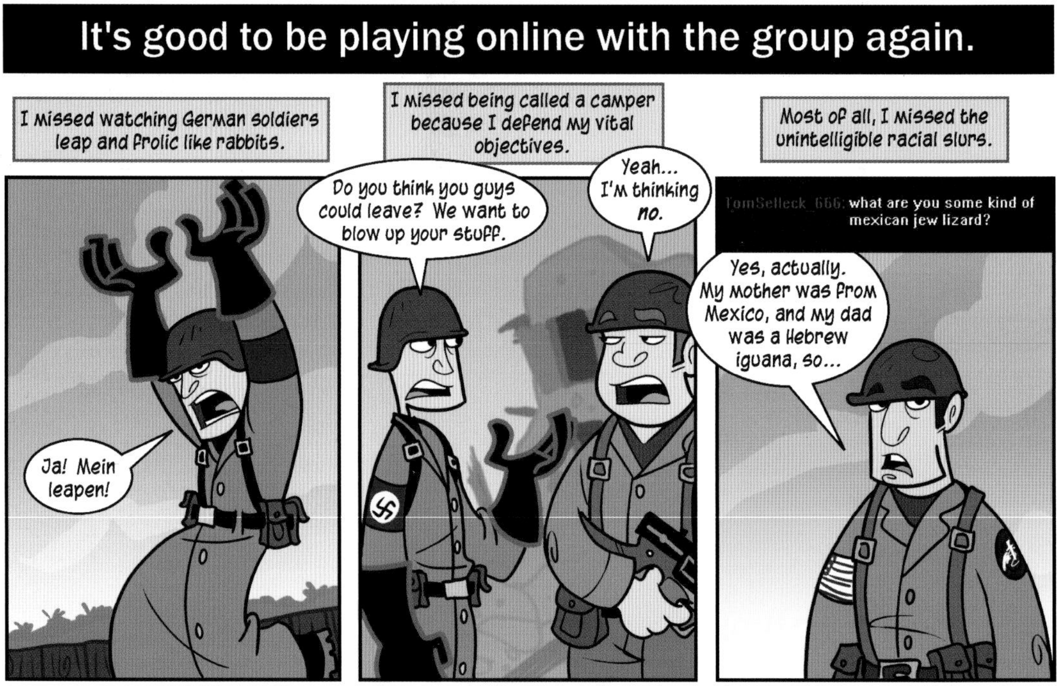
It's good to be playing online with the group again.
I missed watching German soldiers leap and frolic like rabbits.
Ja! Mein leapen!
I missed being called a camper because I defend my vital objectives.
Do you think you guys could leave? We want to blow up your stuff.
Yeah... I'm thinking **no**.
Most of all, I missed the unintelligible racial slurs.
TomSelleck_666: what are you some kind of mexican jew lizard?
Yes, actually. My mother was from Mexico, and my dad was a Hebrew iguana, so...

STRAIGHT TALKIN'

November 5, 2003 Be careful what you wish for, huh? It's hard to believe that there was a period when Electronic Arts simply disregarded the entire Xbox platform as an online venue.

THE NOT SO GOOD OLD DAYS

November 7, 2003 "Mexican Jew Lizard" is, I'm sad to say, a real epithet from those thoroughly exciting days. More lulls in nightly crew play would follow, but I'm overjoyed to say that it's basically rock-solid now. It is the part of the day that everything else hangs from.

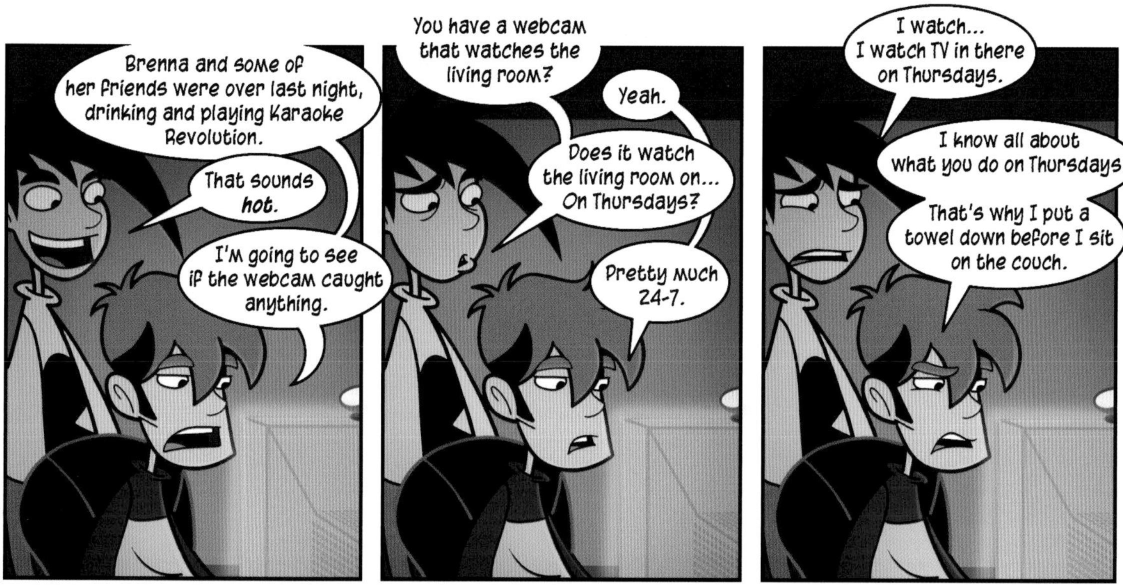
Brenna and some of her friends were over last night, drinking and playing Karaoke Revolution.
That sounds *hot*.
I'm going to see if the webcam caught anything.
You have a webcam that watches the living room?
Yeah.
Does it watch the living room on... On Thursdays?
Pretty much 24-7.
I watch... I watch TV in there on Thursdays.
I know all about what you do on Thursdays.
That's why I put a towel down before I sit on the couch.

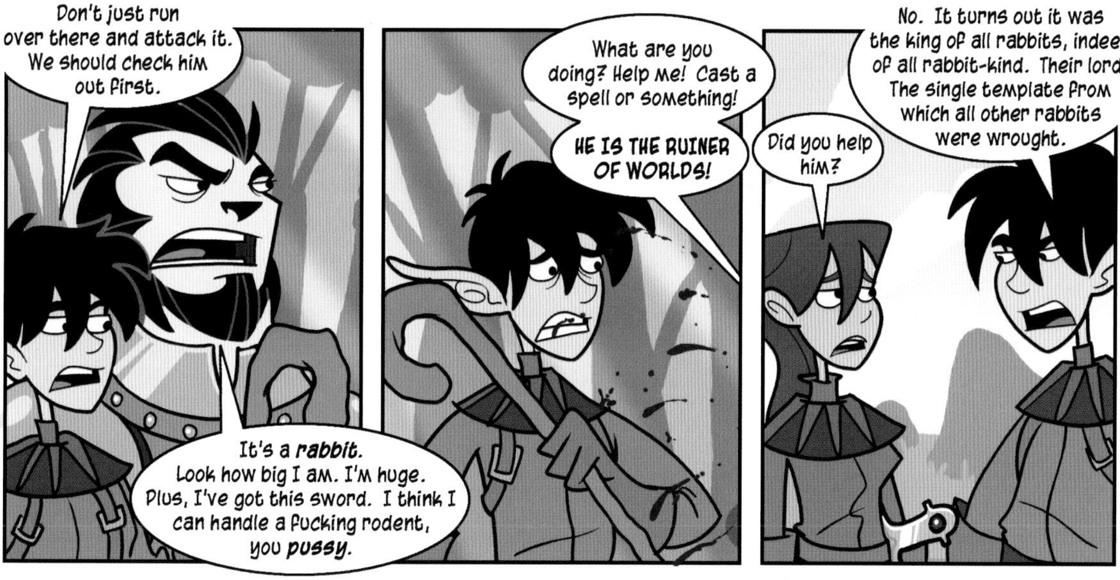
Don't just run over there and attack it. We should check him out first.
It's a *rabbit*. Look how big I am. I'm huge. Plus, I've got this sword. I think I can handle a fucking rodent, you *pussy*.
What are you doing? Help me! Cast a spell or something!
HE IS THE RUINER OF WORLDS!
Did you help him?
No. It turns out it was the king of all rabbits, indeed of all rabbit-kind. Their lord. The single template from which all other rabbits were wrought.

SOMEWHAT UNPLEASANT

November 10, 2003 I'm always trying to encourage Brenna and her friends to just *try* videogames, the way your parents might *try* to get you to eat some broccoli. This was in the ancient times, the 2003 times. I had to use guile and trickery then. These days, I imagine that Wii Sports Tennis would do all the work for me.

THE OMEGA HARE

November 12, 2003 Gabe and Kara didn't stay long in Vana'Diel, what they call the *world* in Final Fantasy XI, but they did stay for a while. Kara was the White Mage, Gabe the Black Mage, and I the burly Galkan Fighter who so *frequently* took one for the team.

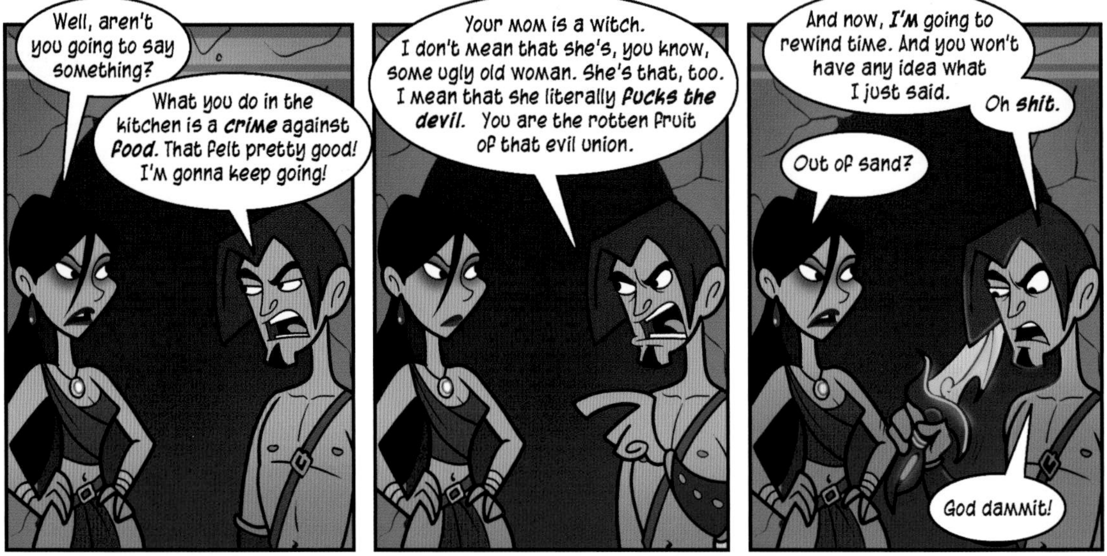
Well, aren't you going to say something?
What you do in the kitchen is a *crime* against *food*. That felt pretty good! I'm gonna keep going!
Your mom is a witch. I don't mean that she's, you know, some ugly old woman. She's that, too. I mean that she literally *fucks the devil*. You are the rotten fruit of that evil union.
And now, *I'm* going to rewind time. And you won't have any idea what I just said.
Oh *shit*.
Out of sand?
God dammit!

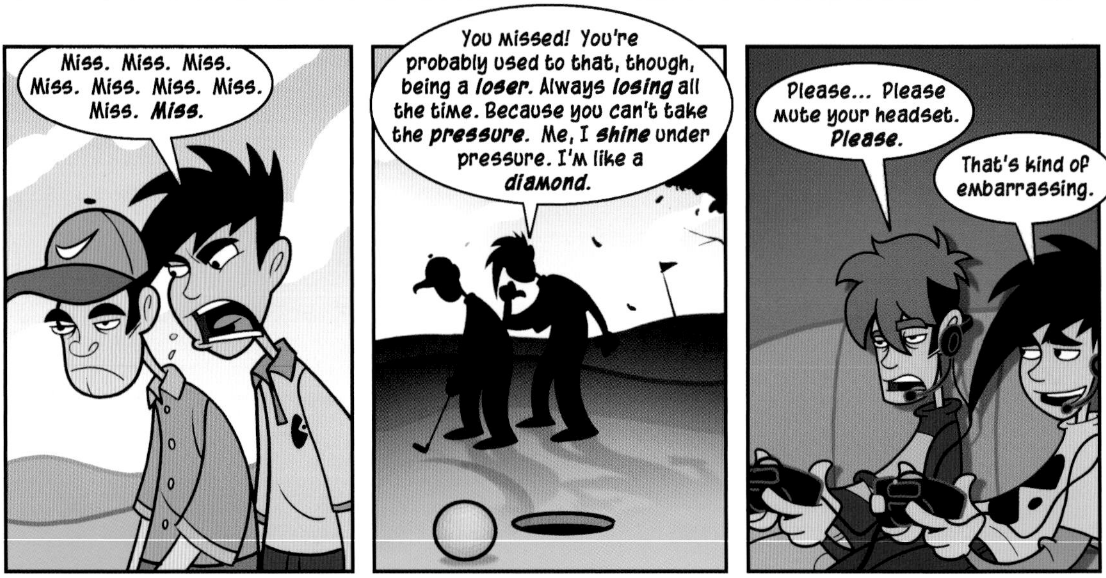
Miss. Miss. Miss. Miss. Miss. Miss. Miss. Miss. *Miss*.
You missed! You're probably used to that, though, being a *loser*. Always *losing* all the time. Because you can't take the *pressure*. Me, I *shine* under pressure. I'm like a *diamond*.
Please... Please mute your headset. *Please*.
That's kind of embarrassing.

DON'T EVER SAY THINGS LIKE THIS

November 14, 2003 When the game takes this ability away from you—I guess that's a spoiler, but seriously, this game is like a million years old—it's like walking a tightrope. I literally tingled in my extremities at the end, where you must scale an entire mountain fortress in a single life. There's a nominal "boss fight" as well, but that's not really the boss. The boss is *getting* there.

A GENTLEMAN'S GAME

November 17, 2003 We whiled away hours playing Links on Xbox Live; though it didn't have the raw polish of an EA presentation, the gameplay itself was very right. This was back when Microsoft was doing a ton of its own sports development. That doesn't happen anymore, and in the resultant shuffle the Links brand got sold away, and the new project based on it was canceled. A moment of silence, please.

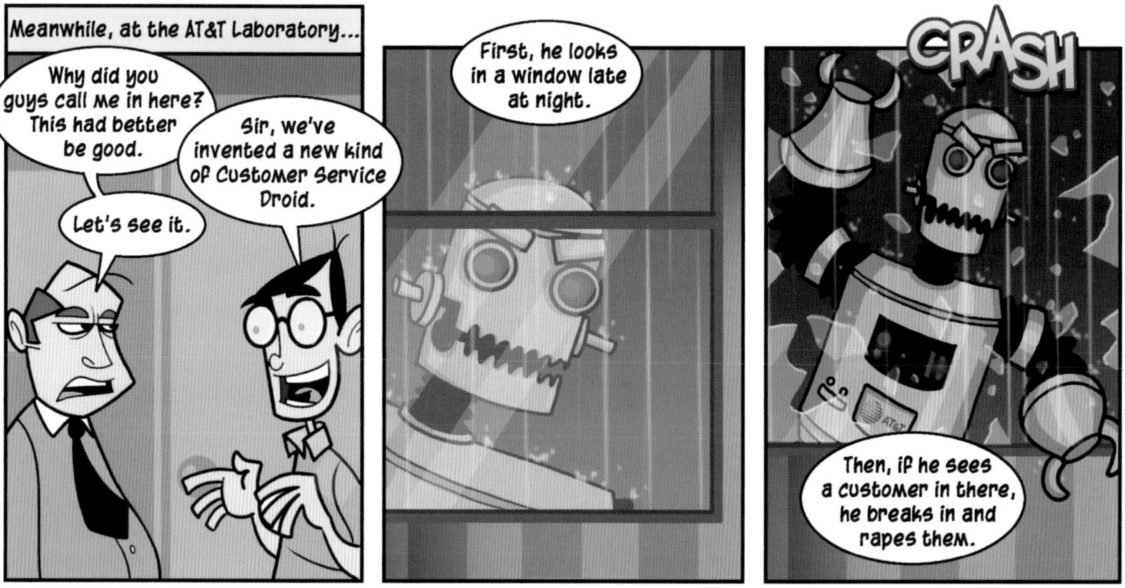
Meanwhile, at the AT&T Laboratory...
Why did you guys call me in here? This had better be good.
Sir, we've invented a new kind of Customer Service Droid.
Let's see it.
First, he looks in a window late at night.
CRASH
Then, if he sees a customer in there, he breaks in and rapes them.

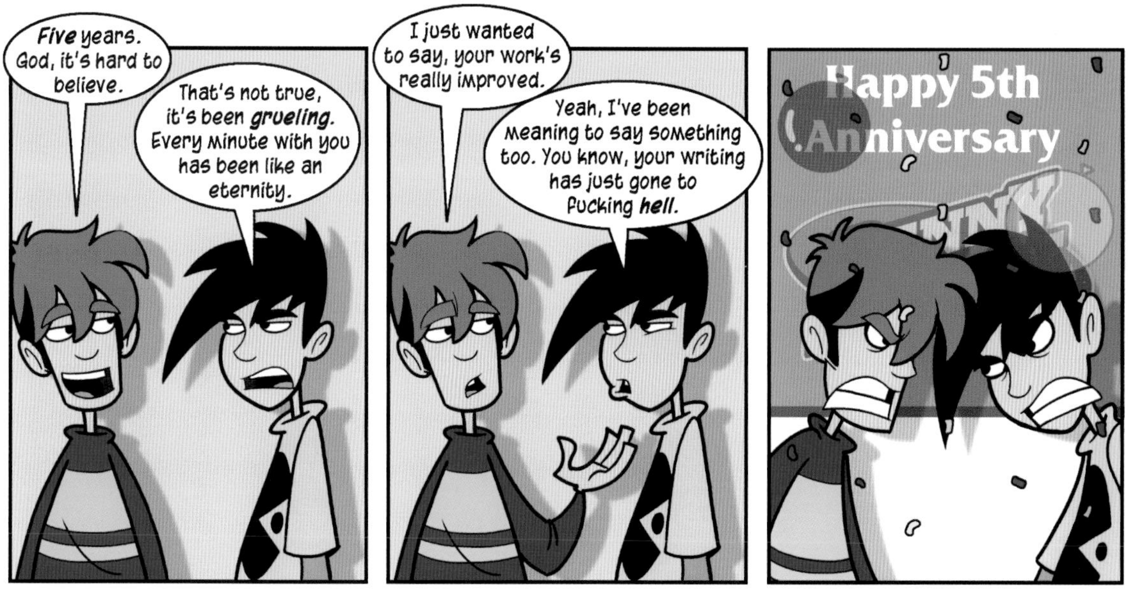
Five years. God, it's hard to believe.
That's not true, it's been grueling. Every minute with you has been like an eternity.
I just wanted to say, your work's really improved.
Yeah, I've been meaning to say something too. You know, your writing has just gone to fucking hell.
Happy 5th Anniversary

REACH OUT AND TOUCH SOMEONE WITH YOUR STEEL PENIS

November 19, 2003 AT&T had recently applied for (and been awarded) a patent for circumventing spam filters, which did not strike us as a noble act, but the reason they had done it was to sue the Spam Kings when they tried to use the same techniques. So this comic is despicable and unfair. We're very sorry, megacorp! Expect a heartfelt fax to your *Feelings Department*.

A CONSTANT FESTIVAL OF MERRYMAKING

November 21, 2003 We have fought a total of four times in the twelve years we've known each other; while the sniping you see in the strip is accurate it rarely escalates to the *gritted teeth phase* depicted in panel three. The first time, we learned that it's really best if we never discuss religion. The other three times were all related to our 1v1 matches in Duke Nukem 3D.

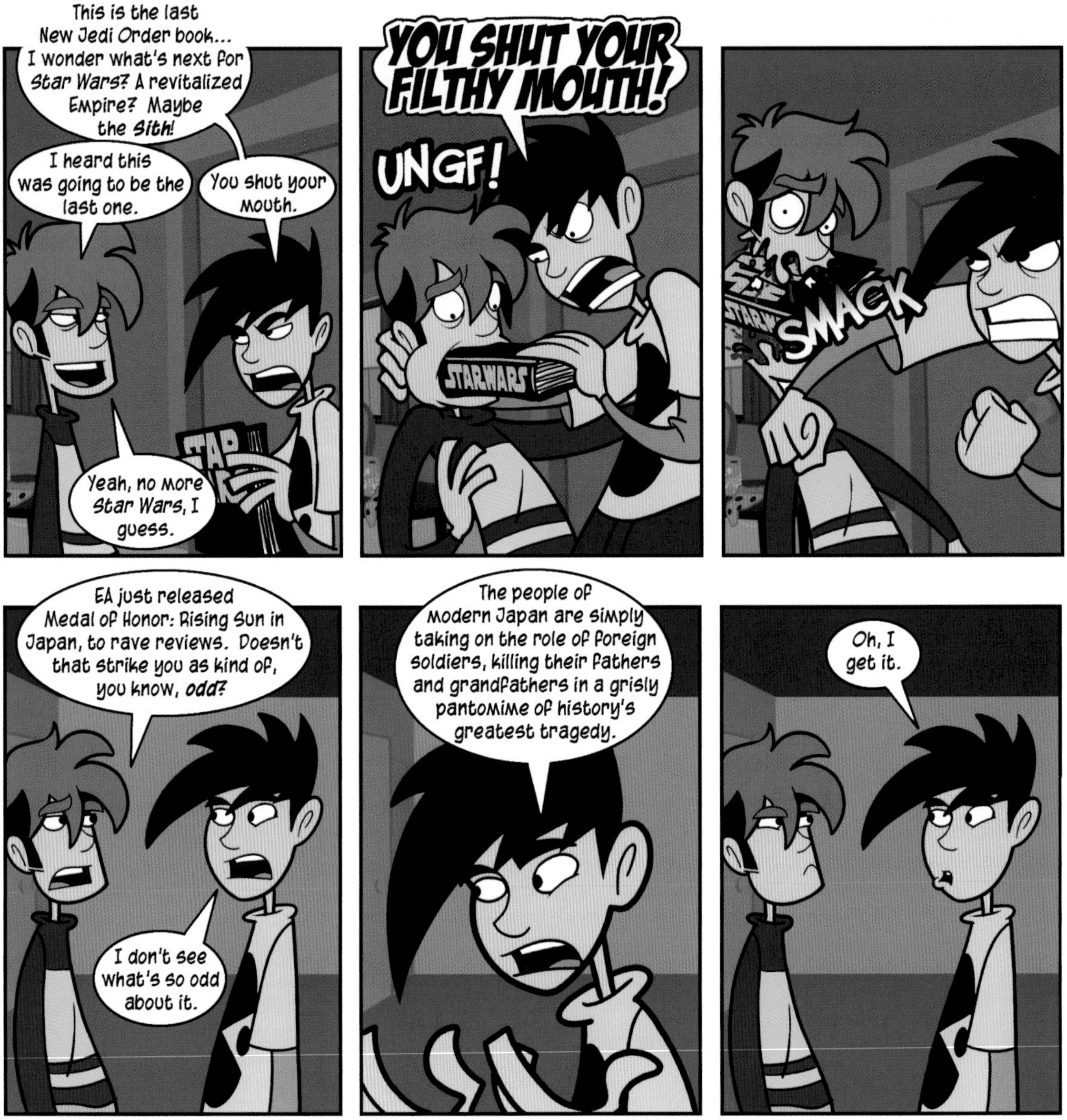
This is the last New Jedi Order book... I wonder what's next for Star Wars? A revitalized Empire? Maybe the Sith!
I heard this was going to be the last one.
You shut your mouth.
Yeah, no more Star Wars, I guess.
STAR WARS
YOU SHUT YOUR FILTHY MOUTH!
UNGF!
STAR WARS
SMACK
EA just released Medal of Honor: Rising Sun in Japan, to rave reviews. Doesn't that strike you as kind of, you know, odd?
I don't see what's so odd about it.
The people of modern Japan are simply taking on the role of foreign soldiers, killing their fathers and grandfathers in a grisly pantomime of history's greatest tragedy.
Oh, I get it.

A VORACIOUS READER

November 24, 2003 This is especially funny now that I'm reading the dog-eared copies he brings to work and carrying on conversations with *Star Wars* authors, one of whom wrote the introduction to this very book. I'm sorry, Karen Traviss, internationally recognized science fiction author! I apologize retroactively!

HELL YEAH, IT'S ODD

November 26, 2003 Yeah, that's a fun fact, huh? *Yeesh*.

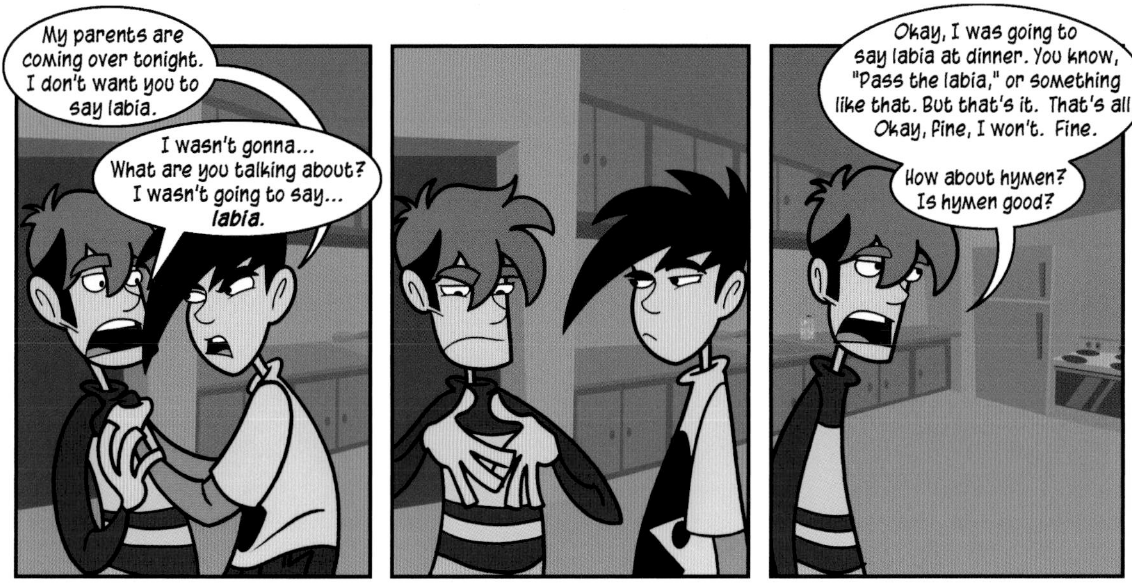
My parents are coming over tonight. I don't want you to say labia.
I wasn't gonna... What are you talking about? I wasn't going to say... *labia.*
Okay, I was going to say labia at dinner. You know, "Pass the labia," or something like that. But that's it. That's all. Okay, fine, I won't. Fine.
How about hymen? Is hymen good?

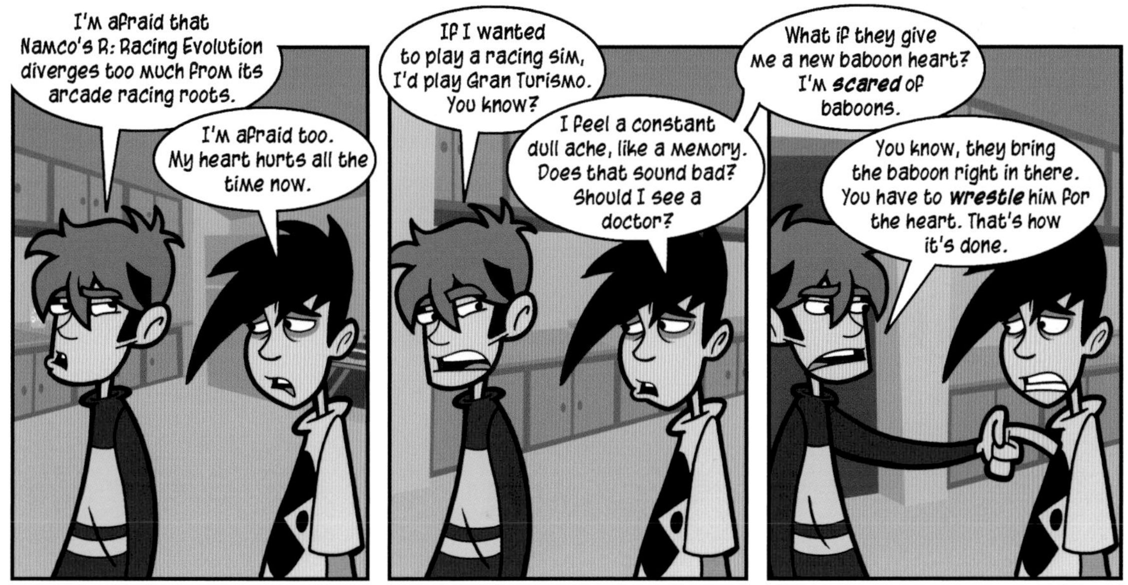
I'm afraid that Namco's R: Racing Evolution diverges too much from its arcade racing roots.
I'm afraid too. My heart hurts all the time now.
If I wanted to play a racing sim, I'd play Gran Turismo. You know?
I feel a constant dull ache, like a memory. Does that sound bad? Should I see a doctor?
What if they give me a new baboon heart? I'm *scared* of baboons.
You know, they bring the baboon right in there. You have to *wrestle* him for the heart. That's how it's done.

PLEASE DON'T READ THIS, MOM

November 28, 2003 I sometimes become addicted to certain words, certain . . . *nouns*, and everyone around me must pay the price. As a young man, I once repeated a word ("whimbly") so many times that my sister swiped at my eye with a letter opener. Man, if I could just get addicted to *heroin* like a normal person.

HE ACTUALLY DOES HURT ALL THE TIME

December 1, 2003 Managing Gabriel's mental and physical crises, talking him down from metaphorical *ledges*, has long been my sacred duty. I'm not actually cruel to him during these crucial ministrations, but a comic in which I treat him gingerly is *no comic at all*.

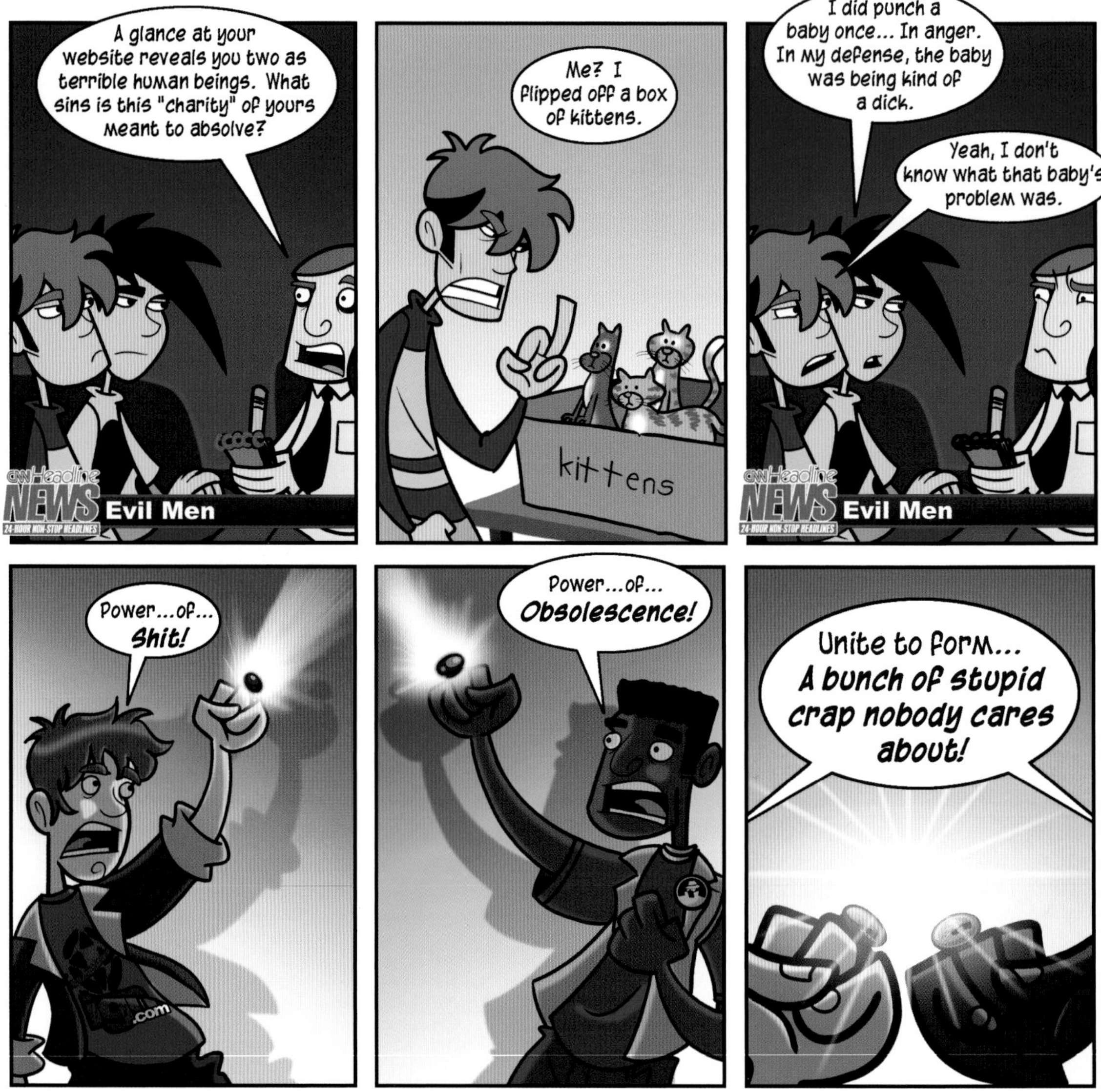
A glance at your website reveals you two as terrible human beings. What sins is this "charity" of yours meant to absolve?
Evil Men
Me? I flipped off a box of kittens.
kittens
I did punch a baby once... In anger. In my defense, the baby was being kind of a dick.
Yeah, I don't know what that baby's problem was.
Evil Men
Power...of... Shit!
Power...of... Obsolescence!
Unite to form... A bunch of stupid crap nobody cares about!

DARK TRUTHS

December 3, 2003 This was the year that Child's Play made its debut. Since then, your total donations have cracked two million dollars. Just think . . . That's one dollar for each of our heinous crimes! I'm not sure why we (of all people) were the ones to start it, but it needed doing, and you agreed. The rest is just trivia.

EVERYBODY'S FAVORITE...THING

December 5, 2003 GameSpy and IGN merged around this time, forming the zzzzzzzzzzzzzzzzzzzzzzzz zzzzzzzzzzzzzzzzzzzzzzzzzzzzzzzzzzzzzzzzzzzzzzzzzzzzzzzzzzzzzzzzzzzzzzzzzzzzzzzzzzzzzzzzzzzzzzzzzzzzzzzzz zzzzzzzzzzzzzzzzzzzzzzzzzzzzzzzzzzzzzzzzzzzzzzzzzzzzzzzzzzzzzzzzzzzzzzzzzzzzzzzzzzzzzzzzzzzzzzzzzzzzz

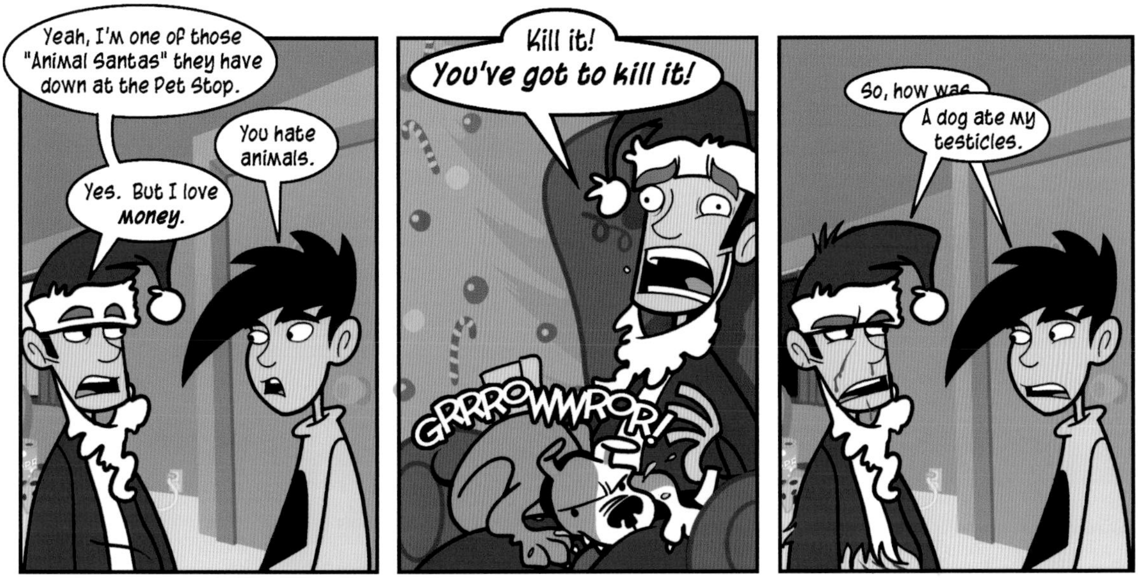
Yeah, I'm one of those "Animal Santas" they have down at the Pet Stop.
You hate animals.
Yes. But I love **money.**
Kill it! **You've got to kill it!**
GRRROWWROR!
So, how wa
A dog ate my testicles.

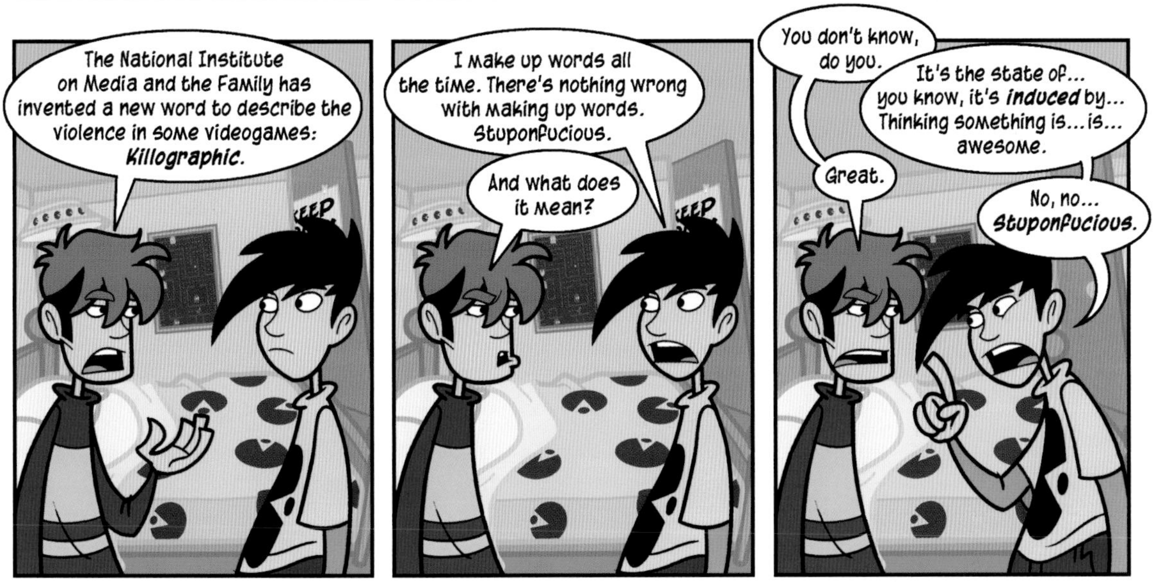
The National Institute on Media and the Family has invented a new word to describe the violence in some videogames: ***Killographic.***
I make up words all the time. There's nothing wrong with making up words. Stuponfucious.
And what does it mean?
You don't know, do you.
It's the state of... you know, it's ***induced*** by... Thinking something is... is... awesome.
Great.
No, no... ***Stuponfucious.***

SANTA'S LITTLE HELPERS

December 8, 2003 If I were compiling a pamphlet entitled "Strips Where Tycho's Balls Are Devoured," it would be very thin indeed, but it would include this strip. In the leftover space, I could provide fun facts ("Did you know there's no cheese in HELL?") or money-saving coupons for area restaurants. If there's any room still available, I've got an idea for a comic about a dog and a cat who dislike one another.

THE WONDERFUL WORLD OF WORDS

December 10, 2003 See, it's like killing and pornography! Because it would be impossible to describe the content of this despicable medium using only the profane and unwieldy *English language*. See, it's a new era, a new cyber era, a . . . *cybera* . . . Hey! Hey, guys! I think I'm getting the hang of it!

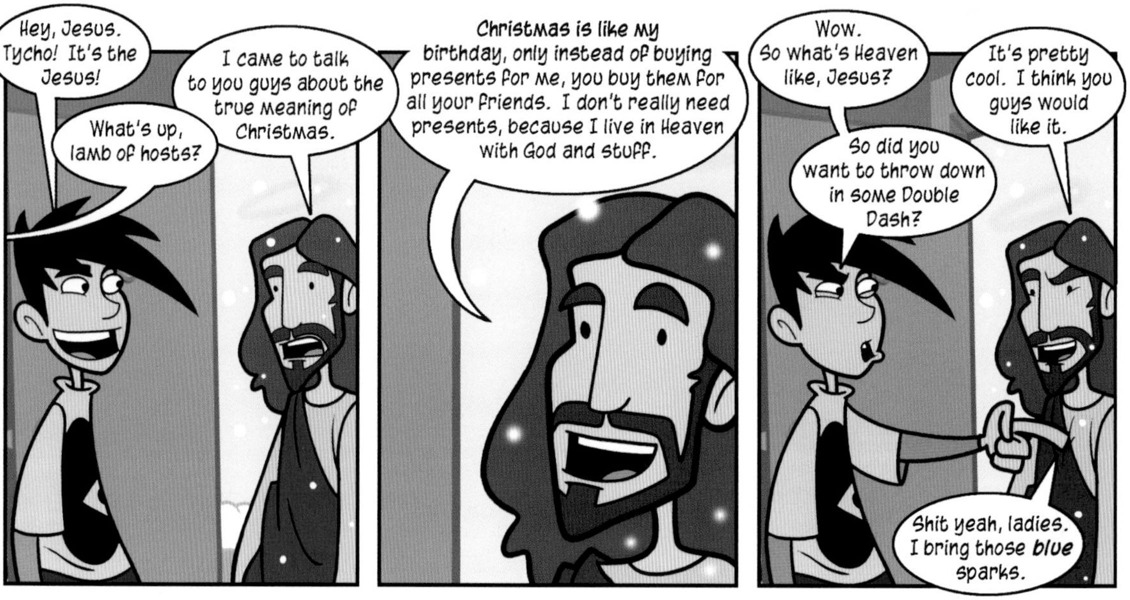
Hey, Jesus. Tycho! It's the Jesus!
What's up, lamb of hosts?
I came to talk to you guys about the true meaning of Christmas.
Christmas is like my birthday, only instead of buying presents for me, you buy them for all your friends. I don't really need presents, because I live in Heaven with God and stuff.
Wow. So what's Heaven like, Jesus?
It's pretty cool. I think you guys would like it.
So did you want to throw down in some Double Dash?
Shit yeah, ladies. I bring those *blue* sparks.

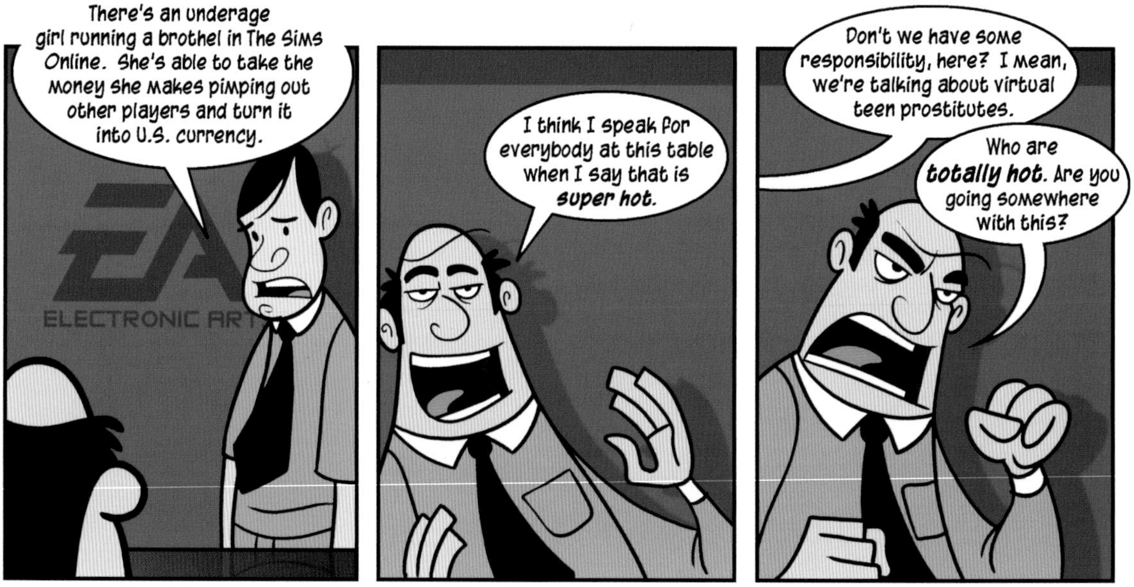
There's an underage girl running a brothel in The Sims Online. She's able to take the money she makes pimping out other players and turn it into U.S. currency.
I think I speak for everybody at this table when I say that is ***super hot.***
Don't we have some responsibility, here? I mean, we're talking about virtual teen prostitutes.
Who are ***totally hot.*** Are you going somewhere with this?

AS FORETOLD IN REVELATIONS

December 12, 2003 Mario Kart on the Cube is still with us. Still! It's surprising how many people come by who have never had a chance to play it in a LAN environment. Gabe hates the Blue Shell—sometimes called "Blue Justice"—because he thinks it places less emphasis on skill. He's right, but I play Nintendo games to have *fun*, something Double Dash continues to deliver.

HOT, AS SUNS ARE HOT

December 15, 2003 We were scandalized to learn the extent of the immoralities on offer in The Sims Online. Of course, all of this is nothing compared to our *modern* multi-user spaces, where players can . . . "innovate," I guess would be the term, to a much greater extent.

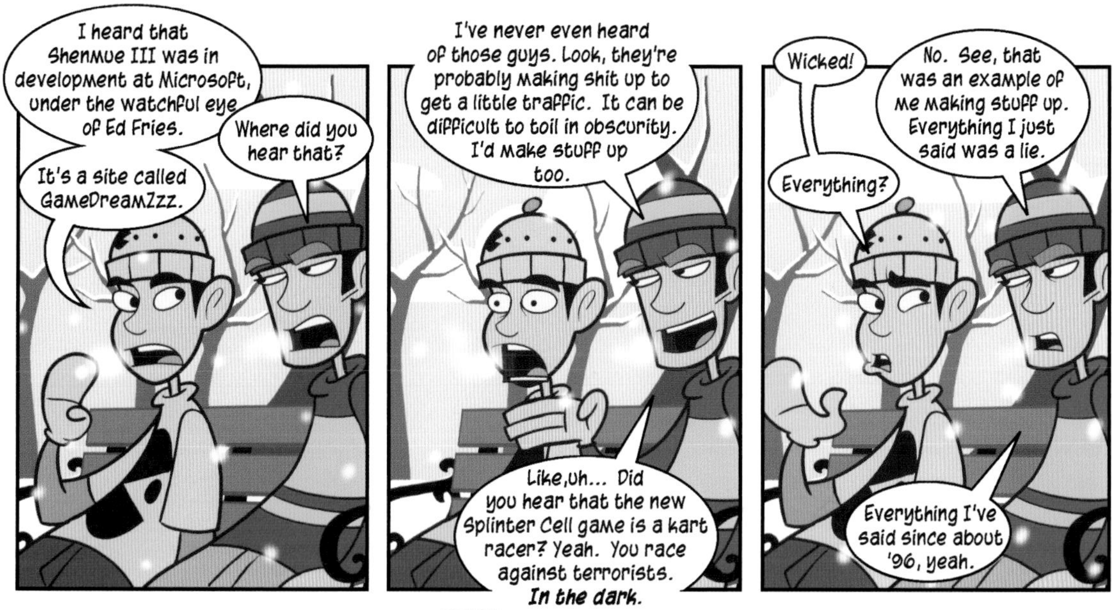
I heard that Shenmue III was in development at Microsoft, under the watchful eye of Ed Fries.
Where did you hear that?
It's a site called GameDreamZzz.
I've never even heard of those guys. Look, they're probably making shit up to get a little traffic. It can be difficult to toil in obscurity. I'd make stuff up too.
Like,uh... Did you hear that the new Splinter Cell game is a kart racer? Yeah. You race against terrorists. *In the dark.*
Wicked!
No. See, that was an example of me making stuff up. Everything I just said was a lie.
Everything?
Everything I've said since about '96, yeah.

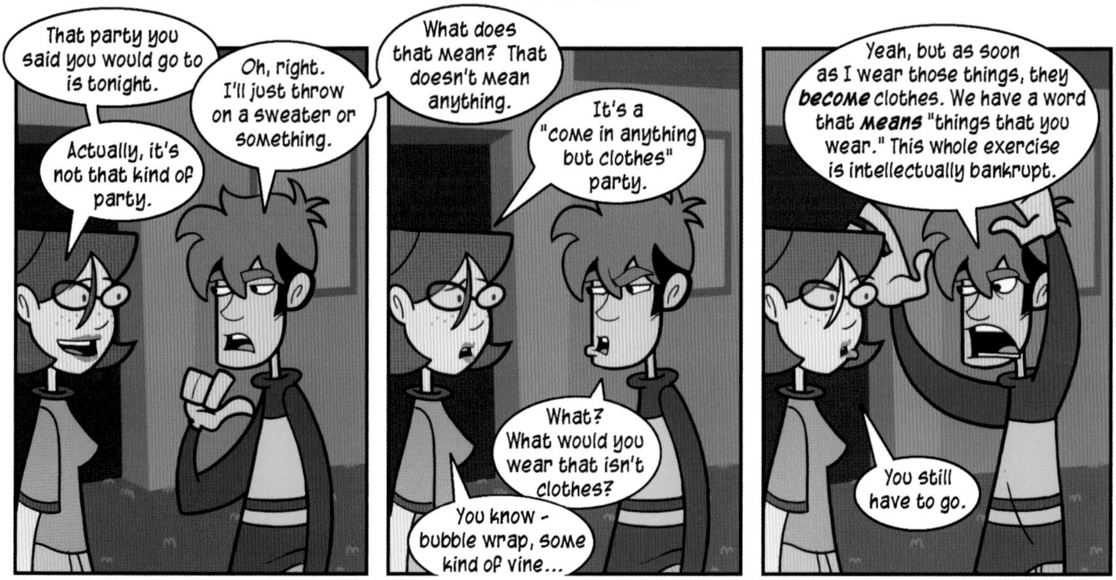
That party you said you would go to is tonight.
Oh, right. I'll just throw on a sweater or something.
Actually, it's not that kind of party.
What does that mean? That doesn't mean anything.
It's a "come in anything but clothes" party.
What? What would you wear that isn't clothes?
You know - bubble wrap, some kind of vine...
Yeah, but as soon as I wear those things, they *become* clothes. We have a word that *means* "things that you wear." This whole exercise is intellectually bankrupt.
You still have to go.

A TRADITION OF DECEIT

December 17, 2003 Nothing came of it, but even given the source I wanted in my heart to believe, to *believe*. There's an online variant coming "soon," but God only knows what that will entail. Shenmue was my favorite game for a very long time. I think I could be very happy just wandering around the docks forever, occasionally asking strangers about the Long Zha.

I LIKE CLOTHED PARTIES, MYSELF

December 19, 2003 You may think that we took liberties here to make the panels flow, but this was the very conversation I related to Gabriel the next day. Does a cobbler see *shoes* everywhere he goes? Do the events of his life conform, he believes, to some kind of underlying *shoe nature*? Because since I began making comic strips, my life has gotten more and more *ridiculous*.

75th annual WE'RE RIGHT AWARDS®

THE TOP TWELVE GAMES OF 2003

Desert Combat

12 I Mean, What Else Are You Going To Do In The Desert?

WarioWare, Inc.

11 Best Game To Play In-Between Breaths

Guilty Gear XX

10 Best Game Featuring Huge Doctors And Rock & Roll Witches

THE 75TH ANNUAL WE'RE RIGHT AWARDS

December 22, 2003 This was the last year we did some variation of the We're Right Awards, choosing in later years to create *actual comics*. It's still nice to know what we thought was important enough to mention back then. I remember DC and WarioWare being big, but I'm only just now remembering what a revolution Guilty Gear was for us. The art, character design, and *impeccable* 2D fighting still endure.

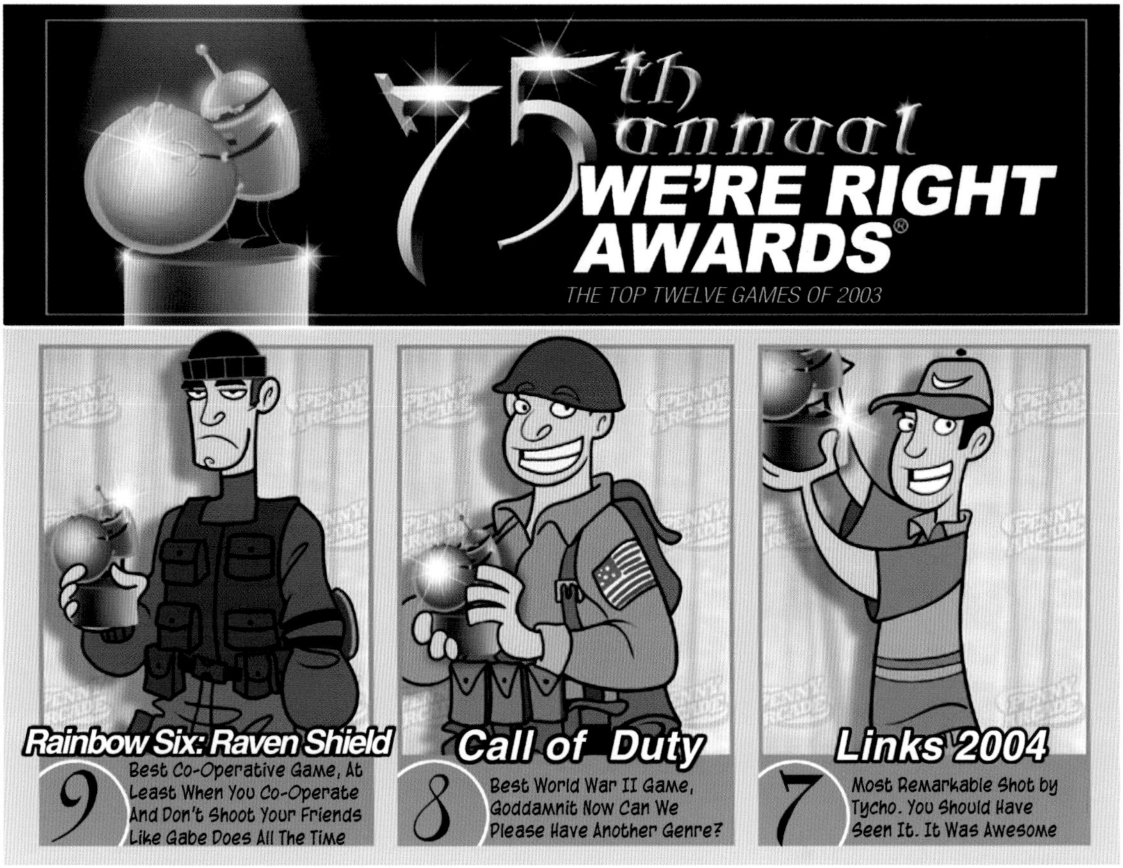
75th annual
WE'RE RIGHT AWARDS®
THE TOP TWELVE GAMES OF 2003
Rainbow Six: Raven Shield
9
Best Co-Operative Game, At Least When You Co-Operate And Don't Shoot Your Friends Like Gabe Does All The Time
Call of Duty
8
Best World War II Game, Goddamnit Now Can We Please Have Another Genre?
Links 2004
7
Most Remarkable Shot by Tycho. You Should Have Seen It. It Was Awesome

WE'RE RIGHT 2003, PART TWO

December 24, 2003 Panels one and three, yes. I support these games wholeheartedly. Raven Shield's modern incarnation, Vegas, has seized us with even greater power, and Links was a confident piece of golf with bring-you-back online savvy. But Call of Duty was odd; we dropped the handles, took ranks, and played online under our own names for the first time. There was something about the quality of the presentation that made it a much more serious experience, and being there under a pseudonym seemed . . . disrespectful, somehow. Weird, right?

75th annual WE'RE RIGHT AWARDS®

THE TOP TWELVE GAMES OF 2003

Mario Kart: Double Dash

6 — Bluest Sparks

FF: Tactics Advance

5 — The "One More Turn, Wow, Is It Really Four In The Morning?" Award

Soul Calibur 2

4 — Most Caliburs

WE'RE STILL RIGHT

December 26, 2003 What a great year. We have here *three great games* that aren't even in the top three. I understand that Final Fantasy Tactics Advance isn't especially well regarded by gamers, even though it reviewed pretty well, but we liked the setting, liked the art, loved the portability. Plus, for all the hatred directed at the Judge system, you have to admit that it laid down the foundation for some of the *coolest adversaries ever* in Final Fantasy XII.

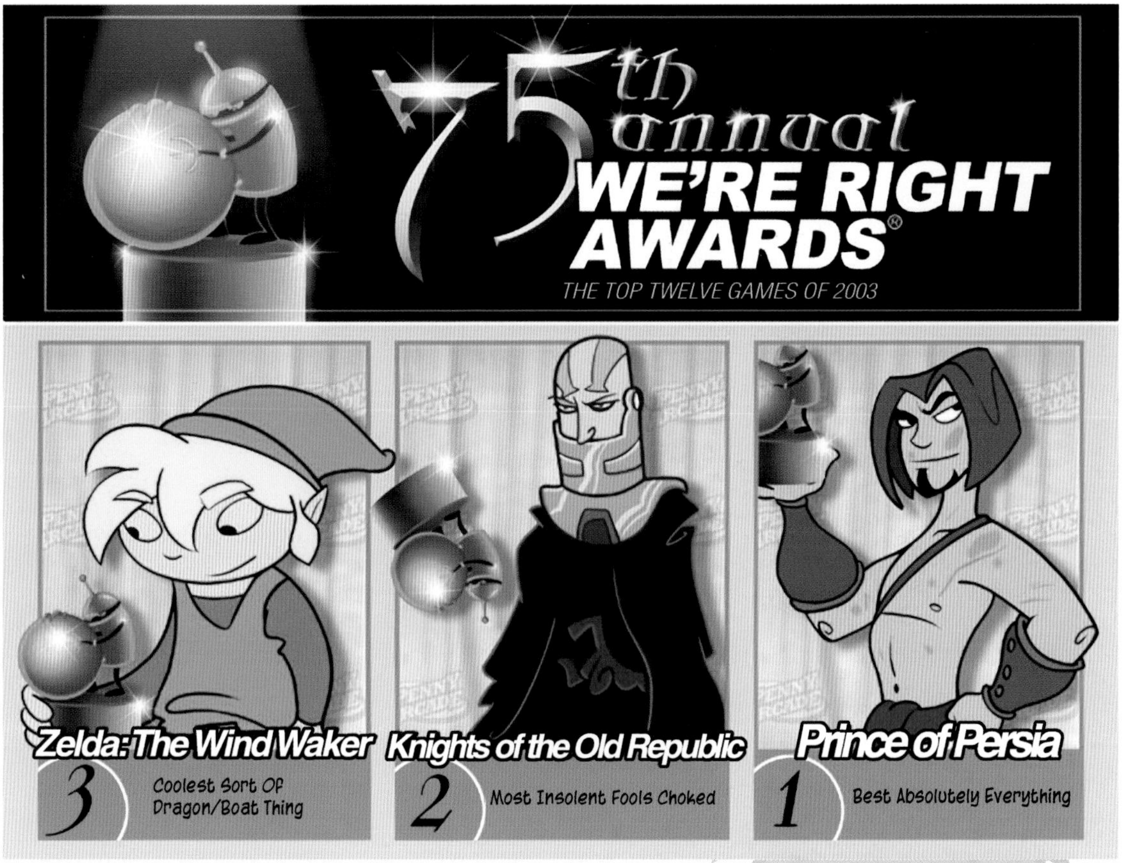
75th annual
WE'RE RIGHT AWARDS®
THE TOP TWELVE GAMES OF 2003
Zelda: The Wind Waker
3
Coolest Sort Of Dragon/Boat Thing
Knights of the Old Republic
2
Most Insolent Fools Choked
Prince of Persia
1
Best Absolutely Everything

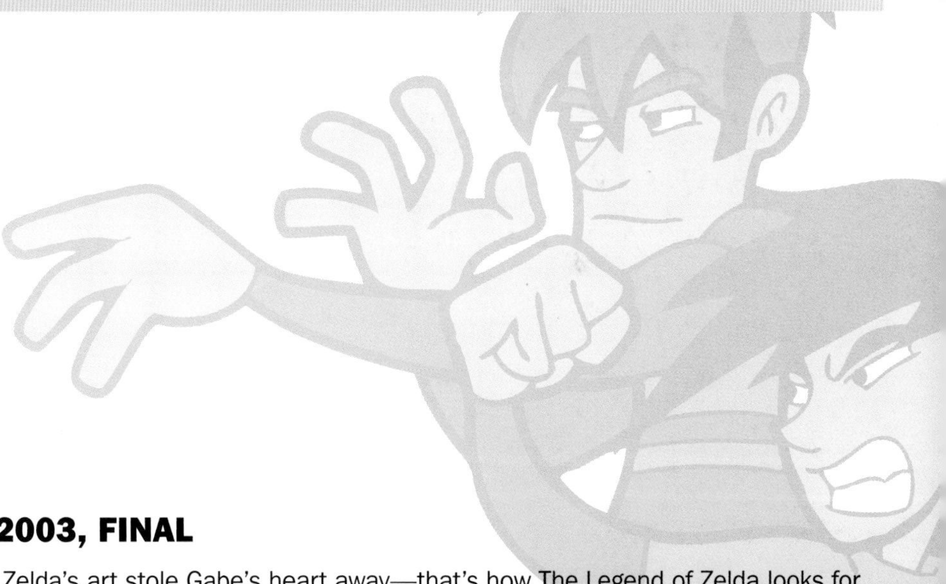

WE'RE RIGHT 2003, FINAL

December 29, 2003 Zelda's art stole Gabe's heart away—that's how The Legend of Zelda looks for him now, so the mature, realistic Link gamers clamored for in Twilight Princess is actually a disappointment. Knights is a *good* RPG with a great twist at the end, which I think leaves you with a good impression that maybe the game doesn't entirely earn. And the Prince, well, you know how I feel about the Prince. It's damn near, *damn* near perfect.

Awkward Holiday Moments

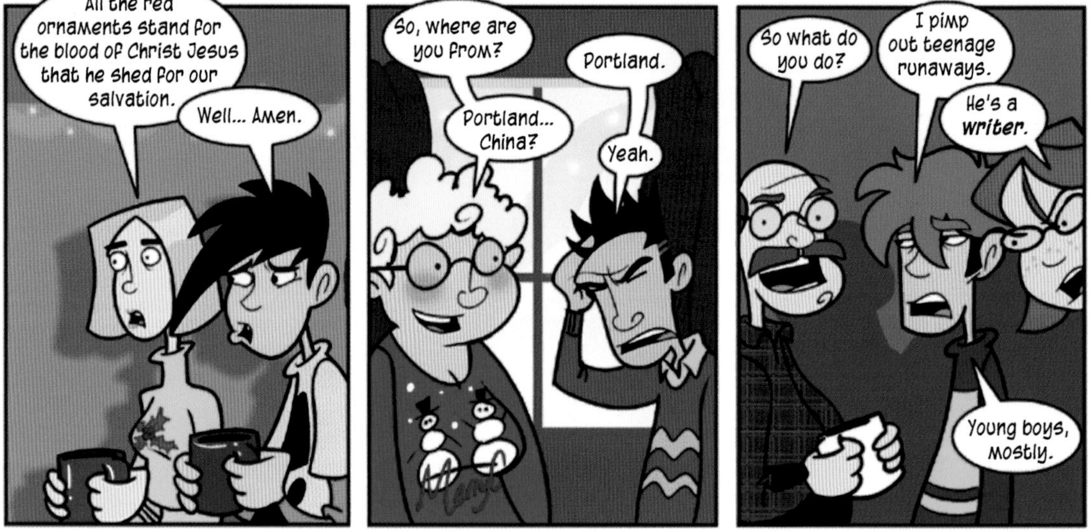
All the red ornaments stand for the blood of Christ Jesus that he shed for our salvation.
Well... Amen.
So, where are you from?
Portland.
Portland... China?
Yeah.
So what do you do?
I pimp out teenage runaways.
He's a ***writer***.
Young boys, mostly.

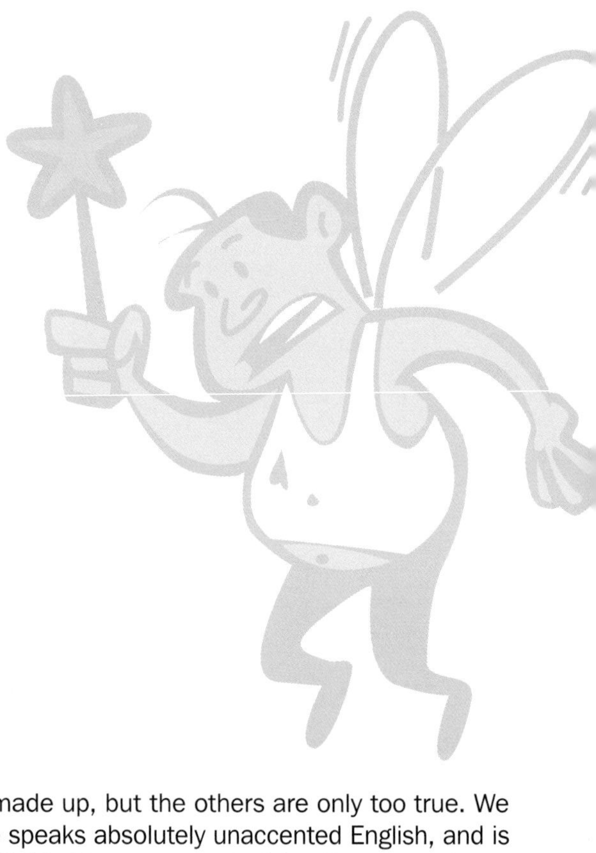

LES MOMENTS AWKWARDS

December 31, 2003 My story in the last panel is made up, but the others are only too true. We couldn't believe Robert when he related it to us. He speaks absolutely unaccented English, and is American, but his girlfriend's family kept offering to "whip him up some rice" for Christmas dinner.

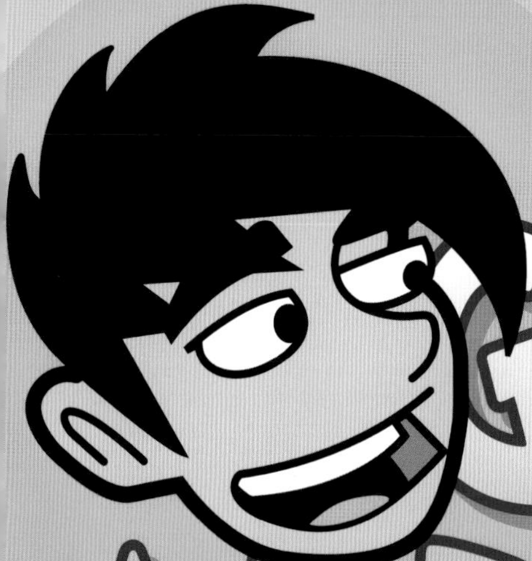

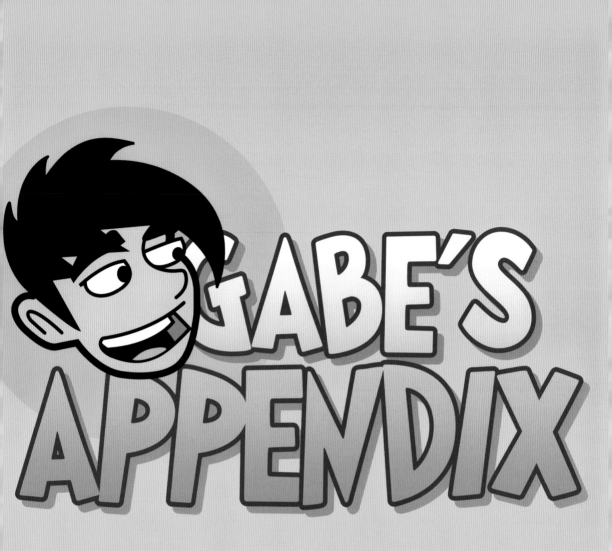

GABE'S APPENDIX

Gabe has a huge bin here at work that contains virtually every picture he's ever drawn.

In the upper strata of this bin you will find things like last week's strips, sketchwork for the games, things he's drawn as gifts, and the like. Below that you'll find the art for every strip going back almost nine years. Beneath those, there are even deeper treasures.

It is those treasures that we explore today . . .

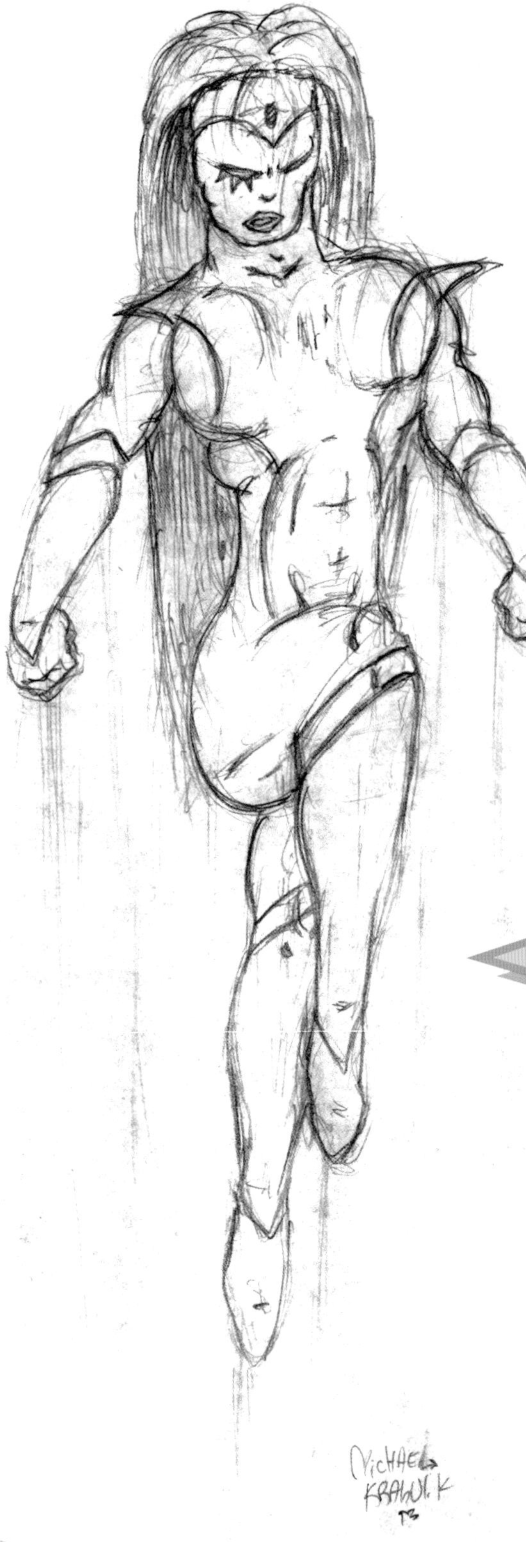

Tycho: Let's begin the appraisal of this period, if we can.

Gabe: Okay.

Tycho: So, this is an orangutan.

Gabe: This is Psy-Fox. She's psychic, but she's also . . .

Tycho: Hot?

Gabe: She's a foxy lady.

Tycho: Was that seriously it?

Gabe: Yeah.

Tycho: I assumed there was some sort of animal. Maybe she had a *totem* animal . . .

Gabe: No. She's a Psy-*Fox*.

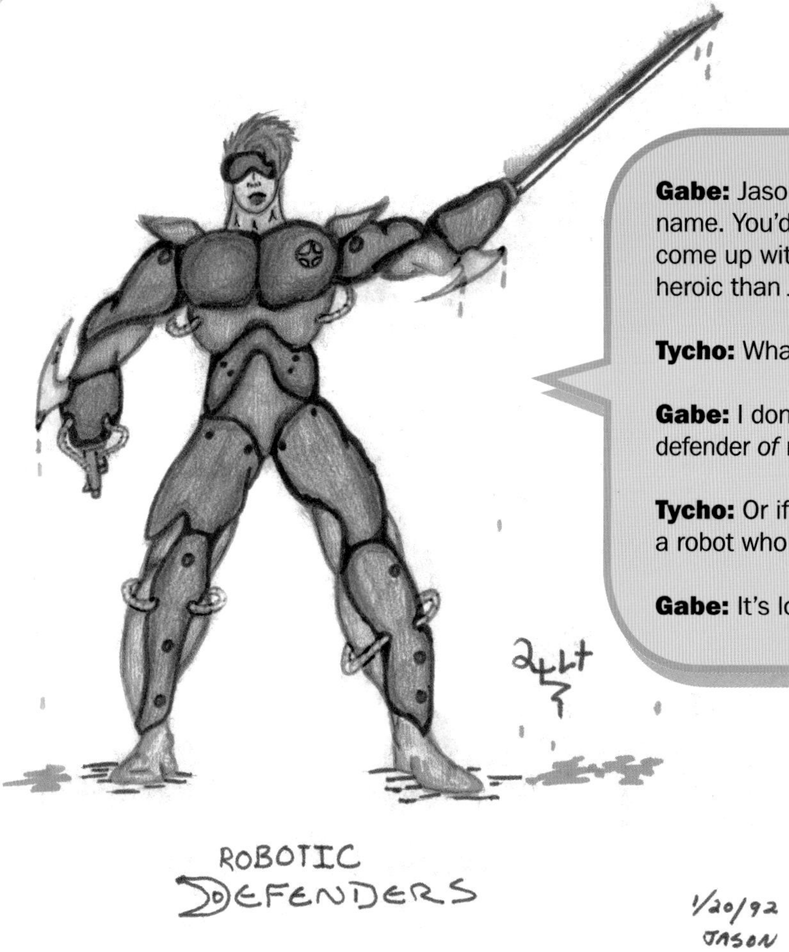

ROBOTIC
DEFENDERS
1/20/92
JASON

Gabe: Jason. What a powerful name. You'd think I could have come up with something more heroic than *Jason*.

Tycho: What was his deal?

Gabe: I don't remember if he was a defender *of* robots, or if he was . . .

Tycho: Or if he was simply a robot who *defended*.

Gabe: It's lost to me, now.

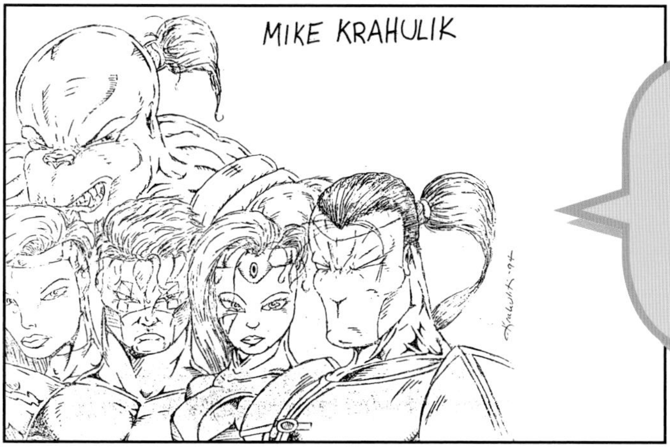

MIKE KRAHULIK

Gabe: This used to be my business card. I would send this out with my portfolio.

Tycho: So these guys are kind of your *sales team*.

Tycho: Real quick, I want to itemize Armageddon's suite of weaponry. On his left arm, there is a belt-fed uzi with a scope, a bracer with two sharp blades that point backward, and he also has two *hot dogs* . . .

Gabe: Those are nunchuks.

Tycho: They are?

Gabe: Or dynamite. I don't remember.

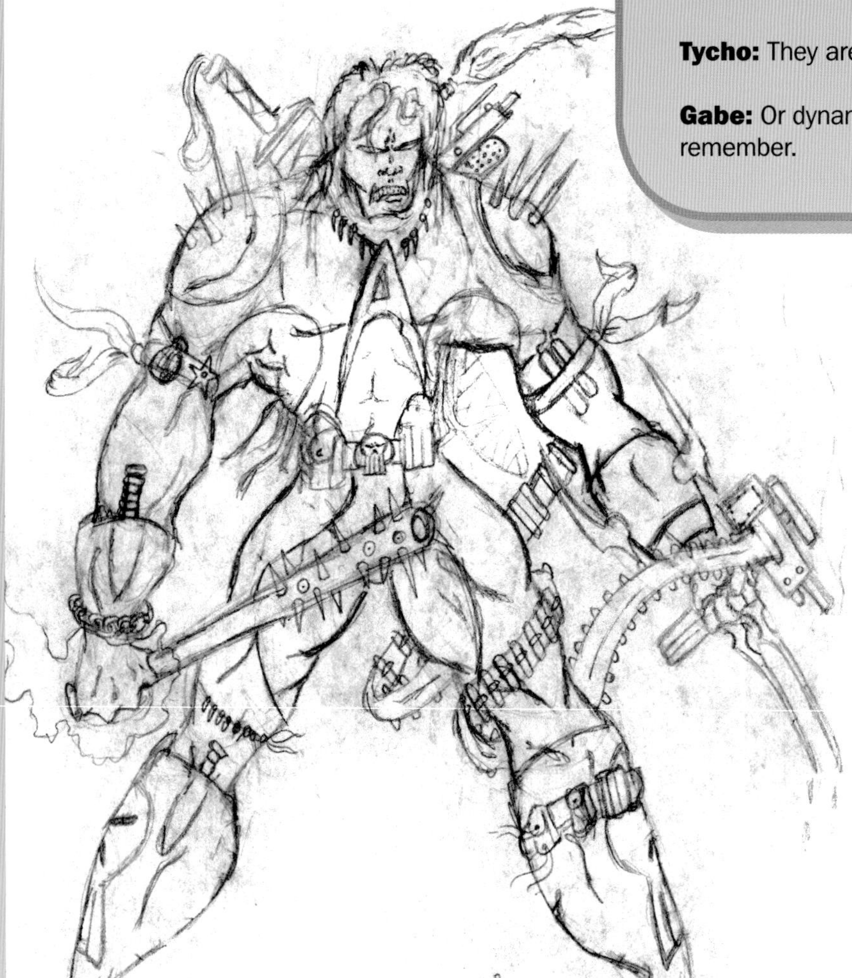
ARMAGEDDON

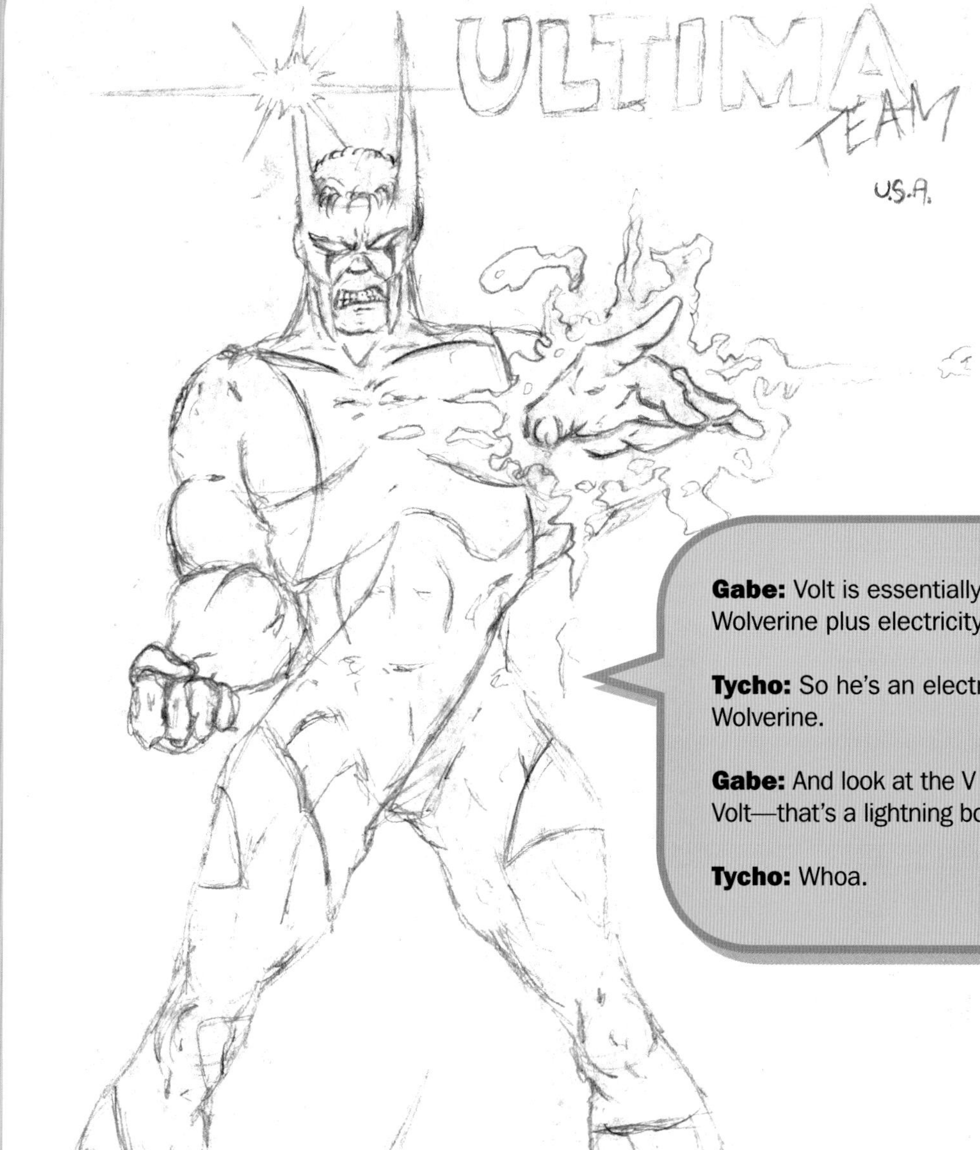
ULTIMA
TEAM
U.S.A.
VOLT

Gabe: Volt is essentially Wolverine plus electricity.

Tycho: So he's an electrical Wolverine.

Gabe: And look at the V in Volt—that's a lightning bolt, too.

Tycho: Whoa.

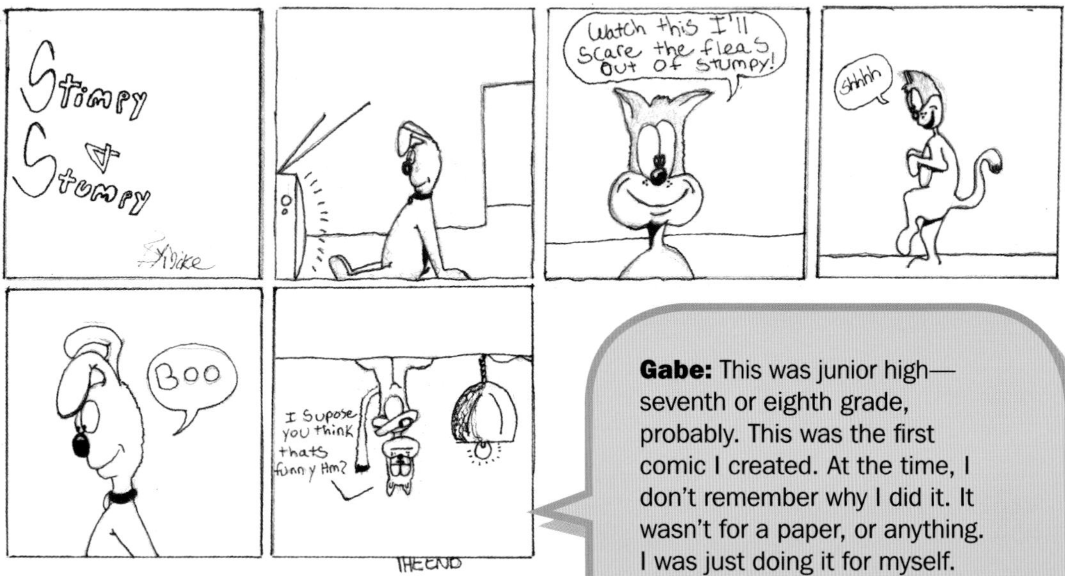
Stimpy
&
Stumpy
Watch this I'll scare the fleas out of Stumpy!
shhhh
Boo
I Supose you think thats funny Hm?
THE END

Gabe: This was junior high—seventh or eighth grade, probably. This was the first comic I created. At the time, I don't remember why I did it. It wasn't for a paper, or anything. I was just doing it for myself.

Tycho: Just to learn?

Gabe: I was just doing it to learn, yeah. And the jokes are *hilarious*.

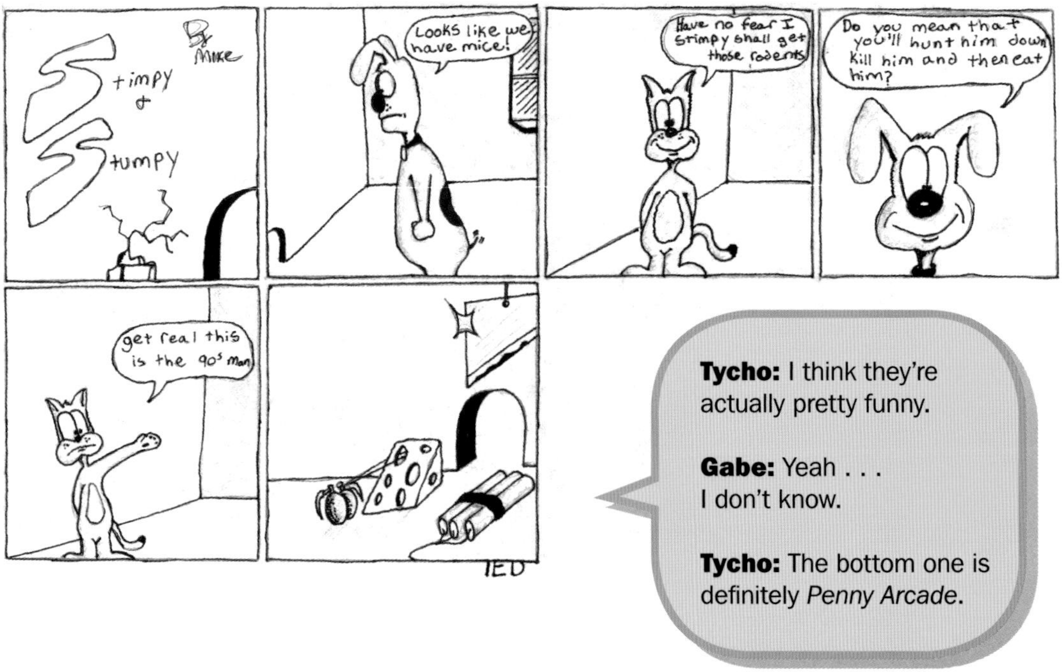
By Mike
Stimpy
&
Stumpy
Looks like we have mice!
Have no fear I Stimpy shall get those rodents
Do you mean that you'll hunt him down kill him and then eat him?
get real this is the 90s man

Tycho: I think they're actually pretty funny.

Gabe: Yeah . . .
I don't know.

Tycho: The bottom one is definitely *Penny Arcade*.

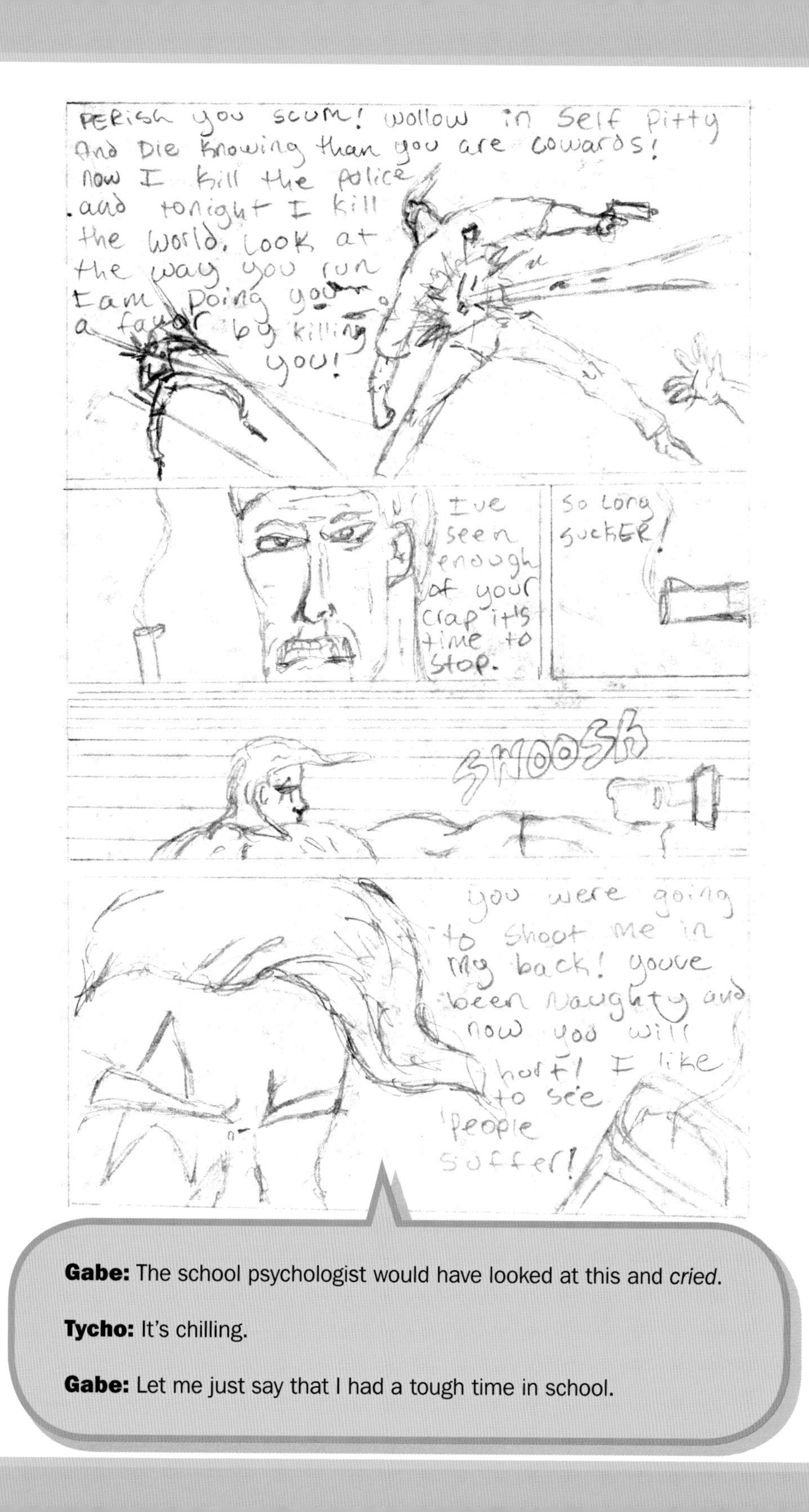
PERish you scum! wollow in Self pitty And Die Knowing than you are cowards! now I kill the police and tonight I kill the world. Look at the way you run I am Doing you a favor by killing you!
Ive seen enough of your crap it's time to stop.
So Long SuckER!
SWOOSH
you were going to Shoot me in my back! youve been Naughty and now you will hurt! I like to see people suffer!

Gabe: The school psychologist would have looked at this and *cried*.

Tycho: It's chilling.

Gabe: Let me just say that I had a tough time in school.

Gabe: This was all you. This was Scythe. You wrote a four or five page story for her that was just . . . garbage.

Tycho: I mean, it was not . . . Yeah. It wasn't very good.

Gabe: How did it start out? "Killing is a lot like . . ."

Tycho: "Killing is a lot like walking, and I've been walking for a long time."

Gabe: I don't feel so bad about the art anymore.

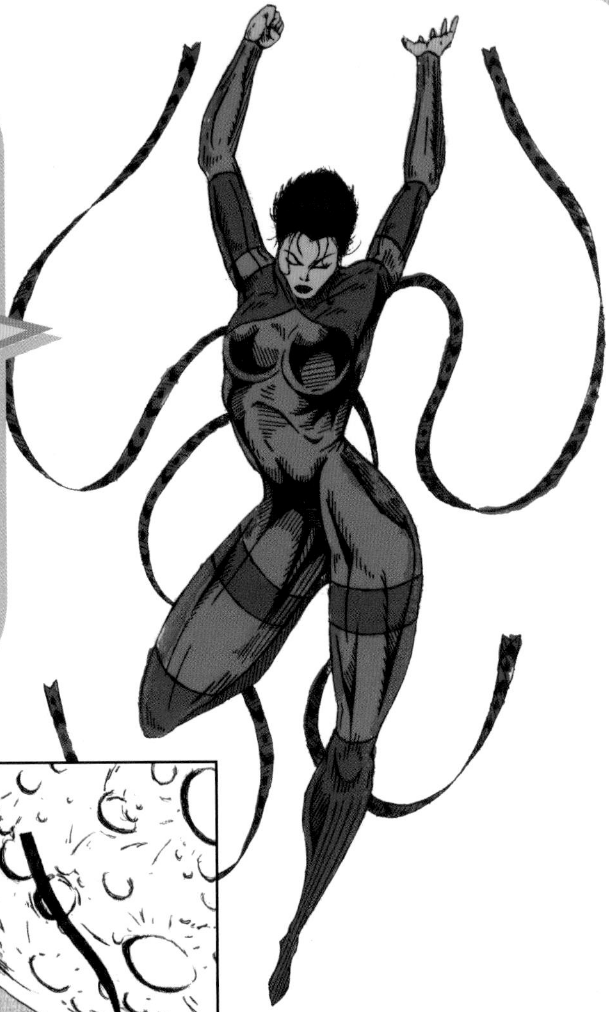

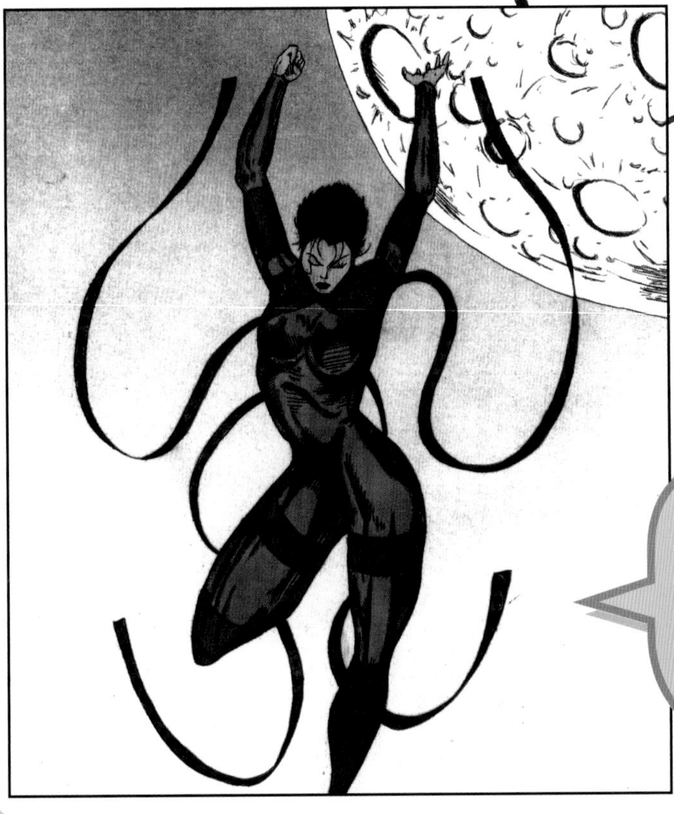

Tycho: And then . . . Night-time shot.

Gabe: This is her at night, yeah.

Gabe: This is a partially inked page of *Sand*. I still think this has some meat. I think we could tell a pretty good story here.

Tycho: This was another project you already had the idea for, and just brought me in near the end to sort of flesh it out. This became an apocalyptic western, eventually—there was some art for *Sand* in volume two, I think.

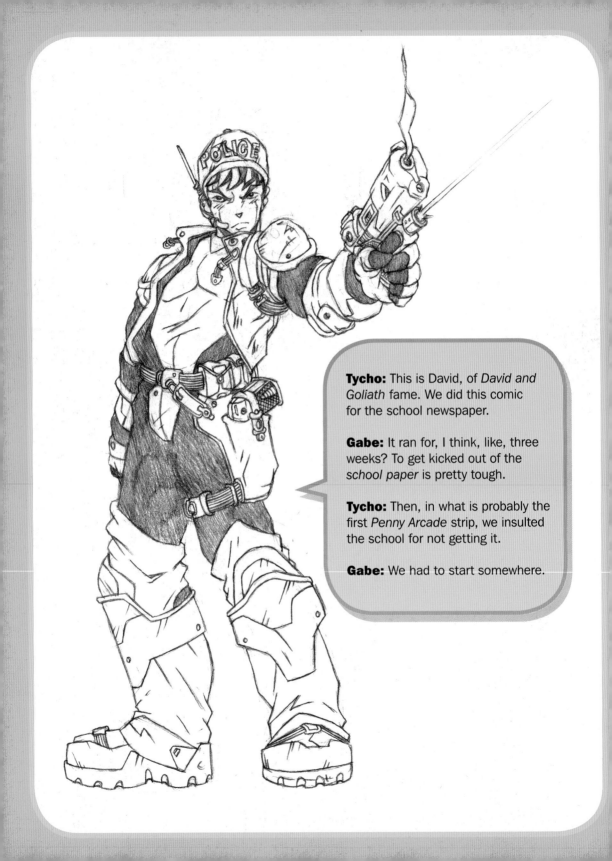

Tycho: This is David, of *David and Goliath* fame. We did this comic for the school newspaper.

Gabe: It ran for, I think, like, three weeks? To get kicked out of the *school paper* is pretty tough.

Tycho: Then, in what is probably the first *Penny Arcade* strip, we insulted the school for not getting it.

Gabe: We had to start somewhere.